NORWEGIAN

DICTIONARY &
PHRASEBOOK

T0275386

Dictionary & Phrasebooks

Albanian
Arabic (Eastern) *Romanized*
Australian
Azerbaijani
Basque
Bosnian
Breton
British
Cajun French
Chechen
Croatian
Czech
Danish
Esperanto
Estonian
Finnish
French
Georgian
German
Greek
Hebrew *Romanized*
Hungarian
Igbo
Ilocano
Irish
Italian
Japanese *Romanized*

Lao *Romanized*
Lingala
Malagasy
Maltese
Mongolian
Nepali
Norwegian
Pashto
Pilipino (Tagalog)
Polish
Québécois
Romanian
Romansch
Russian
Shona
Slovak
Somali
Spanish (Latin American)
Swahili
Swedish
Tajik
Thai *Romanized*
Turkish
Ukrainian
Urdu
Uzbek

NORWEGIAN

DICTIONARY & PHRASEBOOK

Norwegian-English
English-Norwegian

J. GILL HOLLAND

HIPPOCRENE BOOKS, INC.
New York

For information, address:
HIPPOCRENE BOOKS, INC.
171 Madison Avenue
New York, NY 10016

Library of Congress Cataloging-in-Publication Data

Holland, J. Gill
  Norwegian dictionary & phrasebook : Norwegian-
English, English-Norwegian / J. Gill Holland.
      p. cm.
    ISBN-10: 0-7818-0955-X
    ISBN-13: 978-0-7818-0955-9
      1. Norwegian language--Dictionaries--English.
  2. English language--Dictionaries--Norwegian.
  3. Norwegian language--Terms and phrases.
  I. Title: Norwegian dictionary and phrasebook
  II. Title.

PD269.H65 2003
439.8'2321--dc21

                                        2003047171

Printed in the United States of America.

Contents

Acknowledgments

I am indebted to many who helped me put together this handbook. The staff of the E. H. Little Library at Davidson College helped me in my research. Sharon Baggarley and her assistant Jessica Singerman in Instructional Support Services at Davidson College scanned the photograph used for the cover. I consulted regularly with Nancy Mitchell, Assistant to the Department of English at Davidson College, who took care of the marathon of technology needed to produce the manuscript; she made good suggestions about layout and organization. I also want to thank her assistant Ed Rainey for his help. My sister-in-law Inger-Lise Skaar advised me on Norwegian usage. Our daughter Siri Lise Doub, the author of two books published by Hippocrene Books, *Taste of Latvia* and *Tastes and Tales of Norway*, suggested my name to the publisher, helped with the dictionaries and contributed to the text in the section on Norwegian food; her vision and drive inspired hopes for a better handbook for visitors to Norway. I am especially indebted to my brother-in-law Bjørn Lugg for his careful proofreading, suggestions about language and other useful information he provided. At Hippocrene Books I want to thank my editor Nicholas Williams for bringing the project to a successful conclusion. Davidson College has helped fund research trips to Norway for many years. I am grateful to all of these colleagues and friends. Finally I owe a large debt to family and friends in Oslo. Above all I thank my wife Siri.

Introduction

The view from an airliner approaching the coast of Norway—the summer sea, the islands, then the mountains and forests—gives a sublime gateway to **Oslo Lufthavn**, the new Oslo airport at **Gardermoen**. The terminal building at Gardermoen is spacious and open, the customs procedures swift, and the one-hour transportation by bus or train into Oslo convenient. An estimated 17 million passengers enjoy a smooth entry into Norway every year at Gardermoen.

But for me the sea still provides the most dramatic port of entry for Norway. It was my portal on the overnight pleasure ship that sailed from Copenhagen to Oslo under the bright summer sky in 1960. A single figure standing on the bow deck still symbolizes the adventure, a young Spaniard who when asked his destination answered in French, "Je voyage." "I travel!" Visitors to Norway will also breathe that Viking air.

The Copenhagen-Oslo line still runs today, and those two words spoken under the northern sky still capture the spirit of one's first sail out of the open water of the Skagerrack sixty miles up the long fjord to Oslo. As you enter the harbor, the distinctive beacon of the twin towers of the Oslo City Hall is dead ahead. Above the harbor on the right stands the medieval fortress of Akershus. From the deck the princely ski jump at Holmenkollen is visible on the mountainside high above the city of Oslo; the royal family of Norway has been known for excellence in the sports of skiing and sailing. There at the Holmenkollen ski jump an annual international competition is held every March. The view from the 183-foot ski tower where the jumpers launch their flight gives you a stunning view of the harbor and the ships in the fjord below. Everyone remembers the Winter Olympics of 1994 that were held in Lillehammer; in 1952 Oslo also hosted the games. In the 1928 Olympics in Amsterdam, Crown Prince Olav, who reigned as King Olaf V from 1957 to 1991, was a member of the gold medallist crew in yachting.

If you sail to Norway from the English port of Newcastle-upon-Tyne, the harbor of Bergen offers its own charm amid the fjords on the western coast of Norway. The distinctive wooden architecture of the Bergen Wharfs, which are on the World Heritage List of protected structures, dates from the Hanseatic period in the fourteenth century. Every May Bergen hosts **Festspillene**, an international festival of music and dance. The violinist **Ole Bull** and the composer **Edvard Grieg** made Bergen the music capital of Norway. **Grieghallen**, the Bergen concert house, is named for Grieg, whose home is situated by the sea. The cabin where he composed the **Per Gynt Suite** for the poetic masterpiece of Norway's great dramatist **Henrik Ibsen** sits on boulders right over the water's edge.

The best overall view of Bergen and the sea is from **Fløyen**, above the city, which is reached by cable car. Check the visibility first though, for Bergen, like its rainy sister city Seattle, is known for its umbrellas. The saying goes that every newborn in Bergen comes into the world carrying a baby **paraply** (umbrella). From Fløyen you can see **Hurtigruten** (the coastal steamer) leaving for the north. This line of steamers is the principal means of transporting cargo and passengers north along the coast and beyond the Arctic Circle, past the **Lofoten** islands and **Nordkapp** to **Kirkenes** near the Russian border. Steamers sailing into the Lofoten Islands may be met by singers and horn players on the pier. Edgar Allan Poe's short story "Descent into the Maelstrom" takes place off the islands at a giant whirlpool in the Arctic Ocean. This is indeed the land of the midnight sun. Tourists on our ship who went out on deck before midnight to see the sun bounce off the horizon were disappointed; it did not even come close, just hung high in the sky. Some veterans prefer **Hurtigruten** in the dark winter months. Then the coastal cities and towns are ablaze with lights, and the moon and stars shine in the sea. In winter, **Tromsø**, the "Paris of the North," glitters, and its "Arctic Cathedral" is a gleaming miracle of icy glass.

Nordkapp (North Cape) at the northernmost tip of Norway has almost seventy days of utter darkness during winter, just as it has almost seventy days of around the clock sunlight during summer. Yet Norway has an almost unlimited amount of hydroelectric power; windows everywhere shine in the dark. More astonishing, with snow on the ground, starlight is reflected off the white surface of the earth, and the world is illumined from below. When the moon is full, of course the effect is dazzling, but I remember my amazement upon first seeing the brightness of reflected starlight. The vision is magical when the ground is lit only by starlight.

I hope this book will tempt you to go to Norway to discover the wonders of the land and her people, in any season. What follows is a day's walk through the **Sentrum** (downtown) of Oslo, which serves as a more localized introduction to the capital. Then come a dictionary and a phrasebook, which includes special lists of vocabulary devoted to subject such as shopping, food, children's activities, sports, camping, the coast, and so on. Emergency numbers and phrases you need if you run into trouble are here too. As a special treat, our daughter Siri Lise Doub, whose book *Tastes and Tales of Norway* Hippocrene Books published last year, has contributed an introduction to food in Norway. Food is a good introduction to any country. **Tusen takk** (many thanks) are the first words to learn in Norwegian, and the first phrase to learn may well be **Takk for maten** (thank you for the meal). Thus prepared, you will be off to a good start. Welcome to Norway! **Velkommen til Norge!**

A Day in Downtown Oslo: A Stroll Down Karl Johan

Oslo, **hovedstaden** (the capital city), was designed for walkers. The Norse name for Oslo, which was founded in the year 1000, seems to have meant "pasture of the gods" (**Ás** = gods, **lo** = pasture). Natives are proud that the geographical center of the municipality lies far out of the city in **Nordmarka** (North Forest), more than an hour's walk beyond the ski jump, where you can walk in nature for hours, indeed, days.

This short essay will lead you not into the forest but on a walk from the residence of the royal family into the **sentrum.** We begin at **Det Kongelige Slott** (the Royal Palace). The Palace was designed by H. F. D. Listow and built in the years 1824–1851 after the *Empire* or neoclassical style arrived in Norway. The tranquil acres surrounding the Palace are a beautifully landscaped park in the heart of the city. They are open to the public and safe to stroll through in any season. Tickets for a tour of the interior of the palace (when the royal family is not in residence) may be obtained at any of the nearby post offices. Regarding the absence of a heavy guard around the royal residence, the story goes that a foreigner asked **kong** (King) **Olav V** (reigned 1957–1991) about his safety. Pointing to the passers-by, the king responded, "I have four-and-a-half million Norwegians to protect me." Today **kong Harald V** and **dronning** (Queen) **Sonja** and their family are very popular in the constitutional monarchy of Norway. In modern times Norway only got her own king in 1905, when the union with Sweden was dissolved and Prince Carl of Denmark was elected king and crowned Haakon VII (reigned 1905–1957). In ancient times, around the year 900, **Harald Hårfagre** (Fairhair) unified Norway. Denmark held supremacy from 1380 until 1814, when it was forced to cede its claim to Sweden. Karl XIV Johan was king of Sweden and Norway from 1818–1844. The Eidsvoll Constitution Day dates from May 17, 1814. Norwegians began to celebrate the date in the 1820s, much to the displeasure of the king, who fought the celebration unsuccessfully for a decade before giving in.

Constitution Day, **syttende mai** (May 17th), is a day of flags. At the palace elementary and high school students parade to patriotic music under the balcony, where the King and Queen wave to the long line of happy boys and girls. Graduating seniors are divided into the blues and the reds, the colors of the national flag; their faces and garb are colored red for high school students in the humanities line, blue for those in the business line. The national flag of a blue cross on a broader white cross on a field of red is seen flying everyday in Norway. The continuing patriotic tradition of flying the flag owes much to the solidarity the Norwegian people built during World War II under German Occupation and their joy upon the return of the royal family after the German surrender in May of 1945.

The view from the palace over the city extends a cordial invitation to walk down the hill to **Karl Johan's gate** (street), the principal avenue of the city named for kong Karl Johan, whose course through the city center was planned by architect Listow in concord with the site of the Royal Palace. **Karl Johan**, a brilliant boulevard lined with shops, restaurants, parks and fountains, is laid out on a human scale, unlike the vast avenues of Paris or Berlin or Beijing. State buildings are approachable, like **Nationalteatret** (the National Theater), before the doors of which the national literary heroes Ibsen and Bjørnson stand in bronze.

Just outside the theater one passes the bandstand, where a uniformed brass band plays on occasion. At the rear of the building at the subway station (**T-bane**) a fountain is surrounded by bustling street life. The attire of Norwegians is worth observation, from the furs and ski sweaters of the colder months to the light dresses and hiking attire of the warmer months. These people take to vigorous activity in the outdoors, and the complexions of the boys and girls glow in the open air.

Walking toward the harbor, you pass **Norway Designs** (known for its Norwegian jewelry, glassware, clothing and furniture—don't miss the contemporary glass of artist Benny Motzfeldt), an **American Express** office (Fridtjof Nansens plass 6) and the woolens shop **William Schmidt** (ask to see hand-knitted sweaters before deciding to buy the machine-knitted article). You are now standing before the twin red brick towers of the **Rådhus** (city hall), which were completed in 1950 in the Nordic Neo-Renaissance style. The high walls of its interior sala are covered with murals depicting the history of Oslo painted by Henrik Sørenson, Per Krohg and other famous twentieth-century artists. The **Noble Peace Prize** is awarded here every December 10th. A few steps away in the handsome old west railway station is the **Norges Informasjonssenter** (Norway Information Center, Vestbaneplassen 1), where you can pick up a copy of the *Oslo Guide* and the **Oslo Card**; this card will help you save a good deal of money on public transportation and museum entrance fees. The center is a treasure trove of information for visitors to all of Norway.

Behind the Rådhus lies the harbor. First you will see ferries, which will take you to the peninsulas **Nesodden** and **Bygdøy** to visit the **Folk Museum**, the **Viking ships** and the vessels **Kon-Tiki** and **Ra** made famous on the ocean adventures of **Thor Heyerdahl**. At the harbor in the morning, vans from city restaurants shopping for the fresh catch are often parked by fishing boats just in from the sea. A short walk along the pier to the right is **Aker Brygge**, a festival of restaurants, cafes, cinema, apartment houses, shops and businesses; it is a perfect spot to have a cup of coffee or a glass of beer and watch the sea traffic and passers-by. The transformation of the former shipyards of Aker Brygge into this complex reflects the shift of Norwegian business away from a concentration on shipbuilding toward a more diversified economic base.

If you walk left from the city hall past ocean-going vessels you come to **Akershus,** the stately baroque fortress that has overlooked the harbor since its construction began in the fourteenth century. After the old wooden town of Oslo burned in 1624, King Christian IV planned the new city in brick around the walls of the stone fortress. It holds state rooms, the royal crypts, and **Norges Hjemmefront Museet** (the Underground Resistance Museum of Norway), which displays a dramatic record of the underground movement against the German occupation during World War II.

Starting again from **Nationalteatret,** if you cross the street in the opposite direction from the harbor you pass by the august yellow buildings of **Oslo University,** built in 1842–1852. C. H. Grosch designed the university and the **Oslo Bourse** (stock market) in the neo-classical style that reflects the kinship of Norway with the Continent at the time, notably with Germany. Grosch was indebted to the Prussian architect Schinkel, who designed the university of Leipzig and many of the buildings, which give Berlin its neo-classical look. Farther along the street facing antiquarian book and map shops lies **Nasjonalgalleriet** (the National Gallery), which holds monumental nineteenth-century Romantic landscapes of the mountains, glaciers and fjords by **Tidemann** and **Gude.** As you go up the grand staircase you will see the bronze *Hell* (1897) by **Gustav Vigeland,** Norway's famous sculptor; in 1893 Vigeland visited Rodin in Paris, and the allusion to the French master's *Gates of Hell* is powerful. Vigeland's psychological study of Ibsen in marble (1903) is also in the museum collection. In the **Edvard Munch** room the stunning painting *The Sick Girl* awaits you. This painting was Munch's technical breakthrough in the mid-1880s, when he began to scratch the surface of his paintings violently; later this **hestekur** (horse-cure) included setting the paintings outside in the weather to "cure" them. In the Munch room tourists are often found posing for their souvenir snapshot beside the ecstatic *Madonna* or *The*

Scream, now one of the world's most universally recognized icons. With Vincent van Gogh, Munch is considered the father of Expressionism. **Munch-museet** (the Munch Museum), which is the home of the largest collection of Munch's work, is a direct four-stop subway trip away at Tøyen on the eastern side of the city. Munch's fame as a printmaker has been recently celebrated in a *catalogue raisonné* by Gerd Woll, print curator at the museum; the printmaking press from Munch's studio is on display there as well as his artwork and an extensive biography in pictures on the ground floor.

If you continue down Karl Johan from Nationalteatret you pass shops, arcades and open-air cafes. Sidewalk tables are full of pleasure-takers in the summertime. The large bookstore **Tanum Libris** sells books of all sorts in numerous languages; Oslo's many bookstores are a reminder of Norway's highly literate population. Across the street is **Eidsvolls plass**, a park that offers public sculpture and benches beside a pool that becomes a skating rink in the wintertime.

Farther down the street come the **Ticket** travel agency (No. 33) and a large newsstand that sells both domestic and foreign newspapers and magazines from Europe and America. *Aftenposten* (The Evening Post), Oslo's flagship daily, is published in morning and evening editions. *Aftenposten* offers an English edition at its on-line website, but opening the pages of its paper edition twice a day is one of the delights of visiting Norway and an ever-renewed reward for learning to read Norwegian. *Dagbladet* (The Morning Paper) and *Verdens Gang* (The Way of the World) are other dailies of a more sensational nature.

The **Grand Hotel** is one of Oslo's most famous hotels. **Ibsen** walked to the Grand every day and took his place in the seat reserved for him. Locals set their watches by his arrival at noon. Munch's portrait inside shows him lodged in place with his back to the window, one eye seeming to glare out at you and the other to be searching an inner world. The mural, which covers the entire back wall, shows a panorama of luminaries from Oslo's cultural past, including Munch and Ibsen.

The chocolate store a few steps away is the place to buy a box of **Kong Haakon Sjokolade** (chocolates) or a bag of

Twist (Norwegian candies) to bring along as a present to your hostess if you pay a call. You are now at the entrance to the **gågate** (pedestrian street). Opposite the **Storting** (Parliament) sits a bronze statue of **Christian Krohg** in all his rotundity presiding over an outdoor cafe, one of the most famous painters of the 1880s, an early supporter of Munch's and for a time husband of **Oda**, herself a celebrated Bohemian painter whose paintings hang with Krohg's in Nasjonalgalleriet. Krohg's giant canvas *At the Police Physician's* shows a scene from the life of **Albertine**, a poor girl forced onto the streets in the harsh 1880s; Krohg's protest novel of that title tells her moving story.

A block farther down Karl Johan stands **David Andersen**, the famous silver and gold store. Look at the traditional broaches and jewelry patterns that have been handed down from Viking times. A set of tiny enamel spoons makes an elegant wedding gift from Norway. An **ostehøvel** (cheese slicer) makes a unique gift. **Tinn** (pewter) from Norway is renowned. Pewter cups and plates, bottle openers and candlestick holders from Norway are distinctive.

Outside David Andersen street performers from puppeteers to Andean musicians draw crowds. You can turn and look back up Karl Johan all the way to Slottet before proceeding down the hill to **Oslo Domkirke**, the cathedral completed in 1697; Christianity came to Norway in 1000, and with the Reformation in 1536 the state church became Lutheran. Behind the cathedral lies the half circle called the **Basarhallene** (the Bazaar Halls), whose cafes and shops make a charming locale under arches designed by the architect Grosch, the architect of the University; this time he created a romantic style reminiscent of German castles (1849). Below the Bazaar Halls is the marketplace where flowers, fruits, leatherwork and jewelry are sold. Not far away is **Husfliden**, one of the stores across the country that sell Norwegian crafts like **rosemaling** (wooden utensils and furniture painted with floral designs, like the classic corner cupboard) and national costumes like the **bunad** with its distinctive silver broaches.

Below the cathedral stands **Oslo S**, the principal railway station of the capital, which marks the terminus of our walk. We began at the royal palace up the hill at the head of **Karl Johan** and made our way down the cultural, commercial, political and ecclesiastical axis of the capital of the country.

On another day you can go by boat to the peninsula **Bygdøy** to see *Kon Tiki*, the **Viking ships** and the **Folk Museum**, where old and young alike enjoy traditional farm architecture (with grass growing on the sod roofs) and puppet shows based on the folktales of **Asbjørnsen** and **Moe** (like that of **Askeladden**, "the ash-lad," the "cinder-boy" Cinderella). The strong lines of the dark Viking ships with their rising dragon prows almost rekindle the awe surrounding the Northmen in most of Europe during the Viking Age (8th–10th centuries). The ships are evidence that in the science of shipbuilding the pagan Vikings were considered ahead of the Christian countries they invaded. The design of the hull of Viking ship was passed on—turned upside down—in the roof of the medieval stave church, which also continued to use the Viking dragon motif in ornamental wood carvings. The Vikings even reached Constantinople, where they served as mercenaries, and Russia; the very name "Russia" comes from the Old Norse *Rôthsmenn*, "row-men," "seafarers," from the verb *rôthr*, "to row." Leif Eriksson lived the Viking spirit of travel when he sailed to North America, which he called *Vinland*, around the year 1000. The great number of Norwegian young people that work and study abroad must reflect the old spirit too.

Elsewhere in and around Oslo sites worth visiting abound. The **Vigeland sculpture park and museum** and **the ski jump at Holmenkollen** are top tourist attractions. The forty acres of **Vigeland Parken** took forty years to complete. The great fountain of six giants in bronze holding up a bowl of water (designed in 1906), the Monolith granite column of seven meters' height from the 1920s, and the figures on the bridge over the lakes of **Frogner-parken** (the Frogner Park) are three paramount attractions; they depict the human story in dignity and pathos in a range of styles from classic to primitive vitalism. Near Holmenkollen on the mountainside is the **Frognerseter Restaurant**, a striking piece of dark wooden architecture designed by Holm Munthe in 1890 in the so-called romantic dragon style. After your stroll through downtown Oslo, just look for the **trikk (T-bane)** marked "Frognerseteren," and it will take you right up the mountain. The spectacle of the city and fjord beyond from tables outside or inside the picturesque old restaurant is a wonder.

Some Notes on the Norwegian Language

Norwegian is a North Germanic, West Scandinavian language. It is derived from Old Norwegian, which had branched off from other Scandinavian languages by the beginning of the thirteenth century. Under the union of Denmark and Norway, from 1380 to 1814, "Dano-Norwegian" became the principal language of the major cities, and the older forms of Norwegian remained only in certain dialects. In the middle of the nineteenth century during the rise of National Romanticism, Ivar Aasen created a "purer" Norwegian untainted by Danish, which incorporated elements of Norwegian that differed from Danish taken from these dialects. This he called *nynorsk*, "new Norwegian," to distinguish it from *riksmål*, "national language" (later called *bokmål*, "book-language"). In 1885 *nynorsk* became the second official language of the country. Language reforms of 1907, 1917 and 1938 brought elements of *nynorsk* into *riksmål*, and for a time there was a move to combine the two official languages into *samnorsk*, "combined Norwegian." That movement was abandoned and *nynorsk* has lost much ground in many parts of the country and in the media. *Riksmål* is used almost exclusively in this dictionary and phrasebook. Distinctions between the three genders of nouns—masculine, feminine and neuter—which are less important in *riksmål*, are not given; instead nouns are classified by the very important distinction between nouns that take the indefinite article *en* and the post-positional definite article *-en*, and nouns that take the indefinite article *et* and the post-positional definite article *-et*.

The post-positional definite article, which Norwegian shares with other Nordic (Germanic Scandinavian) languages, is simply explained. In English, the definite article precedes the noun: "the book." But in Norwegian "the book" is *boken*, *bok* ("book") plus *en* ("the") at the end of the noun, literally, "book-the." Contrast the indefinite article, which precedes the noun in both English and Norwegian: "a book," *en bok*. Norwegian keeps the same word for both the definite and the indefinite article: *en*. English uses different words, "the" for the definite article, "a" or "an" for the indefinite article.

Norwegian also keeps the same form for the verb for all first-, second- and third-person subjects in both singular and plural. For example, in English we have "I am," "you are," "it is," "we are," and "they are"—three different verb forms. Norwegian, on the other hand, uses *er*, the same form of the verb "to be," for all six pronoun subjects: *jeg er, du er, det er, vi er, dere er* and *de er.*

Speakers of Danish, Norwegian and Swedish can largely understand each other and for the most part speak to each other in their own language. In some ways Norwegian is the middle ground of the three; for example, it is the Nordic language used by SAS (Scandinavian Airline System) on international flights.

Abbreviations

abbrev.	abbreviation
adj.	adjective
adv.	adverb
art.	article
conj.	conjunction
interj.	interjection
n.	noun
n.en	noun that takes 'en'
n.et	noun that takes 'et'
n.pl	plural noun
num.	number
Pln.	place name
prep.	preposition
pron.	pronoun
v.	verb

The Norwegian Alphabet

A   ah

AA   oh (this is the old spelling of *Å* seen today in proper names)

B   beh

C   seh

D   deh (like the *d* in *day*)

E   eh

F   eff

G   geh

H   hoh

I   ee

J   yeh

K   koh

L   ell

M   em

N   enn

O   oh

P   peh

Q   koo (not used in native Norwegian words)

R   ehr (like the English word ***air*** with the *r* rolled)

S   ess

T   teh

U   oo

V   veh

W   dobbelt-veh

X   eks (not used in native Norwegian words)

Y   ü (like the *u* in *huge*)

Z   sett

Æ   a (like the *a* in *after*)

Ø   ur

Å   oh

Norwegian Pronunciation

A (short A): like *a* in *art*

A (long A): like *a* in *father*

AI: like *aye*

AU: like *aow*

B: like *b* in *bear*

C: like S before E and I as in *cider*

C: like K before A, O and U as in *Cuba*

D: as in *do*; D is silent after R, L, N and long vowels
(exception: D is pronounced in Gud [God])

E: as in *ten*

EI: as in **ay-ee** spoken rapidly

F: as in *for*

G (hard G before A, O, Å): as in *get*; G is silent in words
ending in -*ig*

GJ: Y as in *yes*

H: as in *have*

HJ: Y as in *yes*

I (short I): as in *sit*

J: Y as in *yes*

K: as in *keep*; K is pronounced before consonants as well
as vowels

KJ: a combination of the CH in *change* and the SH in *she*
(the J may be dropped before EI, I, and Y)

L: as in *light*

M: as in *may*

N: as in *no*

O (short O): as in *for*

O (long O): as in *too*

P: as in *pop*

R: as in *right*

S: as in *so*

SJ: SH as in *share*

SK: SH as in *share*

SKJ: SH as in *share*

T: as in *true*

U: as in *soothe*

V: as in *vat*

W: as in *vat*

X: eks

Y: yeh as in yellow

Z: S as in *so*

Æ: A as in *mare*

Ø: EA as in *heard*

ØY: OI as in *boy*

Å: OH

A Note on the Pronunciation of Norwegian

Like English, Norwegian is a Germanic language. Though it is a northern Germanic cousin to English, Norwegian follows the same general rule of accenting the first syllable of words, and with fewer exceptions than in English. There are fewer silent consonants in Norwegian. The most common silent consonants are the **d** at the end of a word as in **god** (*good*), the **g** in the suffix -**lig**, as in **rimelig** (*reasonable, inexpensive*), the **t** in **det** (*the*) and the suffix –**et,** as in **landet** (*the land, the country*) and the initial **h** consonant in combinations like **hvem** (*who, whom*) and **hjelp** (*help*).

For English speakers the grammar of modern Norwegian should not be as difficult as the grammar of Romance or Slavic languages. The pronunciation is certainly easier once Norwegian is heard. Although Norwegian has tonal aspects that must be learned at a more advanced stage, these **sample sentences** should guide the new speaker into comprehensible **norsk** (*Norwegian*).

    Norge er et deilig land.

    (nor-ge er et d'eye-lee land)

    Norway is a delightful country.

The **r** slightly rolled in *nor* and *er.* The *eye* in *d'eye* is like our English word *eye.* –**lig** is pronounced *lee.*

Jeg gikk på guttetur på landet.
(y-eye yikk poh gut-uh toor poh land-uh)
I went on a trip with the boys in the country.
The **j** in Norwegian is pronounced like the *y* in English *yes.*

Unnskyld. Kan du hjelpe meg?
(oon-shill. Can doo yelp-uh m'eye)
Excuse me. Can you help me?
Sk is pronounced like *sh* at the beginning of a syllable. **D** is silent after **l, d,** and **r. Hj** is pronounced **y.**

Det er deilig med et frisk bad!
(day er d'eye-lee med et frisk bad)
It is wonderful with a refreshing bath.
Note that with **–sk** at the end of a word the **k** is pronounced forcefully.

Many Norwegians know a great deal of English and most know some English. In a way, this makes it more fun to speak Norwegian because many foreign visitors to Norway simply rely on English. The response you will get from speaking in the language of the land will make you glad you took the initiative. The Norwegians appreciate every bold try **på norsk** (in Norwegian)!

Basic Grammar

Word Order (*Ordstilling*)

The word order in Norwegian is similar to the word order in English.

Subject-verb-object/complements is the normal word order of the declarative sentence in both Norwegian and English.

Vi drar til byen.
We are leaving for town.

Hun leser avisen.
She is reading the newspaper.

But there are differences as well.

In Norwegian, if the declarative sentence begins with an adjective or adverb or the object, the verb still comes second:

Ofte kommer Bjørn på besøk.
Bjørn comes for a visit often.

The negative **ikke** (not) takes third position in questions:

Han får ikke lov.
He does not have permission to.

Får han ikke lov?
Doesn't he have permission? Isn't it okay for him to do it?

The adverb follows the verb in the normal word order:

De spiser ofte aftens.
(Literally: *They eat often supper.*)

In a relative clause, the negative **ikke** (not) follows the subject:

De sa at de ikke kunne bli med.
(Literally: *They said that they not could be with.*) *They said that they could not come along.*

In conversation, one often hears the subject repeated at the end of the sentence, as with **du** (you) in the following case:

Du kommer jo med, du.
You are certainly coming along.

Plural Nouns (*Flertallsformer*)

The usual way to form the simple plural of **en** nouns is by adding **-er**:

> **hest** *horse*; **hester** *horses*

Et nouns of one syllable do not change:

> **et hus** *one house*; **flere hus** *several houses*

Both **en** and **et** nouns that end in an unstressed **-e** add only **-r** as the plural suffix:

> **gruppe** *group*; **grupper** *groups*

Both **en** and **et** nouns that end in a stressed **-e** add **-er** as the plural suffix:

> **kafé** *café*; **kaféer** *cafés*

In some nouns, the plural is formed by a change in vowel as well as by adding a plural suffix:

> **bok** *book*; **bøker** *books*
> **hånd** *hand*; **hender** *hands*
> **mor** *mother*; **mødre** *mothers*
> **tre** *tree*; **trær** *trees*

In some cases, only the vowel changes, as in English:

> **mann** *man*; **menn** *men*

The plural of both **en** and **et** nouns add the definite article suffix **-ne** or **-ene**:

> **ape** *monkey, ape*; **apene** *the monkeys, the apes*
> **hest** *horse*; **hestene** *the horses*

The Article (*Artikkelen*)

In the singular the indefinite article before an **en** noun is **en** and **et** before an **et** noun:

> **en venn** *a friend (male)*
> **et billett** *a ticket*

In the singular the definite article following the noun as a suffix is **-en** after an **en** noun and **-et** after an **et** noun (or only **n** and **t** if the noun ends in an unaccented **e**):

> **venninne** *friend (female)*; **venninnen** *the friend (female)*
> **slott** *palace, castle*; **slottet** *the palace, the castle*

There are exceptions:
øye *eye*; øyne *eyes*

The Norwegian definite article in the plural is -ene (or only -ne if the noun ends in an unaccented -e):
billett *ticket*; **billettene** *the tickets*
følelse *feeling*; **følelsene** *the feelings*

There are exceptions:
øye *eye*; øyne *eyes*

The Adjective (*Adjektivet*)

The Norwegian adjective agrees with the noun it modifies:
en god bok *a good book*
gode bøker *good books*
et gammelt hus *an old house*
de gamle hus *the old houses*
et snilt menneske *a kind person*
snille mennesker *kind people*

Exceptions: adjectives which end in -ig or -sk do not add –t after the definite article when the noun modified is an et noun.
Norge er et deilig land. *Norway is a wonderful country.*
Dette er et norsk bilde. *This is a Norwegian picture.*

Adjectives which end in a stressed vowel add the suffix -tt before et nouns:
et fritt hus *an unoccupied house*

Predicate adjectives follow the same rule:
Huset er fritt. *The house is unoccupied*

The Possessive Pronoun or Personal Adjective (*Det personlige pronomen*)

min, mitt *my*
din, Deres (formal) *your*
dine (before plural nouns) *your*
hans *his*
hennes *her*
dens, dets, sin, sitt *its*
vår; vårt *our*

before plural nouns:
  våre *our*
  deres, Deres *your*
  deres, sine *their*

The subjective personal pronoun singular:
  jeg *I*
  du, De (formal) *you*
  han *he*
  hun *she*
  den, det *it*

The subjective personal pronoun, case, plural:
  vi *we*
  dere, Dere (formal) *you*
  de *they*

The objective personal pronoun, singular:
  meg *me*
  deg, Dem (formal) *you*
  ham *him*
  henne *her*
  det *it*

The objective personal pronoun, plural:
  oss *us*
  dem, Dem *you*
  dem *them*

A note on du and De: The formal second-person personal pronoun **De** (*you*) has been largely replaced by **du**, which in former times was used only in informal conversation with family and friends. **De** may eventually suffer the fate of *Thou* in English, but it still heard occasionally today. All that said, I have found one gains instant respect if one uses the formal form with strangers and the elderly. It is a way of showing respect that I hope will not die out.

The Adverb (*Adverbet*)

Adverbs like **vel** (*indeed, fully*) or **enda** (*still, yet*) are not formed from adjectives. The many adverbs formed from adjectives are usually constructed by simply adding one of two suffixes: **-t** or **-vis**.

With the suffix **-t**: **god** (*good*) becomes **godt** (*well*).

With the suffix -**vis**: **naturlig** (*natural*) becomes **naturligvis** (*naturally*).

In some cases the same word is both adjective and adverb: **selvfølgelig** (adjective: *obvious*; adverb: *obviously*).

The Verb (*Verbumet*)

Like English, Norwegian has weak verbs and strong (that is, irregular) verbs.

The principal parts of the weak verb **å snakke** (*to talk*) are **snakke** (infinitive), **snakket** (past), **snakket** (past participle).

The principal parts of the two common strong verbs **å si** (*to say*) and **å gå** (*to go, to walk*) are **si** (infinitive), **sa** (*said*, past tense), **sagt** (*said*, past participle) and **gå** (infinitive), **gikk** (*went, walked*, past tense), **gått** (*gone, walked*, past participle).

In the active voice for both weak and strong verbs the tenses are formed as follows:
Present tense:
>**Jeg snakker** (*I talk, I am talking*)
>**Jeg sier** (*I say, I am saying*)

Past tense:
>**Jeg snakket** (*I talked, I was talking*)
>**Jeg sa** (*I said, I was saying*)

Present perfect:
>**Jeg har snakket** (*I have talked, I have been taking*)
>**Jeg har sagt** (*I have said, I have been saying*)

Past perfect:
>**Jeg hadde snakket** (*I had talked, I had been talking*)
>**Jeg hadde sagt** (*I had said, I had been saying*)

The present tense for both weak and strong verbs is formed by adding -**r** to the infinitive for first, second and third person, both singular and plural.

jeg snakker	**vi snakker**
I talk, I am talking	*we talk, we are talking*
du snakker	**dere snakker**
you talk, you are talking	*you talk, you are talking*
han/hun/det snakker	**de snakker**
he/she/it talks/is talking	*they talk, they are talking*

The past, present perfect and past perfect keep the same verb form for first, second and third person, both singular and plural.

The PAST TENSE is formed by simply using the second principal part of the verb.

jeg snakket	**vi snakket**
I talked, I was talking	*we talked, we were talking*
du snakket	**dere snakket**
you talked,	*you talked,*
you were talking	*you were talking*
han/hun/det snakket	**de snakket**
he/she/it talked,	*they talked,*
he/she/it was talking	*they were talking*

The PRESENT PERFECT TENSE is made by using the present tense of the helping verb **ha** (*have*) **"har"** before the third principal part of the verb.

jeg har snakket
I have talked, I have been talking

du har snakket
you have talked, you have been talking

han/hun/det har snakket
he/she/it has talked, he/she,it has been talking

vi har snakket
we have talked, we have been talking

dere har snakket
you have talked, you have been talking

de har snakket
they have talked, they have been talking

The PAST PERFECT TENSE is made by using the past tense of the helping verb **ha** (*have*) **"hadde"** before the third principal part of the verb.

jeg hadde snakket
I had talked, I had been talking

du hadde snakket
you had talked, you had been talking

han/hun/det hadde snakket
he/she/it had talked, he/she/it had been talking

vi hadde snakket
we had talked, we had been talking

dere hadde snakket
you had talked, you had been talking

de hadde snakket
they had talked, they had been talking

Other weak verbs add **–dde** and **–dd** instead of **–t** (or **–et** or **–te**): **bo** (*dwell*), **bodde** (dwelt), **bodd** (*dwelt*).

The FUTURE TENSE is expressed by using the helping verb **skal**:
Når skal hun dra hjem?
When will she leave for home?

Vil may be used if intent is implied:
Han vil følge deg til bilen.
He'll accompany you to the car.

Passive Voice

In Norwegian the passive voice is commonly formed in one of two ways for both strong and weak verbs:

1) with the auxiliary verb **bli** [*become*] (**ble** [*became*] past tense, **blitt** [*become*] past participle) plus the past participle of the verb.
   Examples:
   Middag blir laget på kjøkken.
   Dinner is being prepared in the kitchen.

   Middag ble laget etterpå.
   Dinner was prepared afterwards.

2) with the -**s** suffix added to the infinitive. The -**s** passive is usually used after modal auxiliaries.
   Examples:
   Den slags bil kan kjøres lettere.
   That kind of a car can be driven more easily.

   Må kastes.
   Must throw this out. [*This* is the understood subject of the sentence.]

Two final points about Norwegian verbs:
1) The verb **få** (*to get, receive; accomplish; shall*) is often used as a helping verb.
   Examples:
   Vi får se.
   We'll see.

   Vi får vite snart.
   We'll get to find out soon.

2) The present participle and gerund are not used as often in Norwegian as in English.
Example:
Denne pille kan brukkes for å rense drikkevann.
This pill can be used to purify drinking water.
In English we can also say, *This pill can be used for purifying drinking water.* In Norwegian the infinitive **å drikke** is the more common usage. The present participle is also used less often than in English. Notice the participle *drinking* is not used in the example **drikkevann** (*drinking water*).

A Note on Cognates, Look-alike Words, & False Friends
(or, an ekorn is not always an acorn)

As Germanic languages, the cousins Norwegian and English have many cognates, words of shared lineage. Some have the same meaning: **varm** (*warm*) and **kald** (*cold*), **stillhet** (*stillness*) and **stjerne** (*star*). Some look-alike words are simple loan words: restaurant = restaurant.

But beware the false cognate, that false friend who seems to mean the same thing in Norwegian as in English, but doesn't.
Example:
Glad (*glad, happy*) can mean just that, as in Bjørnson's famous novel **En Glad Gutt** (*A Happy Boy*). But the expression **glad i** (*happy in*) can carry a special meaning. **Jeg er glad i henne** looks like I am delighted with her. The phrase really suggests the stronger *I am very fond of her.*

Example:
Korresponderende can mean *corresponding*, but in an airport it can also mean *connecting*, as in *connecting flight* (**korresponderende fly**).

Example:
Aktuell doesn't mean *actual*; it means *up-to-date, current.*

Example:
Kontrollere can mean *to control*, but it is often used to mean *to check*, as in check your passport or check your

trikk (trolley) ticket. The sign for passport inspection is **PASSKONTROLL**. The uniformed **kontroll** may ask to see your ticket and check that you have had it stamped by the machine at the **trikk** stop.

Example:
Skattefri is pronounced almost the same as *scot-free*, as in, "*He got off scot-free,*" with no penalty. Actually **skattefri** means *tax-exempt.*

Example:
Salat can mean *salad,* but it can also mean simply *lettuce.*

Example:
Side can mean *side,* but it can also mean *page in a book.*

Example:
Dusj, which is pronounced *douche,* means *shower, bath.*

Examples of four-letter words:
Skitt is pronounced like the vulgar English word *shit,* but it simply means *dirt* or *trash.* **Fart** looks like a vulgar English word, but it simply means *speed;* **på farten** means *on the go;* **for full fart** means *at full speed.*

Example:
Ekorn in Norwegian, which surely looks like *acorn,* means *SQUIRREL!*

Norwegian-English Dictionary

A

abonnement *n.et* subscription
abonnere *v.* to subscribe
absolutte *adj.* absolute
absorbere *v.* to absorb
abstrakt *adj.* abstract
absurd *adj.* absurd
addere *v.* to add
adelig *adj.* noble
adgang *n.en* admission
adjø *n.et* goodbye
adlyde *v.* to obey
administrere *v.* to administer
adoptere *v.* to adopt
adresse *n.en* address
adressekalender *n.en*
    directory
adskillelse *n.en* separation
adskillig *adj.* considerable
affære *n.en* affair
afrikansk *adj.* African
aften *n.en* evening
aftens *n.en* supper
agent *n.en* agent
agere *v.* to act, plan
agn *n.et* bait
agurk *n.en* cucumber
akademi *n.et* academy
akevitt *n.en* schnapps
akkurat *adj.* accurate; *adv.*
    exactly
aksel *n.en* shoulder
aksent *n.en* accent
aksje *n.en* stock, share
aksjemegler *n.en* stockbroker
aksjon *n.en* action
akt *n.en* nude painting;
    attention
akte *v.* to respect; pay attention
    (*gi akt! = pay attention!*)
aktiv *adj.* active
aktivitet *n.en* activity
aktuell *adj.* current, up-to-date
akvarell *n.en* watercolors
alarm *n.en* alarm
albu *n.en* elbow

album *n.et* album
aldeles *adv.* quite, completely
alder *n.en* age
aldri *adv.* never
alene *adv.* alone
alfabet *n.et* alphabet
alkohol *n.en* alcohol
all, alt, alle *pron.* everybody;
    adj. all
allé *n.en* tree-lined avenue
aller først *adj.* first of all
aller sist *adj.* last of all
aller øverst *adj.* topmost
allianse *n.en* alliance
allikevel *adv.* still, yet, all
    the same
allmektig *adj.* almighty
allslags *adj.* all kinds of
alltid *adv.* always
almanakk *n.en* almanac
almen *adj.* common, public,
    general
almenheten *n.en* the public
alminneglig *adj.* common,
    universal
alt *pron.; adj.* everything
alternativ *adj.* alternative
altfor *adv.* too
alvorlig *adj.* serious
amatør *n.en* amateur
ambassade *n.en* embassy
ambassadør *n.en* ambassador
ambisjon *n.en* ambition
ambulanse *n.en* ambulance
Amerika *Pln.* America
amerikaner *n.en* American
    (*male*)
amerikanerinne *n.en*
    American (*female*)
analyse *n.en* analysis
analysere *v.* to analyze
ananas *n.en* pineapple
anatomi *n.en* anatomy
anbefale *v.* to recommend
and *n.en* duck

27

ane *v.* to suspect (*jeg anner ikke = I haven't a clue*)
anelse *n.en* suspicion, foreboding
anerkjenne *v.* to acknowledge
anerkjennelse *n.en* acknowledgement, recognition
anfall *n.et* attack, fit, seizure
anfalle *v.* to attack
angre *v.* to repent, to be sorry (*jeg angrer meg = I am sorry*)
angrep *n.et* attack
angripe *v.* to attack
angst *n.en* fear, dread, anxiety
angående *prep.* concerning, with regard to
animalsk *adj.* animal
ankel *n.en* ankle
anker *n.et* anchor
ankomst *n.en* arrival
ankre *v.* to anchor
anledning *n.en* occasion, opportunity
anlegg *n.et* construction; building under construction
anlegge *v.* to establish, start, adopt
anmelde *v.* to announce; review (*review a book*)
anmeldelse *n.en* announcement; review
annen *pron.; adj.* other; second
annerledes *adv.* otherwise
annonse *n.en* advertisement
anonym *adj.* anonymous
anordning *n.en* arrangement
anretning *n.en* serving; table setting
anretningsbord *n.et* buffet, serving table
ansett *adj.* esteemed
ansette *v.* to appoint; hire
ansettelse *n.en* appointment, employment; engagement; assessment

ansikt *n.et* face
ansjos *n.en* anchovy
anskaffe *v.* to procure, purchase
anskuelig *adj.* plain, intelligible
anskuelse *n.en* opinion, view
anstalt *n.en* preparation; institution, establishment
anstrengende *adj.* trying, fatiguing, burdensome
ansvar *n.et* responsibility
ansvarlig *adj.* responsible
ansøkning *n.en* application
anta *v.* to adopt; suppose, assume
antagelse *n.en* reception; adoption; assumption
antall *n.et* number
antenne *v.* to kindle, light
antennelig *adj.* combustible
antikk *n.en* antiquity; *adj.* antique
antikvar *n.en* antiquary
antikvariat *n.et* second-hand bookstore
antikvert *adj.* out-of-date
antologi *n.en* anthology
antrekk *n.et* dress, attire
antyde *v.* to hint
anvise *v.* to indicate, direct, show
anvisning *n.en* instruction
ape *n.en* ape, monkey
apekatt *n.en* monkey
apotek *n.et* apothecary, druggist's
apparat *n.et* apparatus
appelsin *n.en* orange
appetitt *n.en* appetite
april *n.* April
arbeid *n.et* work, employment, task
arbeide *v.* to work
arbeider *n.en* worker
arbeidsdag *n.en* working day
arbeidslønn *n.en* wages
arbeidsløs *adj.* unemployed
arbeidsom *adj.* industrious

arbeidstid *n.en* working hours
arbeidsværelse *n.et* study
    (*room*)
argelig *adj.* annoying
argument *n.et* argument
aristokrati *n.et* aristocracy
aritmetikk *n.en* arithmetic
ark *n.en* ark; *n.et* sheet of
    paper
arkitekt *n.en* architect
arkitektur *n.en* architecture
arkiv *n.et* archives
arkivar *n.en* archivist
Arktis *Pln.* the Arctic
arktisk *adj.* arctic
arm *n.en* arm; *adj.* poor
armbånd *n.et* bracelet
armhule *n.en* armpit
armod *n.en* poverty
arne *n.en* hearth
aromatisk *adj.* aromatic
arrangere *v.* to arrange
arrest *n.en* arrest
art *n.en* kind, nature; species
arte seg *v.* to develop, grow;
    behave
arterie *n.en* artery
artig *adj.* curious, amusing
artikkel *n.en* article
artilleri *n.et* artillery
artist *n.en* artist; performer
artium *n.en* junior college
    degree
arv *n.en* inheritance
arve *v.* inherit
arvegods *n.et* heirloom
arvelig *adj.* hereditary
arveløs *adj.* disinherited
arving *n.en* heir, heiress
asiatisk *adj.* Asiatic
asjett *n.en* dessert plate
askebeger *n.et* ashtray
Askeladd *n.* Ashboy (*male
    Cinderella of folktale*)
asparges *n.en* asparagus
aspirant *n.en* candidate
assimilere *v.* to assimilate
assistere *v.* to assist
assortiment *n.et* assortment

assosiasjon *n.en* association
assuranse *n.en* insurance
astma *n.en* asthma
asyl *n.et* asylum
at *conj.* that
ateisme *n.en* atheism
atelier *n.et* atelier, studio
atlantisk *adj.* Atlantic
Atlanteren *Pln.* the Atlantic
atlask *n.en* satin
atlet *n.en* athlete
atletisk *adj.* athletic
atmosfære *n.en* atmosphere
atom *n.et* atom
atomenergi *n.en* atomic
    energy
atomkraft *n.en* atomic power
atomreaktor *n.en* atomic
    reactor
atomvåpen *n.et* atomic
    weapon
atskille *v.* to separate; divide;
    distinguish between
atskillelse *n.en* separation
atskillig *adj.* considerable
atten *num.* eighteen
attentat *n.et* attack;
    assassination attempt
attestere *v.* to certify
attributt *n.et* attribute
audiens *n.en* audience
auditorium *n.et* auditorium
august *n.* August
auksjon *n.en* auction
australsk *adj.* Australian
autentisk *adj.* authentic
automat *n.en* automat
autorisere *v.* to authorize
av *prep.; adv.* of; from; off
avbetale *v.* to pay off
avbryte *v.* to break off,
    interrupt, stop
avdele *v.* to partition off
avdeling *n.en* branch,
    department
avdød *adj.* deceased
avertere *v.* to advertise
avertissement *n.et*
    advertisement

avfall *n.et* refuse, waste
avgang *n.en* departure
avgi *v.* to give, furnish, deliver
avgift *n.en* fee, royalty, tax
avgjøre *v.* to decide, settle
avgjørelse *n.en* decision
avgrund *n.en* abyss
avgud *n.en* idol
avgå *v.* to go, leave; start
avhandling *n.en* thesis, essay,
    dissertation
avhenge *v.* to depend on
avhengig *adj.* dependent
avhold *n.et* abstinence
avholdsmann *n.en* non-
    drinker (*of alcohol*)
avis *n.en* newspaper
avkjøle *v.* to cool, refrigerate
avløsning *n.en* relief
avreise *n.en* departure
avsende *v.* to send, dispatch
avsette *v.* to fire, remove from
    office, dethrone
avsetning *n.en* sale
avsettelse *n.en* firing,
    dismissal, removal
    from office
avsinn *n.et* madness
avskjed *n.en* departure,
    resignation
avskjære *v.* to cut off, interrupt
avskye *v.* to detest
avskyelig *adj.* detestable
avslutning *n.en* conclusion
avslutte *v.* to conclude
avsløre *v.* to unveil
avsnitt *n.et* section, period
avsperring *n.en* roadblock,
    barricade
avstand *n.en* distance
avta *v.* to decrease
avtale *n.en* agreement
avtale *v.* to agree

B

bad *n.et* bath; spa
bade *v.* to bathe
badebukse *n.en* swimming
    trunks

badedrakt *n.en* swimming suit
badehette *n.en* swimming cap;
    shower cap
badekar *n.et* bathtub
badekåpe *n.en* bathrobe
badested *n.et* seaside resort
badestrand *n.en* swimming
    beach
badstubad *n.et* steam bath
bag *n.en* shopping bag
bagasje *n.en* luggage, baggage
bagasjebrett *n.et* bicycle rack
bagasjehylle *n.en* baggage
    rack
bagasjerom *n.et* baggage
    compartment
bagatell *n.en* trifle, something
    of little significance
bak *n.en* behind, posterior;
    adj. behind
bake *v.* to bake
bakeri *n.et* bakery
bakfra *adv.* from behind
bakke *n.en* hill
bakover *adv.* backwards
baktale *v.* to slander
bakvendt *adj.* awkward;
    backwards
balanse *n.en* balance; scales
balansere *v.* to balance
balkong *n.en* balcony
ball *n.en* ball (*å spille ball = to*
    play ball)
ballett *n.en* ballet
ballong *n.en* balloon
banan *n.en* banana
band *n.et* musical band
bandasje *n.en* bandage
bane *n.en* course, track;
    traffic lane
bange *adj.* afraid
bank *n.en* bank
bankboks *n.en* bank box, safe-
    deposit box
banke *v.* to beat, knock
bankerott *n.en* bankruptcy;
    adj. bankrupt
banne *v.* to curse
banner *n.et* banner

barber *n.en* barber
barbere *v.* to shave
barbere seg *v.* to shave oneself
bare *adv.* only, just
bark *n.en* bark on a tree
barmhjertig *adj.* merciful
barmhjertighet *n.en* mercy
barn *n.et* child
barnaktig *adj.* childish
barndom *n.en* childhood
barndåp *n.en* baptism
barnebarn *n.et* grandchild
barnemat *n.en* baby food
barnepark *n.en* playground
barnepike *n.en* nursemaid
barnepleierske *n.en* nurse
    trained in child care
barnerik *adj.* rich in children,
    having many children
barnerim *n.et* nursery rhyme
barneseng *n.en* crib
barnetøy *n.et* children's
    clothing
barnevakt *n.en* babysitter
barnevogn *n.en* baby carriage
barneværelse *n.et* nursery
barnløs *adj.* childless
barnslig *adj.* childish
barometer *n.et* barometer
barsk *adj.* gruff; rough
    (*weather*)
be *v.* to beg, ask; invite; pray
bebo *v.* to inhabit, occupy
bedrage *v.* to deceive
bedre *v.* to better; *adj.* better
bedring *n.en* improvement,
    convalescence
bedrift *n.en* achievement;
    business
befale *v.* to command, order
befatning *n.en* dealing,
    involvement
befolkning *n.en* population
befrielse *n.en* liberation,
    deliverance
begavet *adj.* gifted
begeistre *v.* to inspire
begeistret *adj.* enthusiastic
begivenhet *n.en* event

begjær *n.et* lust
begravelse *n.en* burial, funeral
begynne *v.* to begin
begynnelse *n.en* beginning
behag *n.et* pleasure
behagelig *adj.* pleasant
behandle *v.* to handle, deal
    with
behandling *n.en* treatment
beherske *v.* to control
beholde *v.* to keep
behov *n.et* need, requirement
behove *v.* to need
bekjenne *v.* to confess
bekjennelse *n.en* confession
bekjent *adj.* acquainted;
    famous
bekjentskap *n.et* acquaintance
bekk *n.en* brook
beklage *v.* to regret, be sorry for
beklage seg *v.* to complain
bekvem *adj.* comfortable
bekymre seg *v.* to care about
bekymret *adj.* anxious,
    concerned
belastning *n.en* load, weight;
    debt
beliggende *adj.* situated,
    located
beliggenhet *n.en* site
belte *n.et* belt
belyse *v.* to light up
belysning *n.en* illumination
belønne *v.* to reward
belønning *n.en* reward
bemerke *v.* to notice
ben *n.et* bone, leg, foot
benekte *v.* to deny
benk *n.en* bench
bensin *n.en* petrol, gasoline
benytte *v.* to make use of;
    employ
benåde *v.* to pardon
berede *v.* to prepare
beregne *v.* to calculate
beregning *n.en* calculation
beretning *n.en* account
berette *v.* to relate
berg *n.et* mountain

berge *v.* to save
berike *v.* to enrich
berolige *v.* to soothe, quiet
beruset *adj.* intoxicated
berømme *v.* to praise
berømt *adj.* famous
berøre *v.* to touch
berørende *adj.* moving,
  touching
beskatte *v.* to tax
beskjeden *adj.* modest
beskrive *v.* to describe
beskrivelse *n.en* description
beskytte *v.* to protect
beskyttelse *n.en* protection
bestemme *v.* to decide upon
bestemt *adj.* definite, fixed
bestyrelse *n.en* management,
  board of directors
besvime *v.* to faint
besynderlig *adj.* strange
besørge *v.* to take care of,
  handle, arrange
betenke seg *v.* to reflect upon
betjene *v.* to serve
betjene seg *v.* to serve oneself
betone *v.* to stress, emphasize
bety *v.* to mean, signify
betydning *n.en* meaning;
  importance
beundre *v.* to admire
beundring *n.en* admiration
bevegelse *n.en* movement
bevis *n.et* proof
bevise *v.* to prove
bevissthet *n.en* consciousness
bevisstløs *adj.* unconscious
bevæpne *v.* to arm
beære *v.* to honor
bi *n.en* bee
biholde *v.* to keep
Bibel *n.en* Bible
bibliotek *n.et* library
bidrag *n.et* contribution
bifag *n.et* secondary subject
bifall *n.et* applause; approval
bikkje *n.en* dog
bil *n.en* automobile
bilde *n.et* picture

bile *v.* to motor, drive
bilag *n.et* enclosure; voucher
bilist *n.en* motorist
billede *n.et* picture
billedhugger *n.en* sculptor
billett *n.en* ticket; note
billig *adj.* cheap; reasonable,
  fair
bind *n.et* volume of a book;
  bandage; sanitary napkin
biograf *n.en* biographer
biografi *n.en* biography
bit *n.en* bit, morsel
bitteliten *adj.* tiny
bitter *adj.* bitter
bjelle *n.en* bell
bjørk *n.en* birch
bjørn *n.en* bear
blad *n.et* sheet, page; blade;
  magazine
bråk *n.et* noise
bransje *n.en* department,
  branch; line of business
bratt *adj.* steep
bre *n.en* glacier
bred *adj.* broad
bredd *n.en* bank, shore
bredde *n.en* breadth
brekke *v.* to break
bremse *n.en* brake; *v.* to brake
brenne *v.* to burn
brennende *adj.* hot; ardent
brensel *n.et* fuel
brett *n.et* tray; rack
brev *n.et* letter (*post*)
brevkort *n.et* postcard
brevpapir *n.et* stationery
briller *n.pl.* spectacles, glasses
bringe *v.* to bring, take
britisk *adj.* British
broderi *n.et* embroidery
bror *n.en* brother
brosje *n.en* brooch
brosjyre *n.en* pamphlet
bru *n.en* bridge
brud *n.en* bride
brudd *n.et* rupture, fracture
brudepar *n.et* bridal couple
brudepike *n.en* bridesmaid

brudgom *n.en* bridegroom
bruk *n.en* use; custom
brukbar *adj.* serviceable
bud *n.et* command; commandment; messenger
budsjett *n.et* budget
bue *n.en* bow, arc
buffet *n.en* buffet
bukett *n.en* bouquet
bukse *n.en* trousers
bunn *n.en* bottom, ground
burde *v.* ought to
buskap *n.en* livestock
buss *n.en* bus
butikk *n.en* shop
by *n.en* town, city
bydel *n.en* district
bygge *v.* to build
bygning *n.en* construction; house
byrd *n.en* birth
byrde *n.en* burden
bytte *v.* to exchange
bær *n.et* berry
bære *v.* to carry
bølge *n.en* wave
bønn *n.en* prayer
bønne *n.en* bean
bør *v.* ought to
børs *n.en* stock exchange
børste *n.en* brush
bøtte *n.en* bucket
bøy *n.en* bend
bøye *n.en* buoy
bøye seg *v.* yield
bøyning *n.en* bend, curve
både ... og *conj.* both ... and
bål *n.et* bonfire
bånd *n.et* band, ribbon
båt *n.en* boat

C

charmant *adj.* charming
cicerone *n.en* guide
cirka *adv.* about

D

da *adv.* then; *conj.* when
dag *n.en* day

dagbok *n.en* diary
daggry *n.et* dawn
daglig *adj.* daily; everyday
dal *n.en* valley
dam *n.en* pool; dam
dame *n.en* lady
dameskredder *n.en* dressmaker
damp *n.en* steam
dampbåt *n.en* steamer
Danmark *Pln.* Denmark
danne *v.* to shape
dannelse *n.en* culture, education
dannet *adj.* well-bred, educated
dans *n.en* dance
danse *v.* to dance
dansk *adj.* Danish
danske *n.en* Dane
datere *v.* to date
datter *n.en* daughter
debatt *n.en* debate
debut *n.en* debut
defekt *n.en* defect
defensiv *adj.* defensive
definere *v.* to define
deig *n.en* dough
deilig *adj.* lovely, delicious
dekade *n.en* decade
dekk *n.et* deck, cover
dekke *v.* to cover
dekketøy *n.et* table linen
deklarere *v.* to declare (*at customs*)
deklinere *v.* to decline
dekorere *v.* to decorate
del *n.en* part, share
dele *v.* to divide
dels *adv.* partly
delvis *adv.* partly
demonstrasjon *n.en* demonstration
dempe *v.* to subdue, dampen, lessen
den *pron.* he, she, it; that; *art.* the
dengang *adv.* then; *conj.* when
denne *pron.* this

departement *n.et* department
deponere *v.* to deposit
depresjon *n.en* depression
deprimert *adj.* depressed
der *pron.* who, which; *adv.* there
derfor *adv.* therefore
desember *n.* December
desertere *v.* to desert
desorientert *adj.* disoriented
dessert *n.en* dessert
dessuten *adv.* besides
dessverre *adv.* unfortunately
destillere *v.* to distill
det *pron.* it; *art.* the
detalj *n.en* detail
detektiv *n.en* detective
detektor *n.en* detector
determinert *adj.* determined
detonasjon *n.en* detonation
dette *pron.* this
diakon *n.en* deacon; male
    nurse
diakonisse *n.en* nursing sister
dialekt *n.en* dialect
dialog *n.en* dialogue
diamant *n.en* diamond
diaré *n.en* diarrhea
diet *n.en* diet
differere *v.* to differ
differanse *n.en* difference
dikt *n.et* poem, poetry
dikter *n.en* poet
diktning *n.en* poetry; literature
dikterisk *adj.* poetic
dilettant *n.en* amateur
dinere *v.* to dine
diplom *n.et* diploma
diplomati *n.et* diplomacy
dirigent *n.en* director (*musical*)
dirigere *v.* to direct
disiplin *n.en* discipline
diskonto *n.en* discount;
    discount rate
diskusjon *n.en* discussion
disputen *v.* to argue
dissens *n.en* dissent
distanse *n.en* distance
distingvert *adj.* distinguished
distré *adj.* absent-minded

distrikt *n.et* district
dit *adv.* there
dobbelt *adj.* two-fold
dogmatisk *adj.* dogmatic
dokument *n.en* document
dokumentere *v.* to verify
dom *n.en* cathedral; judgment,
    sentence
dominere *v.* to dominate
domkirke *n.en* cathedral
domstol *n.en* court of law
dosent *n.en* lecturer
doven *adj.* lazy
dra *v.* to pull; leave; attract
drag *n.et* pull, tug; breath;
    puff; haul
drakt *n.en* suit (*of clothes*)
dram *n.en* shot (*of aquavit*)
drama *n.et* drama
dramatiker *n.en* dramatist
drap *n.et* murder
dreie *v.* to turn, rotate
drepe *v.* to kill
drift *n.en* management;
    enterprise
driftende *adj.* energetic
driftig *adj.* enterprising
drikk *n.en* drink, beverage
drikke *v.* to drink
drikkepenger *n.pl.* tip, gratuity
dristig *adj.* daring
drittvær *n.et* foul weather
drive *v.* to drive, operate; as a
    helping verb, to be
    engaged in doing
    something
dronning *n.en* queen
drosje *n.en* taxi
drue *n.en* grape
drukne *v.* to drown
drypp *n.et* drop
dryppe *v.* to drip
drøm *n.en* dream
drømme *v.* to dream
dråpe *n.en* drop
due *n.en* pigeon
duft *n.en* fragrance
dufte *v.* to smell
dug *v.* to be fit, good

duk *n.en* tablecloth; cloth; canvas
dukke *v.* to dive
dum *adj.* foolish
dumhet *n.en* stupidity
dundre *v.* to thunder
dunkel *adj.* dim
dyd *n.en* virtue
dykke *v.* to dive
dyktig *adj.* clever, capable
dyne *n.en* down-filled duvet, comforter
dyp *adj.* deep
dyr *n.et* animal; *adj.* dear, expensive
dyrke *v.* cultivate
dyrkningsland *n.et* cultivated land; arable land
dyrlege *n.en* veterinarian
dyster *adj.* gloomy
dø *v.* to die
død *n.en* death; *adj.* dead
dødelig *adj.* deadly
døgn *n.et* twenty-four hours
dømme *v.* to judge; condemn
døpe *v.* to baptize
dør *n.en* door
døv *adj.* deaf
dåd *n.en* deed, exploit
dåp *n.en* baptism
dårlig *adj.* worthless

E

edderkopp *n.en* spider
eddik *n.en* vinegar
edel *adj.* noble
effekt *n.en* sensation
effektiv *adj.* effective
egen *adj.* own
egg *n.en* egg
eggerøre *n.en* scrambled eggs
eie *v.* to own, possess
eiendom *n.en* property, estate
eik *n.en* oak
ekorn *n.en* squirrel
eksakt *adj.* exact
eksamen *n.en* examination
eksellent *adj.* excellent
eksempel *n.et* example

eksepsjonell *adj.* exceptional
eksistere *v.* to exist
ekskursjon *n.en* excursion
ekspedere *v.* to dispatch, send; kill (*slang*); take care of, dispose of
ekspert *n.en* expert
eksplodere *v.* explode
eksport *n.en* export
eksportere *v.* to export
ekspress *n.en* express; express train
ekstase *n.en* ecstasy
ekstra *adj.* extra
ekstra arbeid *n.et* overtime work
ekstrakt *n.en* extract; summary
ekstratog *n.et* unscheduled train
ekte *adj.* genuine
ektefolk *n.et* married couple
ektepar *n.et* married couple
ekteskap *n.et* marriage
elastisk *adj.* elastic
eldre *adj.* older, elderly
elefant *n.en* elephant
eletriker *n.en* electrician
element *n.et* element
elementær *adj.* elementary
elendig *adj.* miserable
elendighet *n.en* misery
elev *n.en* pupil
elevator *n.en* elevator
elg *n.en* moose
elite *n.en* elite
eller *conj.* or
ellers *adv.* otherwise
elleve *num.* eleven
elske *v.* to love
elsker *n.en* lover (*male*)
elskerinne *n.en* sweetheart; mistress
elskov *n.en* love
elv *n.en* stream, river
emalje *n.en* enamel
emblem *n.et* emblem
emigrant *n.en* emigrant
emne *n.et* subject, topic

en *art.* a, an; *num.* one
enda *adv.* still (*enda bedre* = still better)
ende *n.en* end
ende *v.* to end
endelig *adv.* finally
endre *v.* to alter
energi *n.en* energy
enestående *adj.* unique, exceptional
eng *n.en* meadow
engang *adv.* once
engasjere *v.* to engage
engel *n.en* angel
engelsk *adj.* English
engelskmann *n.en* Englishman
England *Pln.* England
engstelig *adj.* anxious
enhet *n.en* unity
enig *adj.* agreed
enighet *n.en* agreement
enke *n.en* widow
enkel *adj.* plain, simple
enkelt *adj.* single
enkemann *n.en* widower
enquete *n.en* newspaper survey
ensidig *adj.* partial, one-sided
enslig *adj.* solitary
ensom *adj.* lonely
enstemmig *adj.* unanimous
enten ... eller *conj.* either ... or
entré *n.en* entry hall
entusiastisk *adj.* enthusiastic
epidemi *n.en* epidemic
episode *n.en* episode
epistel *n.en* epistle
eple *n.et* apple
eplekake *n.en* apple-cake
eremitt *n.en* hermit
erfaring *n.en* experience
ergerlig *adj.* irritated
erindre *v.* to remember
erindring *n.en* remembrance
erkjenne *v.* to recognize
erkjennelse *n.en* acknowledgement; recognition

erme *n.et* sleeve
ernære *v.* to nourish
erobre *v.* to conquer
erobrer *n.en* conqueror
erobring *n.en* conquest
erotisk *adj.* erotic
erstatning *n.en* replacement; compensation
ert *n.en* pea
erte *v.* to tease
eske *n.en* box, carton
espalier *n.et* trellis
estetisk *adj.* esthetic
establissement *n.et* establishment
et *art.* a, an; *num.* one
etappe *n.en* stage, stretch; military post
etasje *n.en* story, floor (*første etasje* = ground floor)
etikett *n.en* label
etisk *adj.* ethical
etter *prep.* after
etterfølger *n.en* successor
etterlate *v.* to leave behind
etterlyse *v.* to advertise for
etternavn *n.et* surname
etterpå *adv.* afterwards
etterskrift *n.en* postscript
etterslekt *n.en* posterity
ettersøke *v.* to search for
ettertanke *n.en* reflection, consideration
Europa *Pln.* Europe
europeisk *adj.* European
evangelist *n.en* evangelist
evangelium *n.et* gospel
eventyr *n.et* fairytale
evig *adj.* eternal
evighet *n.en* eternity
evne *n.en* power; talent
evnerik *adj.* gifted

F

fabrikk *n.en* factory
fadder *n.en* godparent
fag *n.et* school subject; profession

fagkunnskap *n.en* knowledge of a field or skill
fagmann *n.en* expert
faktisk *adj.* factual; real; *adv.* in fact
fakultet *n.et* faculty
fall *n.et* fall; case, instance
fallskjerm *n.en* parachute
falme *v.* to fade
falsk *adj.* false
familie *n.en* family
familienavn *n.et* family name
fane *n.en* banner
fang *n.et* lap
fange *n.en* prisoner; *v.* to capture
fantasere *v.* to fantasize
fantasi *n.en* fancy, imagination
fantastisk *adj.* fantastic
far *n.en* father
farbror *n.en* uncle, father's brother
fare *n.en* danger; *v.* to travel
farfar *n.en* grandfather, father's father
farge *n.en* color; *v.* to color
farlig *adj.* dangerous
farmor *n.en* grandmother, father's mother
fart *n.en* speed
fartøy *n.et* boat, vessel
farve *n.en* color; *v.* to color
farvel *n.et* farewell
fasade *n.en* façade; surface
fasan *n.en* pheasant
fascinere *v.* to fascinate
fase *n.en* phase
fast *adj.* firm, steady
fastboende *adj.* resident
faste *v.* to fast
fastland *n.et* mainland
fat *n.et* dish, cask
fattig *adj.* poor
fattigdom *n.en* poverty
fatøl *n.et* draft beer
favn *n.en* embrace; fathom
favne *v.* to embrace
fe *n.en* fairy; *n.et* cattle
feber *n.en* fever

februar *n.* February
febrilsk *adj.* agitated
fedme *n.en* obesity
fedreland *n.et* fatherland
feie *v.* to sweep
feiekost *n.en* broom
feig *adj.* cowardly
feighet *n.en* cowardice
feil *n.en* error; defect
feile *v.* to err
feilaktig *adj.* erroneous
feiltagelse *n.en* mistake
feire *v.* to celebrate
feiret *adj.* celebrated
fell *n.en* pelt, fur rug
felles *adj.* collective, common
fellesferie *n.en* general holiday
felt *n.et* field; province; tennis court
feltrop *n.et* password
feltseng *n.en* folding camp bed
feltstol *n.en* camp stool
fem *num.* five
femten *num.* fifteen
femti *num.* fifty
fengsel *n.et* prison
fenomen *n.et* phenomenon
fenomal *adj.* phenomenal
ferd *n.en* expedition
ferdig *adj.* ready; completed
ferie *n.en* vacation; holiday
ferje *n.en* ferry
fersk *adj.* fresh
fersken *n.en* peach
fest *n.en* festival, celebration
feste *v.* to attach
festlig *adj.* festive, jolly; ceremonious
festning *n.en* fortress
festsal *n.en* auditorium
fet *adj.* fat
fett *n.et* grease, fat
fetter *n.en* cousin (*male*)
fiasko *n.en* failure
fiber *n.en* fiber
fiende *n.en* enemy
fiendskap *n.et* enmity
figur *n.en* figure

fiken *n.en* fig
fiksjon *n.en* fiction
film *n.en* film
fin *adj.* excellent; delicate; genteel
finale *n.en* finish
finansiell *adj.* financial
finger *n.en* finger
fingernem *adj.* dexterous
finne *v.* to find
finnes *v.* to exist, be found
finsk *adj.* Finnish
fire *num.* four
firkantet *adj.* square
firma *n.et* firm
fisk *n.en* fish
fiske *v.* to fish
fiskeboller *n.pl.* fishballs
fiskebåt *n.en* fishing boat
fiskefangst *n.en* catch of fish
fiskehandler *n.en* fishmonger
fiskehermetikk *n.en* canned fish
fiskekaker *n.pl.* fishcakes
fiskekrok *n.en* fish hook
fisker *n.en* fisherman
fiskeri *n.et* fishery
fiskesnøre *n.et* fishing line
fiskestang *n.en* fishing pole
fiskesuppe *n.en* fish soup
fisketur *n.en* fishing trip
fiskevann *n.et* good lake for fishing
fiskevær *n.et* good weather for fishing
fjell *n.et* mountain
fjellgård *n.en* mountain farm
fjellkjede *n.en* mountain range
fjellklatrer *n.en* mountain climber
fjellklatring *n.en* mountain climbing
fjellras *n.et* landslide
fjellrygg *n.en* mountain ridge
fjellrype *n.en* ptarmigan
fjellstue *n.en* mountain hostel
fjellvann *n.et* mountain lake
fjerde *num.* fourth
fjern *adj.*; *adv.* far, distant

fjerne *v.* to remove
fjernere *adj.*; *adv.* farther
fjord *n.en* fiord, firth
fjorten *num.* fourteen
flagg *n.et* flag
flagge *v.* to display the flag
flaggermus *n.en* bat (*animal*)
flamme *n.en* flame; *v.* flame
flane *n.en* flirt
flaske *n.en* bottle
flau *adj.* flat, stale; embarrassed
flekk *n.en* spot, speck
flere *adj.* more, several
flerhet *n.en* plurality; plural (*grammar*)
flertall *n.et* majority
flesk *n.et* pork
flest *adj.* most
flestepart *n.en* majority
fletning *n.en* braid
flimre *v.* to glimmer
flink *adj.* smart, clever
flittig *adj.* industrious
flod *n.en* high tide; torrent
flott *n.et* float; *adj.* stylish, extravagant, superb
flue *n.en* housefly
flukt *n.en* escape
fly *n.et* airplane; *v.* to fly
flykte *v.* to flee
flyndre *n.en* sole, flounder (*fish*)
flytende *adj.* liquid; fluent
flytte *v.* to move one's home or job
flørte *v.* to flirt
fløte *n.en* cream; *v.* to float
fløyte *n.en* flute; *v.* to whistle
flåte *n.en* raft; fleet; navy; *v.* to float
folk *n.et* nation, people
folkelig *adj.* popular
folkerike *adj.* populous
folkeskol *n.en* elementary school
folkevandring *n.en* migration
for *adv.* too; *prep.* for, to; *conj.* because

forakt *n.en* contempt
forakte *v.* to despise
foran *prep.* in front of
foranderlig *adj.* changeable
forandre *v.* to change
forandring *n.en* change
forargelig *adj.* shocking, disgusting
forat *conj.* in order to
forbanne *v.* to curse
forbannelse *n.en* curse
forbarme seg *v.* to have pity
forbauset *v.* to be astonished
forbedre *v.* to improve
forberede *v.* to prepare
forberedelse *n.en* preparation
forbi *adv.* past, over
forbindelse *n.en* connection
forbruk *n.et* consumption
forbruker *n.en* consumer
forbrytelse *n.en* crime
forbryter *n.en* criminal
forbud *n.et* prohibition
forby *v.* to forbid
fordel *n.en* advantage
fordelaktig *adj.* advantageous
forderve *v.* to spoil; corrupt
fordervelig *adj.* destructive, pernicious
fordervet *adj.* corrupted
fordi *conj.* because
fordom *n.en* prejudice
fordra *v.* to endure
fordømme *v.* to condemn
forkjølelse *n.en* a cold
forkjølet *adj.* to have a cold
forklare *v.* to explain
forklaring *n.en* explanation
forkle *n.et* apron
forlag *n.et* publisher
forlagsrett *n.en* copyright
forlange *v.* to demand
forlate *v.* to desert, leave; pardon
forlatelse *n.en* pardon
forleden *adv.* recently, the other day
forlegen *adj.* embarrassed
forlenge *v.* to prolong

forlengst *adv.* long ago
forlovet *adj.* engaged to be married
form *n.en* form
formiddag *n.en* morning
formue *n.en* fortune; assets
fornavn *n.et* given name
fornekte *v.* to deny
fornuftig *adj.* reasonable
fornøyd *adj.* satisfied, content
fornøyelse *n.en* pleasure
    (*God fornøyelse! = Have a good time!*)
forord *n.et* preface
forresten *adv.* moreover
forretning *n.en* business
forretningsforbindelse *n.en* business connection
forrige *adj.* previous
forrykt *adj.* crazy
forræder *n.en* traitor
forræderi *n.et* treason
forsalg *n.et* advance sale
forsamle *v.* to assemble
forsikre *v.* to assure
forsikring *n.en* insurance; assurance
forsiktig *adj.* careful
forsinke *v.* to delay
forsinkelse *n.en* delay
forske *v.* to investigate
forsker *n.en* researcher
forskjell *n.en* difference
forskjellig *adj.* different; various
forskning *n.en* research
forslag *n.et* proposal
forsone *v.* to reconcile
forsoning *n.en* reconciliation
forsove *v.* to oversleep
forspill *n.et* prelude
forstand *n.en* intellect
forsterke *v.* to strengthen
forstyrre *v.* to disturb
forstørrelse *n.en* enlargement
forsvar *n.et* defense
forsvare *v.* to defend
forsvinne *v.* to disappear
forsøk *n.et* attempt

forsøke *v.* to attempt
fort *adj.* fast
fortelle *v.* to tell, relate
fortelling *n.en* story, tale
fortid *n.en* past
fortjene *v.* to deserve
fortolke *v.* to interpret
fortrefflig *adj.* excellent
forsette *v.* to continue
fortsettelse *n.en* continuation
fortvilelse *n.en* despair,
     desperation
forundring *n.en* wonder
foruten *adv.* besides
forutsetning *n.en* assumption;
     condition
forutsette *v.* to assume
forventning *n.en* expectation
forvirring *n.en* confusion
forøvrig *adv.* besides
foss *n.en* waterfall
fot *n.en* foot
fotograf *n.en* photographer
fotografere *v.* to photograph
fotografiapparat, fotoapparat
     n.et camera
fra *prep.* from
frakk *n.en* coat
frakt *n.en* freight
fr. *abbrev.* Mrs. or Miss
Frankrike *Pln.* France
fransk *adj.* French
fraskilt *adj.* divorced
fred *n.en* peace
fredag *n.* Friday
fredlig *adj.* peaceful
frekk *adj.* impudent, fresh
frelse *n.en* rescue; salvation;
     v. to rescue
frem *adv.* forth
fremdeles *adv.* still
fremmed *adj.* foreign; strange
fremragende *adj.* eminent
fremskritt *n.et* progress
fremstilling *n.en*
     representation, portrayal
fremtid *n.en* future
fremvise *v.* display, exhibit
fri *adj.* free; unoccupied

fridag *n.en* holiday
frimerke *n.et* postage stamp
frisinn *n.et* broadmindedness;
     liberal views
frisk *adj.* new, fresh; healthy
fristelse *n.en* temptation
frisør *n.en* barber, hairdresser
fritid *n.en* leisure time
fritt *adj.* gratis, for free
frivillig *adj.* voluntary
frokost *n.en* breakfast
from *adj.* pious, devout
frosk *n.en* frog
frossen *adj.* frozen
fru *n.* Mrs. (*abbrev. fr.*)
frukt *n.en* fruit
fruktbar *adj.* fertile
frukthave *n.en* orchard
fryd *n.en* delight
frykt *n.en* fear
fryktelig *adj.* dreadful
fryse *v.* to freeze
frøken *n.* Miss (*abbrev. fr.*)
fugl *n.en* bird
fuktig *adj.* humid
full *adj.* full; drunk
fullføre *v.* carry out
fullstendig *adj.* complete
fundere *v.* to found, base
funke *n.en* spark
funksjon *n.en* function
funn *n.et* discovery
furu *n.en* pine
fy! *interj.* phooey!
fylke *n.et* county
fylle *v.* to fill; complete
fyr *n.en* old chap; fire;
     lighthouse
fyrsten *n.en* prince
fyrstinne *n.en* princess
fyrstikke *n.en* match, light
fyrtårn *n.et* lighthouse
fyrverkeri *n.et* fireworks
fysikk *n.en* physics
fysisk *adj.* physical
føde *v.* give birth
fødested *n.et* birthplace
fødselsdag *n.en* birthday
født *adj.* born

føderasjon *n.en* federation
føle *v.* to feel
følelse *n.en* emotion
følge *n.en* consequence; *v.* to follow; accompany
følsom *adj.* sensitive
før *adv.*; *prep.* before
føre *v.* to guide; *adv.* before
fører *n.en* guide; chief, leader
først *adj.*; *adv.* first
førti *num.* forty
få *v.* to get, receive; *adj.* few

G

gaffel *n.en* fork (*utensil*)
gagn *n.et* benefit
gal *adj.* insane; frantic; incorrect
galant *adj.* polite
galla *n.en* evening dress
galladrakt *n.en* formal attire
galleri *n.et* gallery
gammel *adj.* old
gammeldags *adj.* old-fashioned
gang *n.en* walk, passage; time (*en gang = one time*)
ganske *adv.* quite, entirely
garasje *n.en* garage
garn *n.et* yarn
gasje *n.en* salary
gate *n.en* street
gave *n.en* gift
gebrokken *adj.* broken
geist *n.en* spirit
geit *n.en* goat
geitost *n.en* goat cheese
general *n.en* general
generell *adj.* general
genser *n.en* sweater
geografi *n.en* geography
gevær *n.et* rifle
geværkule *n.en* rifle bullet
gi *v.* to give
gift *n.en* poison; *adj.* married
gifte *v.* to marry
giftig *adj.* poisonous
gips *n.en* plaster
gissel *n.en* hostage

giver *n.en* giver, donor
gjemme *v.* to keep, save
gjenganger *n.en* ghost
gjenkomst *n.en* reappearance, return
gjennon *prep.* through
gjennomgang *n.en* thoroughfare, passage
gjennomsnittlig *adj.* average
gjennomtrekk *n.en* draft
gjenstand *n.en* object
gjerde *n.et* fence
gerne *adv.* gladly
gjespe *v.* to yawn
gjest *n.en* guest
gjestfri *adj.* hospitable
gjette *v.* to guess
gjøre *v.* to do, make
glad *adj.* happy
glane *v.* to stare
glass *n.et* glass
glatt *adj.* smooth; slippery
glede *n.en* joy
glede seg *v.* to be happy
gledelig *adj.* glad, happy
glemme *v.* to forget
glemsom *adj.* forgetful
glossar *n.et* glossary
gni *v.* to rub
god *adj.* good
godhet *n.en* goodness
godhjertet *adj.* kindhearted
gods *n.et* personal property
godta *v.* to accept
godt *adv.* well
godvillig *adj.* willing, voluntary
golf *n.en* golf
golfbane *n.en* golf course
golfkølle *n.en* golf club
grad *n.en* degree
grammatikk *n.en* grammar
grammatisk *adj.* grammatical
gran *n.en* spruce
grann *n.et* particle; trifle
granske *v.* to inquire
gransker *n.en* researcher; scientist
granskning *n.en* research
gras *n.et* grass

grasplen *n.en* lawn
gratulasjon *n.en*
    congratulation
gratulere *v.* to congratulate
grave *v.* to dig
gravere *v.* to engrave
gravsten *n.en* tombstone
gravskrift *n.en* epitaph
gravested *n.et* cemetery plot
grei *adj.* easy; straightforward
grein *n.en* branch; division
Grekenland *Pln.* Greece
greker *n.en* Greek
grense *n.en* boundary
gresk *adj.* Greek
gressplen *n.en* lawn
gripe *v.* to grasp
gris *n.en* pig
gro *v.* to grow
grov *adj.* coarse
grunn *n.en* ground; reason
grunnlag *n.et* foundation
gruppe *n.en* group
grusom *adj.* cruel; terrible
gryteklut *n.et* pot holder
gry *n.et* dawn
grønn *adj.* green
grønsaker *n.pl.* vegetables
grøt *n.en* porridge
grå *adj.* grey
gråte *v.* to weep
gud, Gud *n.en* god, God
gudbarn *n.et* godchild
guddatter *n.en* goddaughter
guddom *n.en* diety, divinity
gudfar *n.en* godfather
gudinne *n.en* goddess
gudmor *n.en* godmother
gudson *n.en* godson
gudstjeneste *n.en* divine
    service
gul *adj.* yellow
gull *n.et* gold
gullsmed *n.en* jeweler
gulrot *n.en* carrot
gult *n.et* yellow
gulv *n.et* floor
gulvteppe *n.et* carpet
gummi *n.en* rubber

gutt *n.en* boy
gyldig *adj.* valid
gyllen *adj.* golden; gilded
gymnasium *n.et* high school,
    junior college
gå *v.* to go; walk
gård *n.en* farmstead; courtyard
gås *n.en* goose
gåte *n.en* puzzle
gåtefull *adj.* enigmatic

H

ha *v.* to have
hai *n.en* shark
hake *n.en* chin; hook; *v.* to hook
hals *n.en* neck
halsbånd *n.et* necklace
halstørkle *n.et* scarf
halt *adj.* lame
halv *adj.* half
halvdel *n.en* half
hammer *n.en* hammer
handel *n.en* commerce
handle *v.* to act; do business
    with, shop
hanske *n.en* glove
hardangerfele *n.en* Hardanger
    fiddle
hare *n.en* hare
hasard *n.en* gambling; hazard
hast *n.en* haste
hastig *adj.* hasty
hat *n.et* hatred
hate *v.* to hate
haug *n.en* hill; heap
hauk *n.en* hawk
hav *n.et* ocean
havbukt *n.en* bay
have *n.en* garden
havfrue *n.en* mermaid
havn *n.en* harbor
havregraut *n.en* oatmeal
    porridge
hedensk *adj.* pagan
hefte *n.et* number, issue of a
    magazine; volume in a set
    of books
heis *n.en* elevator
heks *n.en* witch

hektisk *adj.* hectic
hel *adj.* whole
helbred *n.en* health
heldig *adj.* lucky
heldigvis *adv.* fortunately
hel *adj.* whole
helg *n.en* holiday; weekend
hell *n.et* success
helle *n.en* flagstone
heller *adv.* rather
hellig *adj.* holy
helse *n.en* health
helst *adv.* preferably
helt *n.en* hero
helvete *n.et* hell
hemmelig *adj.* secret
hemmelighet *n.en* secret
hen *adv.* away
hende *v.* to happen
hendelse *n.en* incident
henføre *v.* to refer
henge *v.* to hang
henrette *v.* to execute, put
   to death
henrivende *adj.* charming
henrykt *adj.* delight
hente *v.* to fetch
hentyde *v.* to allude
henvise *v.* to refer
her *adv.* here
herberge *n.et* inn; shelter
herje *v.* to ravage
herkomst *n.en* ancestry
herlig *adj.* glorious
herme *v.* to repeat, copy
hermetikk *n.en* canned goods
herr Mr. (*abbrev.* **hr.**)
herre *n.en* lord, master
herskapelig *adj.* aristocratic
hest *n.en* horse
het *adj.* hot
hete *v.* to be named
hevde *v.* to assert
heve *v.* to raise; cash (*a check*)
hevn *n.en* revenge
hilse *v.* to greet
hilsen *n.en* greetings, regards
himmel *n.en* sky; heaven
hindring *n.en* obstacle

hingst *n.en* stallion
hissig *adj.* inflamed, angry
historie *n.en* history; story
hit *adv.* here, hither
hitte på *v.* to think of
hive *v.* to heave
hjelp *n.en* help
hjelpe *v.* to help
hjem *n.et* home
hjemkomst *n.en* homecoming
hjemlig *adj.* domestic; cozy
hjemover *adv.* homeward
hjerne *n.en* brain
hjertelig *adj.* cordial
hjerteslag *n.et* heart attack;
   heartbeat
hjort *n.en* stag
hjul *n.et* wheel
hjørne *n.et* corner
hode *n.et* head
hodepine *n.en* headache
hoff *n.et* court (*royal*)
hofte *n.en* hip
hogge *v.* to hew
holdbar *adj.* durable
holde *v.* to hold
holdeplass *n.en* bus stop,
   trolley stop, cab stand
hollandsk *adj.* Dutch
holme *n.en* small island
homogen *adj.* homogeneous
honnig *n.en* honey
honnør *n.en* honor
honorar *n.et* fee
hoppe *v.* to jump
hore *n.en* prostitute
horisontal *adj.* horizontal
horn *n.et* horn
horoskop *n.et* horoscope
hos *prep.* at (*hos oss = at our
   place*)
hospital *n.et* hospital
hoste *v.* to cough
hotell *n.et* hotel
hoved- *prefix* chief
hovedfag *n.et* principal line
   of study
hovedsak *n.en* main point
hovedstad *n.en* capital city

hr. *abbrev.* Mr.
hud *n.en* skin
huff da! *interj.* oh dear! ugh!
hukommelse *n.en* memory
hulder, huldra *n.en* fairy, siren
hule *n.en* cave
hull *n.et* hole; cavity; gap
human *adj.* humane
hummer *n.en* lobster
humør *n.et* mood
hund *n.en* dog
hundre *num.* hundred
hurtig *adj.* quick
hurtigtog *n.et* express train
hus *n.et* house
husleie *n.en* rent
hustru *n.en* wife
hva *pron.* what
hval *n.en* whale
hvalfangst *n.en* whaling
hvalp *n.en* puppy, whelp
hvalross *n.en* walrus
hvelv *n.et* arch, vault
hvem *pron.* who, whom
hvem som helst *pron.* anyone
    at all
hverken ... eller *conj.*
    neither ... nor
hvil *n.en* rest
hvile *v.* to rest
hvilken *adj.* which, what
hvis *pron.* whose; *conj.* if
hvit *adj.* white
hvor *adv.* where
hvordan *adv.* how
hvorfor *adv.* why
hvorfra *adv.* from where
hvorhen *adv.* where, whither
hvor som helst *adv.* anywhere
hybel *n.en* rented room
hyggelig *adv.* friendly,
    comfortable
hyrde *n.en* shepherd
hytte *n.en* hut
hær *n.en* army
høflig *adj.* polite
høne *n.en* hen
høre *v.* to hear
høre til *v.* belong to

høst *n.en* autumn
høy *n.et* hay; *adj.* high
høyre *adj.* right
hånd *n.en* hand
håndarbeide *n.et* handicraft;
    needlework
håndkle *n.et* towel
håndskrift *n.en* handwriting
håne *v.* to scorn
håp *n.et* hope
håpe *v.* to hope
hår *n.et* hair

I

i *adv.; prep.* in
i aften *adv.* this evening
i dag *adv.* today
i fjor *adv.* last year
i forgårs *adv.* day before
    yesterday
i går *adv.* yesterday
i morgen *adv.* tomorrow
i morges *adv.* this morning
i natt *adv.* tonight
iakttagelse *n.en* observation
idé *n.en* idea
identisk *adj.* identical
idet *conj.* when; because
idiot *n.en* idiot
idrett *n.en* sports
idrettslag *n.et* athletic club
idrettsplass *n.en* stadium
idrettsstemne *n.et* sports event
igjen *adv.* again
ignorere *v.* to ignore
i hvert fall *adv.* at any rate
ikke *adv.* not
ild, ildebrann *n.en* fire
ille *adj.* bad; *adv.* badly
illegitim *adj.* illegitimate
imellom *adv.; prep.* between
imponere *v.* to impress
imponerende *adj.* impressive
import *n.en* import
inderlig *adj.* heartfelt
indikasjon *n.en* indication
individuell *adj.* individual
indre *n.et* insides; *adj.* inner
industri *n.en* industry

industrialisere *v.* to
industrialize
infeksjon *n.en* infection
infinitiv *n.en* infinitive
inflasjon *n.en* inflation
influensa *n.en* influenza
influere *v.* to influence
informasjon *n.en* information
informere *v.* to inform
ingen *pron.* none; *adj.* no
ingeniør *n.en* engineer
ingensteds *adv.* nowhere
ingenting *pron.* nothing
ingrediens *n.en* ingredient
inklinasjon *n.en* inclination
inkludere *v.* to include
inkompetanse *n.en*
incompetence
inn *adv.* in
inn i *adv.* into
innbille seg *v.* to imagine
innblanding *n.en* meddling
innbrudd *n.et* housebreaking
innby *v.* to invite
innbydelse *n.en* invitation
innbygger *n.en* inhabitant
inne *adv.* inside
inneholde *v.* to contain
innen *prep.; conj.* within
innflytelse *n.en* influence
innfødt *adj.* native
inngang *n.en* entrance
inngravere *v.* to engrave
inngående *adj.* thorough
innhold *n.et* contents
inniblandt *adv.* occasionally;
prep. in between
innland *n.et* inland
innlate *v.* to admit
innledning *n.en* introduction
innlevere *v.* to deliver
innramme *v.* to frame
innrømme *v.* to admit, concede
innsjø *n.en* lake
innskrift *n.en* inscription
innskudd *n.et* contribution;
bank deposit
inntrykk *n.et* impression
innvandrer *n.en* immigrant

innvendig *adj.* internal
innvirkning *n.en* influence
insekt *n.et* insect
innspektør *n.en* inspector
inspirere *v.* to inspire
installere *v.* to install
institutt *n.et* institution
innstruere *v.* to instruct
inntelligens *n.en* intelligence
intens *adj.* intense
interessant *adj.* interesting
interiør *adj.* interior
internasjonal *adj.*
international
intervju *n.et* interview
intervjue *v.* to interview
intim *adj.* intimate
intoleranse *n.en* intolerance
introdusere *v.* to introduce
invitere *v.* to invite
Irland *Pln.* Ireland
ironi *n.en* irony
irritere *v.* to irritate
is *n.en* ice; ice cream
isbjørn *n.en* polar bear
Ishavet *Pln.* the Arctic Ocean
iskald *adj.* ice-cold
Island *Pln.* Iceland
isolere *v.* to isolate
i stand *adj.* in order
istedenfor *prep.* instead of
især *adv.* particularly
ivrig *adj.* eager

J

ja *interj.* yes
jakke *n.en* jacket
jakt *n.en* yacht; sloop; hunt
januar *n.* January
Japan *Pln.* Japan
japaner *n.en* Japanese
japansk *adj.* Japanese
jeg *pron.* I
jeger *n.en* hunter
jente *n.en* girl
jern *n.et* iron
jernbane *n.en* railway
jevn *adj.* level; equal
jo *interj.* yes

jobb *n.en* job
jolle *n.en* dinghy
jomfru *n.en* maiden, virgin
jord *n.en* earth
jordbruk *n.et* agriculture
jordbunn *n.en* soil
jordbær *n.et* strawberry
jorde *n.et* cultivated field
jordisk *adj.* earthly
jordmor *n.en* midwife
jordskjelv *n.en* earthquake
journal *n.en* journal
journalist *n.en* journalist
jubel *n.en* exultation
jubileum *n.et* jubilee,
      anniversary
jul *n.en* Christmas
julaften *n.en* Christmas Eve
julegave *n.en* Christmas gift
juli *n.* July
jungel *n.en* jungle
juni *n.* June
juridisk *adj.* legal
jurist *n.en* law student, lawyer
jus *n.en* law
juvel *n.en* jewel
juveler *n.en* jeweler
jøde *n.en* Jew
jødinne *n.en* Jew (*female*)
jødisk *adj.* Jewish

K

kafé *n.en* café
kaffe *n.en* coffee
kake *n.en* cake; pastry
kald *adj.* cold
kalender *n.en* calender
kalkulere *v.* to calculate
kalkun *n.en* turkey
kalosjer *n.pl.* galoshes
kalv *n.en* calf
kalvkjøtt *n.et* veal
kammer *n.et* room
kamp *n.en* fight
kan *v.* can, may
kanadisk *adj.* Canadian
kandidat *n.en* political
      candidate; graduate, B. A.
kanin *n.en* rabbit

kanne *n.en* can, mug
kano *n.en* canoe
kanskje *adv.* perhaps
kant *n.en* edge, rim
kantre *v.* to capsize
kaos *n.et* chaos
kapell *n.et* chapel
kapital *n.en* capital, stock
kapp *n.et* cape, headland
kaptein *n.en* captain
karaffel *n.en* decanter
karakter *n.en* character
karakteristisk *adj.*
      characteristic
karikatur *n.en* caricature
kart *n.et* map
kartong *n.et* carton
karusell *n.en* merry-go-round
kaserne *n.en* barracks
kasse *n.en* box; cashbox
kassere *v.* to discard; cancel;
      cashier
kastanje *n.en* chestnut
kaste *v.* to throw
katastrofe *n.en* catastrophe
katedral *n.en* cathedral
katolisisme *n.en* Catholicism
katt *n.en* cat
kattøye *n.et* reflector, bicycle
      reflector
kavaler *n.en* escort
kavaleri *n.et* cavalry
kaviar *n.en* caviar
keeper *n.en* goalkeeper
keiser *n.en* emperor
keiserinne *n.en* empress
kelner *n.en* waiter
keramiker *n.en* potter
keramikk *n.en* ceramics;
      pottery
kikke *v.* to peek
kilde *n.en* spring; source
Kina *Pln.* China
kineser *n.en* Chinese
kinesisk *adj.* Chinese
kinn *n.et* cheek
kino *n.en* movie theater
kinobillett *n.en* movie ticket

kinoreklame *n.en* movie advertisement
kiosk *n.en* newsstand; pavilion
kirke *n.en* church
kirkebryllup *n.et* church wedding
kirkegård *n.en* churchyard
kirkeklokke *n.en* church bell
kirkelig *adj.* religious; ecclesiastical
kirketårn *n.et* church steeple
kiropraktor *n.en* chiropractor
kirsebær *n.et* cherry
kirurge *n.en* surgeon
kirurgi *n.en* surgery
kiste *n.en* chest, trunk
kitle *v.* to tickle
kjede *n.en* chain; *v.* to link together
kjedelig *adj.* boring; unpleasant
kjeft *n.en* jaw
kjekk *adj.* cheerful; attractive; brave
kjeller *n.en* cellar
kjelleretasje *n.en* basement
kjemi *n.en* chemistry
kjemikalie *n.et* chemical
kjemiker *n.en* chemist
kjemisk *adj.* chemical
kjemme *v.* to comb
kjempe *v.* to fight; struggle
kjempestor *adj.* enormous
kjenne *v.* to know, recognize
kjenning *n.en* acquaintance
kjennskap *n.et* knowledge
kjent *adj.* familar; well-known
kjerne *n.en* kernal
kjernefysiker *n.en* nuclear physicist
kjernefysikk *n.en* nuclear physics
kjerring *n.en* old woman
kjette *n.en* female cat
kjetting *n.en* chain
kjole *n.en* dress
kjær *adj.* dear
kjæreste *n.en* sweetheart
kjærlighet *n.en* love, affection

kjærlighetsroman *n.en* romantic novel
kjød *n.et* flesh
kjøkken *n.et* kitchen
kjøkkenbenk *n.en* kitchen counter
kjøkkentøy *n.et* kitchen utensils
kjøl *n.en* keel
kjøleskap *n.et* refrigerator
kjølig *adj.* chilly
kjønn *n.et* sex; gender
kjøpe *v.* to buy
kjøpmann *n.en* merchant
kjøpmannskap *n.et* commerce
kjøre *v.* to drive
kjørekort *n.et* driver's licence
kjører *n.en* driver
kjøretid *n.en* driving time
kjøring *n.en* driving, riding
kjøtt *n.et* meat
kjøttbolle *n.en* meatball
kjøttkake *n.en* meatball
kjøttmat *n.en* meat dish
klaffe *v.* to work out well, "come together," "click"
klage *n.en* complaint; *v.* to complain
klamre *v.* to grasp
klang *n.en* sound; ring
klapp *n.et* clap
klappe *v.* to clap, beat
klar *adj.* clear
klare *v.* to clarify
klarhet *n.en* clearness; clarity
klasse *n.en* school or social class
klasserom *n.et* classroom
klassiker *n.en* classic; classic writer or work; classical scholar
klatre *v.* to climb
klatrer *n.en* climber
kle *v.* to dress; cover; become (*hatten kler henne = the hat becomes her*)
klede *v.* to dress
klemme *v.* to squeeze, embrace
klenge *v.* to cling, stick

klikke v. to click
klima n.et climate
klinikk n.en clinic
klippe v. to clip
klo n.en claw
kloakk n.en sewer
klode n.en planet
klohammar n.en claw hammer
klok adj. wise; shrewd
klokke n.en clock; watch; bell
klore v. to scratch
kloster n.et cloister
klovn n.en clown
klubb n.en social club
klump n.en clump
klunke v. to gurgle
klunkeflaske n.en akevitt
    decanter that clucks
    when poured
klynge v. to cling
klær n.pl. clothes
klø v. to scratch
knapp n.en button
knapp adj. scarce; poor; brief
knappe v. to button (knappe
    opp = unbutton)
kne n.et knee
knekke v. to snap; crack open
knekker n.en nutcracker
kniv n.en knife
knivslir n.en knife sheath
knuse v. to smash
knyte v. to tie
kobbe n.en seal
kobbefangst n.en seal hunting
kobber n.et copper
kobbunge n.en young seal
koffert n.en suitcase
kok n.et cooking; boiling
koke v. to boil
kokebok n.en cookbook
kokk n.en cook
kol n.et coal
koldtbord n.et smorgasbord,
    buffet
kollega n.en colleague
kollisjon n.en collision
kolon n.et colon
kolonial n.en grocery store

kolossal adj. colossal
koma n.en coma
kombinasjon n.en
    combination
kombinere v. to combine
komediant n.en comedian
komedie n.en comedy
komfortabel adj. comfortable
komisk adj. comic
komité n.en committee
komma n.et comma
kommandere v. to command
komme v. to come; arrive
kommentar n.en commentary
kommentere v. to give a
    commentary
kommisjon n.en commission
kommode n.en chest of
    drawers
kommunikasjon n.en
    communication
kommunisme n.en
    communism
kommunist n.en Communist
kompani n.et company
komparativ adj. comparative
kompas n.en compass
kompensasjon n.en
    compensation
kompensere v. to compensate
kompetanse n.en competence
kompleks adj. complex
komplimentere v. to
    compliment
komponere v. to compose
kompott n.en stewed fruit
kompromiss n.et compromise
kondisjon n.en condition
konditori n.et confectioner's
    shop
kondolere v. to condole
konduktør n.en conductor
kone n.en wife; woman
konfekt n.en candy
konferere v. to confer;
    compare
konfidensiell adj. confidential
konflikt n.en conflict
konge n.en king

kongelig *adj.* royal
kongerike *n.et* kingdom
kongress *n.en* congress
konjakk *n.en* brandy
konklusjon *n.en* conclusion
konkret *adj.* concrete
konkurranse *n.en* competition
konkurs *n.en* failure,
   bankruptcy (*gå konkurs* =
   go bankrupt)
konsekvens *n.en*
   consequence; consistency
konsekvent *adj.* consistent
konsentrere *v.* to concentrate
konsert *n.en* concert
konservator *n.en* curator
konsis *adj.* concise
konstant *adj.* constant
konstatere *v.* to ascertain;
   declare
konstruere *v.* to design,
   construct
konsulent *n.en* consultant
konsum *n.et* consumption
kontakt *n.en* contact
kontakte *v.* to contact
kontant *adj.* cash
konto *n.en* account
kontor *n.et* office
kontorsjef *n.en* head of
   an office
kontrakt *n.en* contract
kontrast *n.en* contrast
kontroll *n.en* control;
   inspection
kontrollere *v.* to verify, check;
   control
kontur *n.en* contour, outline
konversere *v.* to converse
konvolutt *n.en* envelope
kopi *n.en* copy
kopp *n.en* cup
kor *n.et* chorus
kork *n.en* cork
korketrekker *n.en* corkscrew
korn *n.et* grain; sight on a rifle
korporal *n.en* corporal
korpulent *adj.* obese,
   corpulent

korrekt *adj.* correct
korrespondanse *n.en*
   correspondence; direct
   connection
korrespondere *v.* to
   correspond; connect
korresponderende *adj.*
   connecting (*as in air
   flights*); corresponding
korrigere *v.* to correct
kors *n.et* cross
kort *adj.* short, concise
kort *n.et* card
kose seg *v.* enjoy oneself
koselig *adj.* cozy, pleasant
kost *n.en* broom; food, board
kostbar *adj.* expensive
koste *v.* to cost
kostpenger *n.pl.* per diem
kotelett *n.en* cutlet, chop
krabbe *n.en* crab; *v.* to crawl
kraft *n.en* strength
kraftig *adj.* strong
krage *n.en* collar
krangle *v.* to quarrel
kranglet *adj.* quarrelsome
krans *n.en* wreath
krav *n.et* claim, demand
kreditere *v.* to credit
kreditor *n.en* creditor
kreft *n.en* cancer
krem *n.en* whipped cream;
   facial cream
kreps *n.en* crawfish
krets *n.en* circle
kreve *v.* to demand
krig *n.en* war
krigsskip *n.et* warship
kriminell *adj.* criminal
kringkaste *v.* to broadcast
kringkasting *n.en*
   broadcasting
krise *n.en* crisis
kristelig *adj.* Christian
kristen *n.en* Christian
kristendom *n.en* Christianity
Kristus *n.* Christ
kritiker *n.en* critic
kritikk *n.en* criticism

kritisere *v.* to criticize
kritisk *adj.* critical
kritt *n.et* chalk
krok *n.en* corner; hook;
  bend; trick
kroket *adj.* crooked
kronprins *n.en* crown prince
kronprinsesse *n.en* crown
  princess
kropp *n.en* body
krukke *n.en* jar
krum *adj.* curved, bent
krus *n.et* jug
kruset *adj.* curly
krybbe *n.en* crib; sled
krydder *n.pl.* spices
krykke *n.en* crutch
krype *v.* to creep
krysse *v.* to cross
krystall *n.en* crystal
krøller *n.pl.* curls
krønike *n.en* chronicle
krøpling *n.en* cripple
kråke *n.en* crow
ku *n.en* cow
kulde *n.en* cold
kule *n.en* ball, sphere; bullet
kulisse *n.en* stage wing
  (*bak kulissene = behind
  the scenes*)
kull *n.et* coal
kulminere *v.* to culminate
kultivert *adj.* cultivated
kultur *n.en* culture
kulturarv *n.en* cultural
  heritage
kummerlig *adj.* wretched,
  miserable
kun *adv.* only
kunde *n.en* customer
kunne *v.* to be able to
kunnskap *n.en* knowledge
kunst *n.en* art
kunstig *adj.* artificial
kunstner *n.en* artist
kunsterinne *n.en* female artist
kunstnerisk *adj.* artistic
kunstverk *n.et* work of art
kupé *n.en* compartment

kupong *n.en* coupon
kur *n.en* cure
kurere *v.* to cure
kuriositet *n.en* curiosity
kurs *n.en* course
kurv *n.en* basket
kusine *n.en* female cousin
kval *n.en* agony
kvalifisere *v.* to qualify
kvalm *adj.* nauseated
kvart *n.en* quarter
kvarter *n.et* quarter of an hour;
  district; quarter; watch
  (*on ship*)
kveld *n.en* evening
kvele *v.* to choke
kvikk *adj.* lively, witty
kvinne *n.en* woman
kvinnelig *adj.* womanly
kvinnfolk *n.et* womankind
kvitt *adv.* quits (*å bli kvitt av =
  to get rid of*)
kvittering *n.en* receipt
kylling *n.en* chicken
kynisk *adj.* cynical
kyskhet *n.en* chastity
kyss *n.et* kiss
kysse *v.* to kiss
kyst *n.en* coast
kø *n.en* queue, waiting line
kål *n.en* cabbage
kåpe *n.en* woman's coat

L

lage *v.* to make
laken *n.et* sheet
lakris *n.en* licorice
laks *n.en* salmon
lam *adj.* lame
lammekjøtt *n.et* roast lamb
lampe *n.en* lamp
land *n.et* land, country
landbruk *n.et* agriculture
lande *v.* to land
landevei *n.en* highway
landflyktighet *n.en* exile
landgang *n.en* disem-
  barkation; gangplank
landsby *n.en* village

landskap *n.et* landscape
landsmål (nynorsk) *n.et* New
  Norwegian language
landsmann *n.en* compatriot
landsted *n.et* cottage in the
  countryside
lang *adj.* long, distant
langfredag *n.* Good Friday
langmodig *adj.* patient
langsom *adj.* slow
langvarig *adj.* prolonged
lansere *v.* to start
lanterne *n.en* lamp
lapp *n.en* Laplander (*official
  name "Same"*)
Lappland *Pln.* Lapland
lapskaus *n.en* stew
larm *n.en* noise
last *n.en* cargo; vice; burden
lastebil *n.en* truck, van
lastebåt *n.en* freighter
latter *n.en* laughter
latterlig *adj.* ridiculous
lauv *n.et* foliage
lav *adj.* low; mean
lavendel *n.en* lavender
le *v.* to laugh; *adj., adv.* leeward
lede *v.* to lead
leder *n.en* guide, leader
ledig *adj.* unoccupied
lefse *n.en* thin pancake
legalisere *v.* to legalize
lege *n.en* physician
legeme *n.et* body
legemlig *adj.* bodily
legende *n.en* legend
legge *v.* to lay, put
lege seg *v.* to go to bed
legitim *adj.* legitimate
lei *adj.* tired; sorry
leie *v.* to rent
leieboer *n.en* lodger
leilighet *n.en* opportunity
leilighetsvis *adv.* occasionally
leir *n.en* camp
lek *n.en* game
leke *v.* to play
lekse *n.en* lesson
leksikon *n.et* dictionary

lektor *n.en* teacher, lecturer
lem *n.et* limb (*of the body*)
lenestol *n.en* easy chair
lengde *n.en* length (*for lenge
  siden = a long time ago*)
lenge *adv.* long
lengsel *n.en* longing
lenke *n.en* chain; *v.* to chain,
  fetter
lerret *n.et* painter's canvas
lese *v.* to read
lespe *v.* to lisp
lete *v.* to search
lett *adj.* light; easy
lette *v.* to ease, relieve
lettelse *n.en* relief
lettsindig *adj.* frivolous
lettvint *adj.* easy (*bare
  lettvint = no problem*)
leve *v.* to live
levende *adj.* alive; lively
levere *v.* to deliver
lide *v.* to suffer
lidenskapelig *adj.* passionate
liderlig *adj.* vulgar; lewd
ligge *v.* to lie, rest; be located
ligne *v.* to resemble
lik *n.et* corpse
lik *adj.* like, similar
like *adj.* equal; *adv.* equally
likeglad *adj.* indifferent
liksom *adv.; conj.* as, like
likør *n.en* liqueur
lilje *n.en* lily
lim *n.et* glue
line *n.en* rope
lite, liten *adj.* little
litografi *n.en* lithography
litt *adv.* a little
litteratur *n.en* literature
litterær *adj.* literary
liturgi *n.en* liturgy
liv *n.et* life; waist
livaktig *adj.* lifelike; vivid
livlig *adj.* lively
livsglad *adj.* happy
livsvarig *adj.* lifelong
livvakt *n.en* bodyguard
loddrett *adj.* vertical

loft *n.et* ceiling; attic
logisk *adj.* logical
lokal *adj.* local
lokk *n.en* lock (*lokker* = *tresses*)
lokke *v.* to allure, tempt
lokkende *adj.* attractive
lomme *n.en* pocket
lommeur *n.et* pocket watch
losje *n.en* theater box, loge
losjere *v.* to lodge
losjerende *n.en* lodger
lotteri *n.et* lottery
lov *n.en* law
love *v.* to promise
lovlig *adj.* lawful
lue *n.en* cap
luft *n.en* air
lugar *n.en* cabin, berth
lugge *v.* to pull by the hair
lukke *v.* to shut, close
lukrativ *adj.* lucrative
luksus *n.en* luxury
lukte *v.* to smell
lumpen *adj.* paltry; mean
lun *adj.* genial
lund *n.en* grove
lune *n.et* mood
lunge *n.en* lung
lunsj *n.en* lunch
lur *adj.* tricky, sly
lure *v.* to waylay; spy
ly *n.et* shelter
lyd *n.en* sound
lydelig *adj.* loud; clearly
    audible
lydlig *adj.* obedient
lydløs *adj.* silent, without
    a sound
lykke *n.en* luck, happiness
lykkelig *adj.* happy; lucky
lyn *n.et* lightning
lys *n.et* light; candle; *adj.* light,
    light-colored
lyse *v.* to shine
lysning *n.en* light
lyst *n.en* pleasure; wish
lystig *adj.* merry
lystspill *n.et* comedy
lytte *v.* to listen

lyve *v.* to lie, tell a lie
lær *n.et* leather
lærdom *n.en* learning
lære *n.en* doctrine; teaching;
    lesson; *v.* to learn, teach
lærer *n.en* teacher
lærerik *adj.* informative
lærerinne *n.en* female teacher
løft *n.et* weight; big effort
løfte *n.et* promise; *v.* lift
løgn *n.en* lie, falsehood
løk *n.en* onion
lønn *n.en* compensation;
    salary
lønne seg *v.* to be worth it;
    yield profit
løp *n.et* race; course (*of events*)
løpe *v.* to run
lørdag *n.* Saturday
løs *adj.* loose, slack; relaxed
løslate *v.* to release
løsne *v.* to loosen, relax
løsning *n.en* solution
løsrive seg *v.* to break away
løve *n.en* lion
løvetann *n.en* dandelion
løvinne *n.en* lioness
løytnant *n.en* lieutenant
lån *n.et* loan
låne *v.* to lend; borrow
lår *n.et* thigh
låse *v.* to lock
låse opp *v.* to unlock
låve *n.en* barn

M

madrass *n.en* mattress
magasin *n.et* storehouse;
    department store;
    magazine
mager *adj.* lean
magisk *adj.* magical
magister *n.en* M. A., master
    of arts
magnetisk *adj.* magnetic
mahogni *n.en* mahogany
mai *n.* May
mais *n.en* maize, corn
majestisk *adj.* majestic

majoritet *n.en* majority
make *n.en* mate; match, peer
makrell *n.en* mackerel
makt *n.en* power
male *v.* to paint
malebarisk *adj.* outlandish
maler *n.en* painter
maleri *n.et* picture
malerinne *n.en* female painter
malerisk *adj.* artistic;
  picturesque
mamma *n.en* mamma
man *pron.* one, people (*man
  sier = people say*)
mandag *n.* Monday
mandel *n.en* almond
manér *n.en* manner, fashion
manet *n.en* jellyfish
mange *adj.* many
mangel *n.en* scarcity, shortage;
  flaw
mangesidig *adj.* versatile,
  many-sided
mani *n.en* mania
mann *n.en* man; husband
mannfolk *n.et* men
mannlig *adj.* male
mannskap *n.et* ship's crew;
  troops
manntal *n.et* census
mansjett *n.en* cuff
mansjettknapper *n.pl.*
  cufflinks
manuell *adj.* manual
manuskript *n.et* manuscript
mareritt *n.et* nightmare
marg *n.en* margin; marrow
maritim *adj* maritime
mark *n.en* field
marked *n.et* market
markere *v.* to mark
marmelade *n.en* marmalade
marsipan *n.en* marzipan
  (*almond paste*)
marsipangris *n.en* marzipan pig
marsj *n.* March
mas *n.et* bother, fuss
maske *n.en* mask
maskin *n.en* machine

maskineri *n.et* machinery
maskinist *n.en* machinist
maskulin *adj.* masculine
massakre *n.en* massacre
masse *n.en* mass; multitude;
  crowd
mast *n.en* mast
mat *n.en* food; meal
mate *v.* to feed
matematiker *n.en*
  mathematician
matematikk *n.en* mathematics
materiale *n.et* materials
materiell *adj.* material
matiné *n.en* matinée
matros *n.en* sailor
matrosdress *n.en* sailor suit
matt *adj.* dull; feeble; mate
  (*chess*) (*gjøre matt =
  checkmate*)
maur *n.en* ant
mave *n.en* stomach
med *prep.; adv.* with
medalje *n.en* medal
meddele *v.* to announce;
  communicate
meddelelse *n.en* announcement; communication
medfødt *adj.* innate
medfølelse *n.en* sympathy
medisin *n.en* medicine
medisintran *n.en* codliver oil
medlem *n.et* member
medlemskort *n.et*
  membership card
medlidenhet *n.en* pity
medvind *n.en* tail wind
medynk *n.en* sympathy, pity
megen, meget *adj.* much
megler *n.en* stockbroker
meieri *n.et* dairy
mekaniker *n.en* mechanical
  engineer; mechanic
mektig *adj.* powerful
mel *n.et* meal; flour
melde *v.* to announce, delcare
melde seg *v.* to announce
  oneself; become a
  candidate

melding *n.en* report;
declaration
melk *n.en* milk
mellom *prep.* between
melodi *n.en* melody
melon *n.en* melon
memoarer *n.pl.* memoirs
memorandum *n.et*
memorandum
men *conj.* but
mene *v.* to mean, be of the
opinion
mengde *n.en* multitude;
quantity
menneske *n.et* human being
menneskealder *n.en*
generation
menneskehet *n.en* mankind
menneskelig *adj.* human;
humane
mens *conj.* while
mentalitet *n.en* mentality
meny *n.en* menu
mer *adj.* more
merkbar *adj.* noticeable
merke *n.et* brand, label, mark;
v. to mark; to notice;
to pay attention
merkelig *adj.* remarkable;
peculiar
merkverdig *adj.* extraordinary
merr *n.en* mare
meslinger *n.pl.* measles
messing *n.en* brass
mest *adv.* most; mostly
mester *n.en* master; champion
mesterlig *adj.* masterful
mesterskap *n.et* championship; mastery
mesterverk *n.et* masterpiece
mestre *v.* to master
metall *n.et* metal
meter *n.en* meter
metier *n.en* trade, specialty
metode *n.en* method
metodisk *adj.* methodical
mett *adj.* full (*of food*), satisfied
middag *n.en* midday; dinner
middagshvil *n.en* siesta

middagsmat *n.en* dinner
middel *n.et* means; remedy
middel- *prefix* middle-
middelaldersk *adj.* medieval
middelaldrende *adj.* middle-
aged
Middelhavet *Pln.* the
Mediterranean
middels *adj.* average, middling
midsommer *n.en* midsummer
midt i *adv.* in the middle of
mil *n.en* mile (*Norwegian
mile = 10 km. = 6.2 U. S.
miles*)
mild *adj.* mild; gentle
militær *n.en* soldier; army;
adj. military
miljøn *n.et* milieu
millionær *n.en* millionaire
milorg *n.*
Militærorganisasjonen,
WW II underground
resistance
min *pron.* my, mine
mindre *adj.* less, lesser, smaller
mindretal *n.et* minority
mindreårig *adj.* underage,
minor
mineral *n.et* mineral
minister *n.en* cabinet minister,
envoy
minne *n.et* remembrance,
memory; keepsake; *v.* to
remind, suggest (*minnes
meg om = reminds me of*);
remember
minnes *v.* to commemorate
minoritet *n.en* minority
minst *adj.* least, smallest
minutt *n.et* minute
mirakel *n.et* miracle
misbruk *n.en* abuse
misbruke *v.* to abuse
misfornøyd *adj.* displeased
misforstå *v.* to misunderstand
misjonær *n.en* missionary
mislykket *adj.* unsuccessful
misteltein *n.en* mistletoe
mistenke *v.* to suspect

mistenksom *adj.* suspicious
mistro *n.en* distrust
misunne *v.* to envy
moden *adj.* ripe
moderat *adj.* moderate
moderne *adj.* modern
modig *adj.* courageous
molte *n.en* cloudberry
montere *v.* to install, mount
mor *n.en* mother
morbror *n.en* mother's
    brother, uncle
mord *n.et* murder
morgen *n.en* morning
    (*i morgen* = *tomorrow;*
    i morgen tidlig = *tomorrow*
    morning early)
moro *n.en* fun
morskap *n.en* motherhood
morsom *adj.* amusing
mosjon *n.en* exercise
moskito *n.en* mosquito
most *n.en* cider
mot *n.et* courage; meeting;
    prep. against; toward;
    versus
mote *n.en* fashion
motgang *n.en* adversity
motiv *n.et* motive; motif,
    theme
motor *n.en* motor
motsatt *adj.* opposite
motsetning *n.en* opposite;
    contrast
motstand *n.en* resistance
motta *v.* to receive; welcome
mottagelse, mottakelse *n.en*
    reception; receipt;
    acceptance
motvillig *adj.* reluctant
mugge *n.en* jug
mulig *adj.* possible
muligens *adv.* possibly
mulighet *n.en* possibility
multiplisere *v.* to multiply
mumle *v.* to mumble
munn *n.en* mouth
munter *adj.* cheerful
muntig *adj.* oral

mur *n.en* wall
murstein *n.en* brick
mus *n.en* mouse
museum *n.et* museum
musikalsk *adj.* musical
musikant *n.en* musician
musikk *n.en* music
musikkkorp *n.et* brass band
muskat *n.en* nutmeg
muskel *n.en* muscle
mustasje *n.en* moustache
mye *adj.; adv.* much, more
mygg *n.en* gnat
myndighet *n.en* authority
mynt *n.en* coin
myrde *v.* to murder
mysterium *n.et* mystery
møbel *n.et* furniture
møbelsnekker *n.en*
    cabinetmaker
møblere *v.* to furnish
mødre *n.pl.* mothers
møll *n.et* moth
mønster *n.et* model; pattern
mør *adj.* tender; weakened
mørk *adj.* dark
mørke *n.et* darkness
møte *n.et* meeting
må *v.* must, may
mål *n.et* language; voice; end,
    purpose; goal (*in sports*);
    measure
måle *v.* to measure
måltid *n.et* meal
måne *n.en* moon
måned *n.en* month
måte *n.en* manner
måtte *v.* have to

N

nabo *n.en* neighbor
nagle *n.en* nail
naiv *adj.* naive
naken *adj.* naked
narkoman *n.en* drug addict
narkomani *n.en* addiction to
    narcotics
narkotikum *n.et* narcotic
narr *n.en* fool

nasjon *n.en* nation
nasjonal *adj.* national
nasjonalitet *n.en* nationality
natt *n.en* night
nattevakt *n.en* night
    watchman
natur *n.en* nature
naturligvis *adv.* naturally
nautisk *adj.* nautical
navigasjon *n.en* navigation
navigatør *n.en* navigator
navn *n.et* name
ned *adv.* down
nedbrent *adj.* burnt down
nede *adv.* down
nedenfor *prep.* below
nederlag *n.et* defeat
Nederland *Pl.n.* Holland
nederlandsk *adj.* Dutch
nederlender *n.en* Dutchman
nederst *adj.* lowest
nedgang *n.en* descent,
    entrance; decline
nedrive *v.* to tear down,
    demolish
nedrustning *n.en*
    disarmament, arms
    reduction
nedskrive *v.* to write down
nedtrykt *adj.* depressed,
    discouraged
negativ *n.et* negative image;
    adj. negative
negl *n.en* fingernail, toenail
nei *interj.* no
nekrolog *n.en* obituary
nekte *v.* to deny; refuse
nemlig *adv.* namely
nepe *n.en* turnip
nerve *n.en* nerve
nervøs *adj.* nervous
nes *n.et* headland
nese *n.en* nose
nest *adj.* next
nesten *adv.* almost
nett *adj.* pretty; tidy
netto *adv.* net
nettopp *adv.* just
nevne *v.* to mention

nevø *n.en* nephew
ni *num.* nine
niende *num.* ninth
niese *n.en* niece
nifs *adj.* uncanny
nipp *n.et* sip
nippe *v.* to sip
nisse *n.en* pixie, goblin
nitten *num.* nineteen
nivå *n.et* level
nobel *adj.* noble
noen, noe *pron.* somebody;
    something; any
noe som helst *pron.* anybody
    at all
noensteds *adv.* anywhere
nok *adv.* enough
nokså *adv.* rather
nonsens *n.et* nonsense
nord *adv.* north
nordisk *adj.* northern; Nordic
nordlig *adj.* northerly
nordpol *n.en* north pole
norm *n.en* standard
norsk *adj.* Norwegian
note *n.en* note
notere *v.* to note down
notisbok *n.en* notebook
novelle *n.en* short story
november *n.* November
null *n.en* zero
nullpunkt *n.et* zero
nummer *n.et* number; size
nutid *n.en* present day
nyanse *n.en* nuance
nybakt *adj.* freshly baked;
    novel
nydelig *adj.* charming
nyfødt *adj.* newborn
nygift *adj.* newly married
nyhet *n.en* news
nylig *adv.* recently
nyre *n.en* kidney
nyte *v.* to enjoy; taste
nytid *n.en* present day
nyttår *n.et* New Year
nyttårsaften *n.en* New Year's
    Eve
nytte *v.* to utilize

nær *adj.*; *prep.* near
nære *v.* to nourish
nærhet *n.en* vicinity, proximity
nærliggende *adj.* nearby
nærme *v.* to bring near
nærme seg *v.* to draw near, approach
nød *n.en* need, want; distress
nødvendig *adj.* necessary
nøkkel *n.en* doorkey; clue; musical clef; wrench
nøtt *n.en* nut (*food*)
nøyaktig *adj.* exact
nøytral *adj.* neutral
nå *v.* arrive at; *adv.* now
nåde *n.en* mercy
nådig *adj.* merciful
nål *n.en* needle
når *adv.*; *conj.* when; if
når som helst *adv.* whenever
nåtid *n.en* present
nåtidlig *adj.* contemporary
nåværende *adj.* current

O

objekt *n.et* objekt
objektiv *adj.* objective
obscur *adj.* obscure
odør *n.en* odor
offensiv *adj.* offensive
offentlig *adj.* public
offentliggjøre *v.* to make public; publish
offer *n.et* sacrifice; victim
offerere *v.* to offer
offiser *n.en* officer
offisiell *adj.* official
ofre *v.* to sacrifice
ofte *adv.* often
og *adv.* also; *conj.* and
okkupere *v.* to occupy
okse *n.en* ox
oksekjøtt *n.et* beef
oksestek *n.en* roast beef
oktober *n.* October
oldefar *n.en* great-grandfather
olding *n.en* old man
oldsaker *n.pl.* antiquities
oldtid *n.en* antiquity

oliven *n.en* olive
olje *n.en* oil
om *adv.* again; *conj.* if; during (*om dagen = during the day*); in (*om en uke = in a week*)
ombestemme seg *v.* change one's mind
ombord *adv.* on board
ombudsmann *n.en* grievance officer
ombygge *v.* to rebuild
omelett *n.en* omelette
omfattende *adj.* comprehensive
omfavne *v.* to embrace
omhu *n.en* care, solicitude
omkomme *v.* to perish
omkring *prep.* about
omringe *v.* to surround
område *n.et* territory
omslag *n.et* dust jacket; wrapping
omsorg *n.en* care
omtrent *adv.* about
omvei *n.en* detour
omvendt *adj.* the other way around
ond *adj.* evil
onde *n.et* evil
ondskap *n.en* wickedness
onkel *n.en* uncle
onsdag *n.* Wednesday
opera *n.en* opera
operasjon *n.en* operation
operatør *n.en* operator
operere *v.* to operate
opp *prep.* up
oppdage *v.* to discover
oppdagelse *n.en* discovery
oppdra *v.* to bring up, educate
oppdragelse *n.en* upbringing; education
oppe *adj.* out of bed; upstairs; *adv.* up
oppfatning *n.en* interpretation, view
oppfinne *v.* to invent
oppfinnelse *n.en* invention

oppfinnsom *adj.* inventive, resourceful
omflamme *v.* to inflame
oppgang *n.en* stairs; ascent
oppgave *n.en* task; school assignment
oppgi *v.* to give up
opphisse *v.* to excite
opphold *n.et* pause, intermission; sustenance; stay
oppholde *v.* to hold up; stay
opplag *n.et* edition, issue; supplies
opplyse *v.* to light up
opplysning *n.en* lighting; information
oppmerksom *adj.* attentive; considerate
oppmerksomhet *n.en* attentiveness; thoughtfulness
oppmuntre *v.* to encourage
oppmuntring *n.en* encouragement
opprette *v.* to establish
opprettelse *n.en* foundation; institution
opprinnelig *adj.* original
opprinnelse *n.en* origin
oppsette *v.* to postpone
oppsettelse *n.en* delay
oppsi *v.* to give notice
oppskrift *n.en* recipe
oppstyr *n.et* uproar
opptа *v.* to take up
opptatt *adj.* engaged, busy; occupied
oppvarme *v.* to warm up
oppvask *n.en* dishwashing
optikk *n.en* optics
opptimistisk *adj.* optimistic
oransje *n.en; adj.* orange
ord *n.et* word
ordbok *n.en* dictionary
ordfører *n.en* spokesman
ordne, ordne opp *v.* to put in order
ordspill *n.et* pun
ordspråk *n.et* proverb

organ *n.et* organ of the body; agency of a political body
organisasjon *n.en* organization
orientere seg *v.* to orient oneself
original *n.en; adj.* original; eccentric
orkan *n.en* hurricane
orke *v.* to bear, stand, endure
orkester *v.* orchestra
orm *n.en* worm
ornament *n.et* ornament
ortodoks *adj.* orthodox
osean *n.et* ocean
oss *pron.* us; ourselves
ost *n.en* cheese
oter *n.en* otter
oven *adv.* above
ovenfor *prep.* above, higher up
ovenfra *prep.* from above
over *prep.* over, above
overalt *adv.* everywhere
overbefolket *adj.* overpopulated
overbevise *v.* to convince; convict
overblikk *n.et* panorama; general view
overbord *adv.* overboard
overdreven *adj.* exaggerated
overdrive *v.* to exaggerate
overdrivelse *n.en* exaggeration
overdådighet *n.en* luxury
overfall *n.et* assault
overfalle *v.* to assault
overfladisk *adj.* superficial
overflate *n.en* surface
overflødig *adj.* abundant; superfluous
overfylt *adj.* overcrowded
overføre *v.* to transfer
overgang *n.en* crossing; transition
overgi *v.* to hand over
overgivelse *n.en* surrender
overgrodd *adj.* overgrown
overhodet *adv.* at all, altogether

overjordisk *adj.* supernatural
overklasse *n.en* upper class
overlate *v.* to turn over to, leave to
overleve *v.* to outlive
overmenneskelig *adj.* superhuman
overmot *n.et* arrogance, pride
overnatte *v.* to spend the night
overraske *v.* to surprise
overraskelse *n.en* surprise
overse *v.* to survey, assess; overlook, forgive
oversette *v.* to translate
oversettelse *n.en* translation
oversikt *n.en* survey, view; summary
overskrift *n.en* heading, headline
overskudd *n.et* surplus; profit
overskyet *adj.* overcast
overskygge *v.* to overshadow
overstryke *v.* to cross out
overta *v.* to undertake; take over, take charge of
overtagelse *n.en* undertaking
overtale *v.* to persuade
overtro *n.en* superstition
overtroisk *adj.* superstitious
overvinne *v.* to conquer
overvurdere *v.* to overvalue
ovn *n.en* oven; stove; kiln

P

padde *n.en* toad
paddel *n.en* paddle
padle *v.* paddle
pakke *n.en* parcel; *v.* to pack, wrap (*pakke inn = wrap up; pakke opp = unpack*)
pakt *n.en* covenant; agreement
palett *n.en* palette
palmesøndag *n.* Palm Sunday
panikk *n.en* panic
panne *n.en* forehead
panter *n.en* panther
papegøye *n.en* parrot
papir *n.et* paper
paradoks *n.et* paradox

parafin *n.en* kerosene
paragraf *n.en* paragraph; section
parallell *adj.* parallel
paraply *n.en* umbrella
parat *adj.* prepared, ready
parfyme *n.en* perfume
park *n.en* park
parkere *v.* to park
parodi *n.en* parody
part *n.en* share, portion
pasient *n.en* patient
pass *n.et* passport; care
passasje *n.en* passage
passasjer *n.en* passenger
passasjerbåt *n.en* ocean liner
passe *v.* to fit
passe seg *v.* to take care, watch out
passende *adj.* becoming, suitable
passere *v.* to pass by; happen
passiv *adj.* passive
pastor *n.* The Rev., pastor
patologisk *adj.* pathological
patos *n.en* pathos
patruljere *v.* to patrol
pause *v.* to rest
pave *n.en* pope
paviljong *n.en* pavilion
pedal *n.en* pedal
peis *n.en* fireplace
peke *v.* to point
pekefinger *n.en* forefinger
pelikan *n.en* pelican
pels *n.en* fur
pelsfrakk *n.en* fur coat
pelshandler *n.en* furrier
pelskåpe *n.en* fur cloak
pen *adj.* good-looking
penger *n.pl.* money
pengeseddel *n.en* paper money
penn *n.en* pen
pensjon *n.en* pension
pensjonat *n.et* boarding house
pensjonere *v.* to pension
pepper *n.en* pepper
perfekt *adj.* perfect
periode *n.en* period

perle *n.en* pearl
permanent *n.en* permanent
   wave; *adj.* permanent
perpendikulær *adj.*
   perpendicular
perpleks *adj.* perplexed
person *n.en* person; character
   (*in a literary work*)
personlig *adj.* personal
perspektiv *n.et* perspective
pessimisme *n.en* pessimism
pest *n.en* pestilence
piano *n.et* piano
pidestall *n.en* pedestal
piggtråd *n.en* barbed wire
pike *n.en* girl
pikenavn *n.et* maiden name
pil *n.en* arrow; willow
pille *n.en* pill; column; *v.* pluck,
   pick, shell, peel
pinaktig *adj.* painful
pine *n.en* torture; *v.* to torture
pingvin *n.en* penguin
pinlig *adj.* painful
pinse *n.* Pentecost, Whitsuntide
pioner *n.en* pioneer
pipe *n.en* pipe; chimney;
   v. whistle
pirat *n.en* pirate
pisk *n.en* whip
piske *v.* to whip
pissoar *n.et* urinal
pistol *n.en* pistol
pjolter *n.en* whiskey and soda
plage *n.en* trouble, worry;
   plague; *v.* to trouble
plagsom *adj.* annoying
plakat *n.en* placard, poster
plan *n.en* project; *n.et* plane;
   design; blueprint; *adj.* level
planet *n.en* planet
planlegge *v.* to plan
plante *n.en*; *v.* to plant
plassere *v.* to place
plass *n.en* place, situation;
   space, room; city square
plast *n.en* plastic
plaster *n.et* plaster

plattform *n.en* platform
pleie *n.en* nursing care; *v.* to
   be accustomed to doing;
   to nurse
plen *n.en* lawn
plikt *n.en* duty
plissé *n.en* pleating
plukke *v.* to pick, pluck
pluss *prep.* plus
plutselig *adj.* sudden;
   adv. suddenly
plyndre *v.* to plunder
plystre *v.* to whistle
poeng *n.et* point
poesi *n.en* poetry
poetisk *adj.* poetic
pol *n.en* pole
polakk *n.en* Pole
polemikk *n.en* controversy
Polen *Pln.* Poland
polere *v.* to polish
politi *n.et* police
politikk *n.en* politics
polsk *adv.* Polish
pomp *n.en* pomp
popularitet *n.en* popularity
porselen *n.et* porcelain
porsjon *n.et* portion
port *n.en* gate, doorway
portiere *n.en* curtain
portrett *n.et* portrait
portrettere *v.* to portray
pose *n.en* bag
posisjon *n.en* position
post *n.en* post, situation
postbud *n.et* postman
posthus *n.et* post office
postkasse *n.en* letterbox
postkontor *n.et* post office
postombæring *n.en* mail
   delivery
postskriptum *n.et* postscript
potens *n.en* potency
potet *n.en* potato
potte *n.en* pot
prakisere *v.* to practice
praksis *n.en* practice
prakt *n.en* splendor
praktfull *adj.* splendid, elegant

praktisk *adj.* practical
prat *n.en* chat
prate *v.* to chat
pratsom *adj.* chatty
predikant *n.en* preacher
predike *v.* to preach
preke *v.* to preach
premie *n.en* prize
premiere *v.* to award a prize to
première *n.en* first night
preparat *n.et* preparation
preparere *v.* to prepare;
    preserve
presedens *n.en* precedent
presentere *v.* to present
president *n.en* president
presidere *v.* to preside
presis *adj.* precise
press *n.en* pressure, strain;
    influence
presse *v.* to press, squeeze
presende *adj.* urgent
prest *n.en* priest, clergyman
prestelig *adj.* priestly
prestisje *n.en* prestige
pretendere *v.* to pretend
prevensjon *n.en* contraceptive
preventiv *adj.* preventive;
    prophylactic
prima *adj.* very fine, of first
    class quality
primitiv *adj.* primitive
primær *adj.* primary
prins *n.en* prince
prinselig *adj.* princely
prinsesse *n.en* princess
prinsipiell *adj.* principal
prinsipp *n.et* principle
prioritet *n.en* priority
pris *n.en* price; prize
privat *adj.* private
probere *v.* to try
problem *n.et* problem
problematisk *adj.* problematic
produksjon *n.et* production
produkt *n.et* product
produsere *v.* to produce
profan *adj.* profane
profesjon *n.en* profession

profesjonell *adj.* professional
profet *n.en* prophet
profil *n.en* profile
profitt *n.en* profit
program *n.et* program
proklamere *v.* to proclaim
proletariat *n.et* proletariat
prolog *n.en* prologue
prolongere *v.* to prolong
promenade *n.en* promenade
proponere *v.* to propose
proprietær *n.en* landowner
prosa *n.en* prose
proselytt *n.en* convert
prosent *n.en* percent
prosess *n.en* lawsuit; process
prosjekt *n.et* project
prospekt *n.et* prospect
prospektkort *n.et* picture
    postcard
protest *n.en* protest
protestant *adj.* Protestant
protokoll *n.en* protocol; ledger
provins *n.en* province
pryd *n.en* ornament
prøve *n.en* test; *v.* to try
psykolog *n.en* psychologist
pubertet *n.en* puberty
publikasjon *n.en* publication
publikum *n.et* public
publisere *v.* to publish
pudre *v.* to powder, dust
puls *n.en* pulse
pulver *n.et* powder
pumpe *n.en* pump; *v.* to pump
punkt *n.et* point; spot
punktere *v.* to puncture
punktlig *adj.* punctual
punktum *n.et* period, full stop
punsj *n.en* punch *(drink)*
pupill *n.en* pupil *(in the eye)*
pur *adj.* pure
purpur *n.et* purple
pusleri *n.et* busy work
pusse *v.* to polish
pussig *adj.* funny
pust *n.en* breath; puff of wind
puste *v.* to breathe
pute *n.en* pillow; cushion

pynte seg v. to dress up
pære n.en pear; light bulb
pøbel n.en mob
pøbelaktig adj. vulgar
pølse n.en sausage
på prep.; adv. on, at
påfallende adj. striking
pågripe v. to seize
pågående adj. aggressive
påle n.en pole; v. to drive stakes
pålegg n.et sandwich spreads;
     increase; duty; added-on
     charges
påny adv. afresh
påpeke v. to point out
påregne v. to rely on
påske n. Easter
påskelilje n.en daffodil
påskrift n.en inscription
påstand n.en assertion
påstå v. to insist, claim
påtå v. to assume, take up
     oneself; undertake
påvirke v. to influence
påvirkning n.en influence
påvise v. to demonstrate
påvisning n.en demonstration

R

rabarbra n.en rhubarb
rad n.en row, tier; string of
     beads
radere v. to etch
radering n.en etching
radiator n.en radiator
radikal adj. radical
radioapparat n.et radio
raffinert adj. refined
rake n.en poker; rake; v. to rake
rakett n.en rocket
ramme n.en frame;
     framework; glasses frame;
     v. to strike; to frame a
     picture
rammende adj. pertinent
ran n.et robbery
rand n.en stripe; edge, brink
rang n.en rank
rangel n.en carousal

rangle v. to carouse
ransake v. to search
rapsodi n.en rhapsody
rar adj. peculiar, odd
raritet n.en curiosity
ras n.et avalanche
rase n.en race, breed; v. to
     rage; slide; rush
rasende adj. furious
rasjon n.en ration
rasjonell adj. rational
rask adj. quick
rast n.en rest
raste v. to halt
rastløs adj. restless
ratifisere v. to ratify
ratt n.et steering wheel
reagere v. to react
reaksjon n.en reaction
reaksjonær adj. reactionary
realisme n.en realism
realistisk adj. realistic
realitet n.en reality
rebell n.en rebel
rebelsk adj. rebellious
redaksjon n.en editorial board
redaktør n.en editor
redd adj. afraid
redde v. to rescue
reddik n.en radish
rede n.et nest; v. clarify;
     adj. ready
reder n.en ship owner
redigere v. to edit
redning n.en rescue
redningsbåt n.en lifeboat
redsel n.en horror
redselsfull adj. horrible
redusere v. to reduce
reell adj. real
referanse n.en reference
referat n.et report; summary
referere v. to refer; report
refleksjon n.en reflection
refundere v. to refund
regel n.en rule
regelmessig adj. regular
regiment n.et regiment
region n.en region

regissør *n.en* director; stage manager
register *n.et* register; table of contents
regjere *v.* to govern
regjering *n.en* government
reglement *n.et* regulations
regn *n.et* rain
regnbue *n.en* rainbow
regne *v.* to rain; calculate
regnkappe *n.en* raincoat
regnskap *n.et* account; score
regnskapsfører *n.en* accountant; treasurer
regnvær *n.et* rain (*weather*)
regulere *v.* to regulate
regulær *adj.* regular
rein *n.en* reindeer
reinsdyr *n.et* reindeer
reise *n.en* journey; *v.* to travel; depart; raise
reise seg *v.* stand up; revolt
reisebyrå *n.et* travel agency
reiser *n.pl.* travels
reke *n.en* shrimp
rekke *n.en* row, series, column; ship's rail; *v.* to reach, hand
reklame *n.en* advertisement
rekord *n.en* record (*top performance*)
rektor *n.en* headmaster, principal; president
rekvisitt *adj.* requisite
relativ *adj.* relative
relieff *n.et* relief
religion *n.en* religion
religiøs *adj.* religious
remisse *n.en* remittance
remittere *v.* to remit
ren *adj.* clean; pure; blank
renessanse *n.en* renaissance
rengjøre *v.* to clean
rengjøring *n.en* cleaning
renhet *n.en* purity
renn *n.et* race
renne *v.* to run; flow; thrust
rense *v.* to clean
rente *n.en* interest; dividends
rentefot *n.en* rate of interest

reorganisere *v.* to reorganize
reparere *v.* to repair
replikk *n.en* reply
reportasje *n.en* news reporting
representant *n.en* representative
representere *v.* to represent
reprimande *n.en* reprimand
reprodusere *v.* to reproduce
reptil *n.et* reptile
republikk *n.en* republic
resept *n.en* recipe; prescription
reseptiv *adj.* receptive
reservasjon *n.en* doubts
reserve *n.en* reserves
residens *n.en* residence
resignasjon *n.en* resignation
resignere *v.* to resign
resitere *v.* to recite
resolutt *adj.* resolute
resong *n.en* reason
resonnement *n.et* reasoning
resonnere *v.* to argue
respekt *n.en* respect
respektabel *adj.* respectable
respektere *v.* to respect
ressurser *n.pl.* resources
rest *n.en* remnant
restaurant *n.en* restaurant
restaurasjon *n.en* restoration
resultat *n.et* result
resultere *v.* to result
resymé *n.et* résumé; summary
retning *n.en* direction
retrett *n.en* retreat
rett *n.en* right; law; court of law; dinner course
rette *v.* to correct
rettelse *n.en* correction
rettferdig *adj.* just
retthet *n.en* justice
rettmessig *adj.* lawful
rettsgyldig *adj.* valid
rettsindig *adj.* honest, upright
rettskaffenhet *n.en* honesty, integrity
rettssak *n.en* lawsuit

rettsvitenskap *n.en* jurisprudence
retur *n.en* return
returnere *v.* to return
rev *n.en* fox
revansje *n.en* revenge
revers *n.en* reverse
revidere *v.* to revise
revisor *n.en* auditor
revne *v.* to split
revolte *n.en* revolt
revolusjonær *adj.* revolutionary
revolver *n.en* revolver
revy *n.en* review
ribbe *n.en* rib
ridder *n.en* knight
ridderlig *adj.* chivalrous
ride *v.* to ride
rifle *n.en* rifle; rut; furrow
rik *adj.* rich (*wealthy*)
rikdom *n.en* wealth
riktig *adj.* correct
rim *n.en* frost; *n.et* rhyme
rimelig *adj.* reasonable
rimligvis *adv.* probably
ring *n.en* circle
ringe *v.* to ring
ris *n.et* rice; twigs; child's punishment
risikere *v.* to risk
risikabel *adj.* risky
riste *v.* to roast; toast, shake
rival *n.en* rival
rive *v.* to pull down
ro *n.en* rest; *v.* to row
rokke *v.* to rock
rolig *adj.* calm
rolighet *n.en* calm
rolle *n.en* part
rom *n.et* room
roman *n.en* novel
romanforfatter *n.en* novelist
romantikk *adj.* romantic
romersk *adj.* Roman
rop *n.et* shout
rope *v.* to shout
ror *n.en* rudder
ros *n.en* praise

rose *v.* to praise
rosin *n.en* raisin
rostbiff *n.en* roast beef
rosverdig *adj.* praiseworthy
rot *n.en* root
rotet *adj.* disordered
rovdyr *n.et* prey (*animal*)
ruin *n.en* ruin
ruinere *v.* to ruin
rull *n.en* roll
rulle *v.* to roll
rullestol *n.en* wheelchair
rumpe *n.en* rump
rund *adj.* round
rundstykke *n.et* roll, breakfast roll
rus *n.en* intoxication
russ *n.en* freshman
Russland *Pln.* Russia
russer *n.en* Russian
russisk *adj.* Russian
rust *n.en* rust
ruste *v.* to rust
rustning *n.en* armament; armor
rutebåt *n.en* ocean liner; steamer
rutine *n.en* routine
ry *n.et* fame
rydde *v.* to clear
rygg *n.en* back; ridge
ryggsekk *n.en* backpack
ryke *n.et* rumor; reputation; *v.* to smoke; burst; rush
rynke *v.* to wrinkle; to frown
rype *n.en* ptarmigan, grouse
rytme *n.en* rhythm
rytter *n.en* horseman
rød *adj.* red
rødme *v.* to blush
røk *n.en* smoke
røke *v.* to smoke
rømning *n.en* desertion; evacuation
rør *n.et* tube; reed; telephone receiver
røre *v.* to touch; to move
røre seg *v.* to move oneself
rørig *adj.* active

rørende *adj.* touching, emotionally moving
røst *n.en* voice
røve *v.* to steal
røveri *n.et* robbery
røyk *n.en* smoke
rå *adj.* raw
råd *n.et* advice
råde *v.* to advise
rådgiver *n.en* adviser
rådhus *n.et* townhall
rådyr *n.et* roe deer
råtne *v.* to rot
råtten *adj.* rotten

S

saft *n.en* juice
sag *n.en* saw
sagbruk *n.et* sawmill
sage *v.* to saw
sagn *n.et* legend; tradition
sak *n.en* lawsuit; cause; matter
saks *n.en* scissors
sakte *adj.* slow; soft, gentle
salat *n.en* salad; lettuce
salg *n.et* sale
salig *adj.* blessed
salme *n.en* hymn
salong *n.en* drawing room
salt *n.et* salt
salutt *n.en* salute
salutere *v.* to salute
salve *n.en* ointment
samarbeid *n.et* cooperation
samfund *n.et* society
samhold *n.et* agreement; unity
samle, samle seg *v.* to collect, gather
samling *n.en* collection
samliv *n.et* life together
samme *adj.* same
sammen *adj.* together
sammenligne *v.* to compare
samt *prep.* together with; at the same time
samtale *n.en* conversation
samtidig *adj.* at the same time
samvittighet *n.en* conscience
sand *n.en* sand

sandkasse *n.en* sandbox
sandal *n.en* sandal
sang *n.en* song, singing
sangkor *n.en* choir
sanitær *adj.* sanitary
sankt *n.en* saint
sann *adj.* true
sannhet *n.en* truth
sansynlig *adj.* probable
sannsynligvis *adv.* probably
sans *n.en* sense
sardin *n.en* sardine
sarkastisk *adj.* sarcastic
sart *adj.* tender
satire *n.en* satire
sats *n.en* assertion; proverb
sau *n.en* sheep
saus *n.en* sauce
savne *v.* to lack; miss, regret the absence of
scene *n.en* scene
se *v.* to see
seddel *n.en* slip of paper; banknote
sedelig *adj.* virtuous
segl *n.et* seal, signet
seil *n.et* sail
seile *v.* to sail
seier *n.en* victory
sekk *n.en* sack
sekretær *n.en* secretary
seks *num.* six
seksjon *n.en* section
seksten *num.* sixteen
seksti *num.* sixty
seksuell *adj.* sexual
sekt *n.et* sect
sekund *n.en* second
sel *n.en* seal (*animal*)
selge *v.* to sell
selleri *n.en* celery
selskap *n.et* company, party
selskapelig *adj.* convivial, festive
selsom *adj.* strange
selters *n.en* seltzer
selv *pron.* self
selvfølgelig *adj.* obvious; inevitable; *adv.* of course

selvmord *n.et* suicide
selvstendig *adj.* independent
selvstendighet *n.en*
   independence
selvstyre *n.et* self-government
sement *n.en* cement
semester *n.et* term
sen *adj.* late; slow
senat *n.et* senate
sende *v.* to send
seng *n.en* bed
sengeteppe *n.et* bedspread
senil *adj.* senile
senke *v.* to sink
sennep *n.en* mustard
sensasjonell *adj.* sensational
sentens *n.en* sentence
sentimental *adj.* sentimental
sentral *adj.* central
sentralisere *v.* to centralize
sentrum *n.et* center;
   downtown
separere *v.* to separate
separasjon *n.en* separation;
   divorce
seremoni *n.en* ceremony
sersjant *n.en* sergeant
sertifikat *n.et* certificate
servere *v.* to serve
serviett *n.en* napkin
sesjon *n.en* session
sesong *n.en* season
sete *n.en* seat
seter *n.en* mountain farm
setning *n.en* sentence
sette *v.* to set, put
sette seg *v.* to sit down
sfære *n.en* sphere
si *v.* to say, tell
side *n.en* side; book page
siden *adv.; conj.* since
sigarett *n.en* cigarette
signal *n.et* signal
signatur *n.en* signature
sigøyner *n.en* gypsy
sikker *adj.* secure, safe; certain;
   reliable
sikkert *adv.* assuredly
sikt *n.en* sight

silke *n.en* silk
simpel *adj.* simple; mean,
   common
simulere *v.* to simulate
sinn *n.et* mind; disposition
sinnssyk *adj.* insane
sint *adj.* angry
sirene *n.en* siren
sirkel *n.en* circle
sirkulere *v.* to circulate
sirkus *n.et* circus
sist *adj.; adv.* last
sitat *n.et* quotation
sitere *v.* to quote
sitron *n.en* lemon
sitte *v.* to sit
situasjon *n.en* situation
situert *adj.* situated
sivil *adj.* civil, civilian
sjakk *n.en* chess
sjal *n.et* shawl
sjalu *adj.* jealous
sjalusi *n.en* jealousy
sjampinjong *n.en* mushroom
sjargong *n.en* jargon
sjarlatan *n.en* charlatan
sjef *n.en* chief
sjel *n.en* soul
sjelden *adv.* seldom
sjelelig *adj.* mental; spiritual
sjenert *adj.* embarrassed
sjenerøs *adj.* generous
sjenever *n.en* gin (*alcohol*)
sjofel *adj.* mean, low
sjokk *n.et* shock
sjokolade *n.en* chocolate
sjø *n.en* sea
sjøfart *n.en* navigation
sjømann *n.en* sailor
sjøreise *n.en* sea voyage
sjøsyk *adj.* seasick
sjåfør *n.en* chauffeur
sjåvinisme *n.en* chauvinism
skade *n.en* harm, damage;
   v. to harm, injure, damage
skadelig *adj.* harmful
skaffe *v.* to procure, obtain
skall *n.en* shell, skin
skam *n.en* shame

skamløs *adj.* shameless
skamme seg *v.* to be ashamed
skammelig *adj.* shameful
skandale *n.en* scandal
skandaløs *adj.* scandalous
skandinavisk *adj.*
   Scandinavian
skap *n.et* cabinet; wardrobe
skape *v.* to create
skapelse *n.en* creation
skarp *adj.* sharp; keen
skatt *n.en* tax; treasure
skattbar *adj.* taxable
skepsis *n.en* skepticism
ski *n.en* ski
skiløp *n.et* skiing
skifte *v.* to shift
skikk *n.en* custom
skikkelig *adj.* respectable
skikkelse *n.en* shape
skildring *n.en* description
skilt *n.et* badge; sign;
   nameplate; *adj.* divorced
skinn *n.et* leather, skin; gleam
skinne *v.* to gleam, shine
skip *n.et* ship
skipsbyggeri *n.en* shipyard
skipsfart *n.en* navigation;
   shipping industry
skipper *n.en* skipper
skisse *v.* to sketch
skitne *v.* to soil
skitt *n.en* filth
skje *n.en* spoon
skjebne *n.en* fate
skjegg *n.et* beard
skjelett *n.et* skeleton
skjelve *v.* to tremble
skjenke *v.* to pour out
skjerf *n.et* scarf
skjorte *n.en* shirt
skjule *v.* to conceal
skjær *n.et* reef
skjønn *adj.* beautiful
skjønne *v.* to understand
skjønt *conj.* although
skjørt *n.et* skirt
sko *n.en* shoe
skog *n.en* forest

skogbruk *n.et* forestry
skole *n.en* school
skolegutt *n.en* schoolboy
skolepike *n.en* schoolgirl
skomaker *n.en* shoemaker
skorpe *n.en* crust
skotsk *adj.* Scottish
Scottland *Pln.* Scotland
skotte *n.en* Scot
skotøy *n.et* footwear
skral *adj.* scant, poor; sick
skredder *n.en* tailor
skrekkelig *adj.* frightful
skremme *v.* to frighten
skremsel *n.et* terror, fright
skrift *n.en* writing
skriftlig *adj.* in writing
skrik *n.et* scream
skrike *v.* to scream
skritt *n.et* step
skrive *v.* to write
skrivmaskin *n.en* typewriter
skrue *n.en* propeller; *v.* to screw
skryte *v.* to brag
skrøpelig *adj.* infirm
skrå *adj.* diagonally
skudd *n.et* gunshot; shoot,
   sprout
skue *n.et* appearance; scene;
   spectacle
skuespill *n.et* stage play;
   spectacle
skuespiller *n.en* actor
skuespillerinne *n.en* actress
skuffende *adj.* disappointing
skulder *n.en* shoulder
skulle *v.* to have to; to be
   about to
skulptur *n.en* sculpture
skum *n.et* foam
skummel *adj.* gloomy; sinister
skumring *n.en* dusk
skurk *n.en* villain
skute *n.en* vessel
sky *n.en* cloud; *v.* to shun
skyld *n.en* blame; sin
skylde *v.* to owe; blame
skyldig *adj.* guilty; in debt

skynde *v.* to speed up (*skynde seg* = *to hurry up*)
skyte *v.* to shoot
skyve *v.* to push
skøyeraktig *adj.* mischievous
skål *n.en* bowl; toast
skåle *v.* to drink a toast
skåre *v.* to cut, hack
sladder *n.en* gossip
slag *n.et* blow, hit; battle, game
slags *n.en* sort (*all slags* = *all kinds of*)
slagord *n.et* catchword; motto
slakter *n.en* butcher
slange *n.en* snake; garden hose
slank *adj.* slender
slanke seg *v.* to slim, lose weight
slappe *v.* to relax (*slapp av!* = *relax!*)
slave *n.en* slave
slekt *n.en* lineage
slekting *n.en* relative, kinfolk
slem *adj.* naughty
slett *adv.* absolutely
slik *adj.* such; *adv.* in such a way
slippe *v.* to avoid, escape
slips *n.et* necktie
slitsom *adj.* tiring
slokke *v.* to extinguish, turn off
slott *n.et* palace
sludder *n.et* nonsense
sluke *v.* to swallow
slumre *v.* to slumber
slurk *n.en* gulp
slutning *n.en* conclusion
slutt *n.en* end (*til slutt* = *at last*)
slutte *v.* to end
slør *n.et* veil
sløyfe *v.* to demolish; slur; discard; discontinue
slå *v.* to beat, strike; mow
slåss *v.* to fight
smak *n.en* taste
smakløs *adj.* tasteless, in bad taste
smal *adj.* narrow
smed *n.en* blacksmith
smell *n.en* bang (*report of a gun*)

smelte *v.* to melt, blend
smerte *n.en* pain
smertelig *adj.* painful
smiger *n.en* flattery
smigre *v.* to flatter
smil *n.en* smile
smile *v.* to smile
smitte *n.en* contagion; *v.* to infect
smittsom *adj.* contagious
smoking *n.en* dinner jacket, tuxedo
smukk *adj.* pretty
smykke *n.et* ornament; *v.* to adorn
smør *n.et* butter
smørbrød *n.et* open-faced sandwich
små *adj.* small
småbarn *n.pl.* babies
småpenger *n.pl.* small change
småting *n.en* trifle
snakk *n.et* talk
snakke *v.* to talk
snaps *n.en* aquavit (*alcohol*)
snar *adj.* quick
snart *adv.* soon
snegl *n.en* snail
snekke *n.en* sailboat
snekker *n.en* cabinetmaker; carpenter
snill *adj.* good
snitt *n.et* cut
snitte *v.* to cut
snor *n.en* cord, string
snorke *v.* to snore
snuble *v.* to stumble
snø *n.en* snow; *v.* to snow
soaré *n.en* soirée, get-together
sogn *n.et* parish
sognprest *n.en* parish minister
soignert *adj.* well-groomed
sokk *n.en* sock
sol *n.en* sun
soldat *n.en* soldier
sole seg *v.* to sunbathe
solid *adj.* solid
solist *n.en* soloist
solnedgang *n.en* sunset

soloppgang *n.en* sunrise
som *pron.* who, which, that;
    conj. like
sommer *n.en* summer
sommerfugl *n.en* butterfly
sone *n.en* zone; *v.* to atone for
sonett *n.en* sonnet
sope *v.* to sweep
sopelime *n.en* broom
sopp *n.en* mushroom
sorg *n.en* sorrow
sorgfull *adj.* sad
sort *adj.* black
sosial *adj.* social
sosialist *n.en* socialist
sot *n.en* soot
sove *v.* to sleep
soveplass *n.en* berth
sovevogn *n.en* Pullman,
    sleeping car
soveværelse *n.et* bedroom
sovne *v.* to fall asleep
spalte *v.* to split
spandere *v.* to spend; pay for
spanier *n.en* Spaniard
Spania *Pln.* Spain
spansk *adj.* Spanish
spare *v.* to save, economize
sparepenger *n.pl.* savings
sparke *adj.* to kick
sparsom *adj.* scarce
spas *n.en* joke
spase *v.* to joke
spasere *v.* to walk
spebarn *n.et* infant
speide *v.* to observe, spy
speider *n.en* scout
speil *n.et* mirror
speile *v.* to fry an egg; reflect
spekemat *n.en* cured fish
    or meat
spennende *adj.* thrilling
spent *adj.* tense
sperre *v.* to close, block
sperret *adj.* blocked off
spesial *adj.* special
spesialisere *v.* to specialize
spesialitet *n.en* specialty
spesiell *adj.* special

spill *n.et* play, game; gambling;
    acting
spille *v.* to play, act
spillebord *n.et* card table
spinat *n.en* spinach
spion *n.en* spy
spire *v.* to sprout
spise *v.* to eat
spisekart *n.et* menu
spiselig *adj.* edible
spisevogn *n.en* dining car
spiss *n.en* tip, point; *adj.* sharp;
    sarcastic
spontan *adj.* spontaneous
spor *n.et* footprint; trace;
    railroad track
sport *n.en* sport
sporvei *n.en* trolley line
spott *n.en* ridicule
spotte *v.* to ridicule
spotsk *adj.* contemptuous
sprang *n.et* leap
sprede *v.* to spread
spredt *adj.* scattered
sprek *adj.* spry
sprenge *v.* to burst, blast
sprettende *adj.* lively
springe *v.* to explode; jump,
    run; gush
sprit *n.en* alcohol
sprute *v.* to spurt
sprø *adj.* crisp, brittle; crazy
sprøyte *n.en* hypodermic;
    watering can; fire engine
språk *n.et* language
spurv *n.en* sparrow
spy *v.* to vomit
spydig *adj.* sarcastic
spytt *n.et* spit
spytte *v.* to spit
spøk *n.en* joke
spøke *v.* to joke; haunt
spøkelse *n.et* ghost
spørre *v.* to ask
spørsmål *n.et* question
spådom *n.en* prediction
stab *n.en* staff
stabbur *n.et* storehouse
stabilisere *v.* to stabilize

stad *n.en* place
stadig *adj.* steady; continuous
stadighet *n.en* stability
stagnere *v.* to stagnate
stake *n.en* stake
stakkar! *n.en* poor creature!
stakkars *adj.* pitiable
stamme *n.en* trunk; tribe; *v.* to
    be descended from; stutter
stand *n.en* condition
standpunkt *n.et* standpoint
stang *n.en* pole; fishing pole
stans *n.en* pause
stanse *v.* to stop
starte *v.* to start
stas *n.en* pleasure, fun;
    decoration; celebration
staselig *adj.* handsome
stasjon *n.en* station
stasjonær *adj.* stationary
stat *n.en* state
statistikk *n.en* statistics
statsborger *n.en* citizen
statskirke *n.en* state church
statskunst *n.en* statecraft
statsminister *n.en* prime
    minister
statue *n.en* statue
stebarn *n.et* stepchild
sted *n.et* place
stedlig *adj.* local
stefar *n.en* stepfather
stein *n.en* stone
steke *v.* to roast, fry
stekeovn *n.en* baking oven
stekepanne *n.en* frying pan
stell *n.et* management; order
stelle *v.* to take care of; do the
    housework; prepare (*stelle
    mat = prepare food*)
stelle seg *v.* get ready
stemme *n.en* voice; vote;
    v. to vote
stemning *n.en* atmosphere,
    mood
stemningsfull *adj.* full of
    feeling, emotional
stemor *n.en* stepmother
stemorsblomst *n.en* pansy

stemple *v.* to stamp
stenge *v.* to lock
stengt *adj.* closed
sterk *adj.* strong
stevne *n.et* rally, meeting
sti *n.en* path
stiftelse *n.en* foundation,
    institution
stige *v.* to ascend; stride
stige av *v.* to get off
stikk *n.et* bite, sting
stikkelsbær *n.et* gooseberry
stil *n.en* style
stille *adj.* silent
Stillehavet *Pln.* the Pacific
    Ocean
stillestående *adj.* stationary;
    stagnant
stillhet *n.en* stillness, calmness
stilling *n.en* position;
    employment
stimulans *n.en* stimulus
stimulere *v.* to stimulate
stipend *n.et* scholarship
stirre *v.* to stare
stiv *adj.* stiff
stivhet *n.en* stiffness; formality
stivne *v.* to stiffen
stjele *v.* to steal
stjerne *n.en* star
stoff *n.et* matter, substance;
    theme; fabric
stokk *n.en* log; tree trunk;
    walking stick
stol *n.en* chair
stole på *v.* to rely on
stolt *adj.* proud
stolthet *n.en* pride
stopp *n.en* stop
stoppe *v.* to stop; darn
stoppenål *n.en* darning needle
stor *adj.* big; tall
storartet *adj.* grand; first-rate
stork *n.en* stork
storm *n.en* storm
straff *n.en* punishment
straffe *v.* to punish
straks *adv.* at once
stram *adj.* strict

strand *n.en* shore, beach
strategi *n.en* strategy
strebe *v.* to strive for
streike *v.* to go on strike
strek *n.en* line, stroke
streke over *v.* to delete,
  strike over
streng *adj.* severe, strict
stress *n.en* stress
streve *v.* to strive
strevsom *adj.* hardworking
strid *n.en* fight, dispute
strikk *n.en* rubber band
strikke *v.* to knit
strikkepinne *n.en* knitting
  needle
strikketøy *n.et* knitting
stripet *adj.* striped
strofe *n.en* stanza
struktur *n.en* structure
struts *n.en* ostrich
stryke *v.* to stroke; iron clothes;
  flunk
strøk *n.et* stroke; district
strøm *n.en* stream; electric
  current
strømme *v.* to stream, flow
strå *n.et* straw
strålende *adj.* radiant
student *n.en* student
studere *v.* to study
stue *n.en* living room
stum *adj.* mute
stund *n.en* time, while (*en
  stund = a while*)
stupe *v.* to dive
stupid *adj.* stupid
stygg *adj.* ugly; bad
stykke *n.et* piece, bit
styre *v.* to steer, guide
styrke *n.en* strength
stønn *n.et* moan, moaning
stønne *v.* to moan
størrelse *n.en* size
støte *v.* to push
støtte *v.* to support
støv *n.et* dust
støvbriller *n.pl.* goggles
støvel *n.en* boot

støy *n.en* noise
støyende *adj.* noisy
stå *v.* to stand
stål *n.et* steel
subjekt *n.et* subject
subskribere *v.* to subscribe
substans *n.en* substance
suge *v.* to suck
sukke *v.* to sigh
sukker *n.et* sugar
suksess *n.en* success
sult *n.en* hunger
sulten *adj.* hungry
sump *n.en* swamp
sund *n.et* sound
sunn *adj.* healthy
sunnhet *n.en* health
superb *adj.* superb
suppe *n.en* soup
sur *adj.* sour
suspendere *v.* to suspend
suveren *n.en; adj.* sovereign
svak *adj.* weak
svanger *adj.* pregnant
svar *n.et* answer
svare *v.* to answer
svart *adj.* black
Sveits *Pln.* Switzerland
sveitser *n.en* Swiss
sveitsisk *adj.* Swiss
svekke *v.* to weaken
svekkelse *n.en* weakness
svelle *v.* to swell
svensk *adj.* Swedish
svenske *n.en* Swede
svepe *n.en* whip
sverd *n.et* sword
sverge *v.* to swear
Sverige *Pln.* Sweden
sverm *n.en* swarm
svermeri *n.et* enthusiasm;
  fanatacism
svette *n.en* sweat
svigerfar *n.en* father-in-law
svigerinne *n.en* sister-in-law
svik *n.et* deceit
svimmel *adj.* dizzy
svin *n.et* pig
svinesteik *n.en* roast pork

svindel *n.en* swindle
svoger *n.en* brother-in-law
svulme *v.* to swell
svulst *n.en* tumor; bombast
svær *adj.* huge
svømme *v.* to swim
sy *v.* to sew
syd *adv.* south
Syden *Pln.* the South
sydlig *adj.* southern
Sydpolen *Pln.* the South Pole
syk *adj.* sick
sykdom *n.en* illness
sykepleierske *n.en* female
    nurse
sykkel *n.en* bicycle
sykmeldt *adj.* on sick leave
syltetøy *n.et* sweets
symbol *n.et* symbol
sympati *n.en* sympathy
syn *n.et* sight, vision;
    apparition; outlook
synagoge *n.en* synagogue
synd *n.en* sin
synes *v.* to think; seem
synge *v.* to sing
synke *v.* to sink
synlig *adj.* visible
syntese *n.en* synthesis
sypike *n.en* seamstress
syrin *n.en* lilac
sysle *v.* to be busy
system *n.et* system
sytten *num.* seventeen
sytti *num.* seventy
syv *num.* seven
særdeles *adj.* special;
    adv. especially
særlig *adj.* special;
    adv. especially
søke *v.* to seek; attempt
søknad *n.en* application
søle *v.* to soil
sølv *n.et* silver
søndag *n.* Sunday
sønn *n.en* son
søppel *n.et* garbage
søppelkasse *n.en* garbage can
sørfra *adv.* from the south

sørover *adv.* toward the south
sørge *v.* to grieve; provide for
sørgelig *adj.* sad
søsken *n.pl.* brothers and
    sisters
søster *n.en* sister
søt *adj.* sweet
søvn *n.en* sleep
søvnig *adj.* sleepy
søyle *n.en* column
så *adv.; conj.* so, such
således *adv.* thus, in this
    manner
sånn *adv.* like that, in such
    a way
såpe *n.en* soap
sår *n.et* wound
såre *v.* to wound

T

ta *v.* to take; hold; catch
tak *n.et* roof; ceiling
takk *n.en* thanks
takknemlig *adj.* grateful
taktfull *adj.* discreet
taktikk *n.en* tactics
tale *n.en* speech
talent *n.en* talent
tall *n.en* number
tangere *v.* to touch
tanke *n.en* thought, idea
tankefull *adj.* thoughtful
tann *n.en* tooth
tannbørste *n.en* toothbrush
tannlege *n.en* dentist
tannpasta *n.en* toothpaste
tannpine *n.en* toothache
tante *n.en* aunt
tap *n.et* loss
tape *v.* to lose
tapper *adj.* brave
tarm *n.en* intestines
tarvelig *adj.* modest; shabby
tau *n.et* rope
taus *adj.* silent
tavle *n.en* tablet; blackboard;
    chart
T-bane *n.en* subway; city train
te *n.en* tea

teater *n.et* theater
teaterstykke *n.et* play
tegn *n.et* sign; badge
tegne *v.* to draw
tegnebok *n.en* drawing book
tegning *n.en* drawing
teknikk *n. en* technique
teknisk *adj.* technical
tekst *n.en* text
tekstil *n.en* textile
telefon *n.en* telphone
telefonere *v.* to telephone
telefonkatalog *n.en* telephone directory
telefonkiosk *n.en* telephone booth
telegraf *n.en* telegraph
teleskop *n.et* telescope
telle *v.* to count
telt *n.et* tent
tema *n.et* theme
temme *v.* to tame
tempel *n.et* temple
temperament *n.et* temperament
temperatur *n.en* temperature
tempo *n.et* pace
tempus *n.et* verb tense
tendens *n.en* tendency
tenke *v.* to think
tenke seg om *v.* to think over
tenkelig *adj.* conceivable
tenkning *n.en* thinking; philosophy
tenksom *adj.* reflective
tenne *v.* to light, ignite
tenning *n.en* igniting; automobile ignition
tennplug *n.en* spark plug
teologi *n.en* theology
teoretisk *adj.* theoretical
teori *n.en* theory
teppe *n.et* carpet; tapestry; theater curtain
termin *n.en* term, semester
termometer *n.et* thermometer
terrasse *n.en* terrace
terreng *n.et* terrain
terrin *n.en* tureen

terrorisere *v.* terrorize
testamente *n.et* testament; will
testamentere *v.* to bequeath, will
tett *adj.* tight; dense
ti *num.* ten
tid *n.en* time
tidlig *adj.* early
tidligere *adj.* earlier, former
tidsalder *n.en* age
tidsnok *adv.* in time, soon enough
tidspunkt *n.et* point in time
tidsskrift *n.et* periodical
tie *v.* to be silent
tiger *n.en* tiger
tigge *v.* to beg
tigger *n.en* beggar
til *prep.* to, toward; *conj.* until
tilbake *adv.* back
tilbehør *n.et* belongings; equipment
tilberede *v.* to prepare
tilberedelse *n.en* preparation
tilbringe *v.* to spend (*time*)
tilbud *n.et* offer
tiby *v.* to offer
tildels *adv.* partly
tilegnelse *n.en* dedication
tilfeldig *adj.* accidental; *adv.* by chance
tilfeldighet *n.en* accident, coincidence
tilfeldigvis *adv.* by chance
tilfreds *adj.* satisfied
tilfredshet *n.en* satisfacion
tilgi *v.* to forgive
tilhenger *n.en* follower
tilhøre *v.* to belong to
tilhørende *adj.* belonging to
tilhørere *n.en* audience
tillate *v.* to permit
tillatelig *adj.* permissable
tillatelse *n.en* permission
tillegg *n.et* addition; surcharge; increase
tillit *n.en* trust, confidence
tillitsfull *adj.* trusting
tillokkende *adj.* tempting

tilråde *v.* to advise
tilsagn *n.et* promise
tilsalgs *adv.* for sale
tilsammen *adv.* together
tilskudd *n.et* contribution
tilskuer *n.en* spectator
tilslutt *adv.* at last
tilstand *n.en* condition
tilsyn *n.et* supervison
tilta *v.* to increase
tiltrekkende *adj.* attractive
tilværelse *n.en* existence
time *n.en* hour
ting *n.en* thing; court;
   parliament
tirsdag *n.* Tuesday
titte *v.* to peep
tjene *v.* to serve; earn
tjener *n.en* servant
tjenerinne *n.en* maid, servant
tjeneste *n.en* a favor, good turn
tjue *num.* twenty
to *num.* two
toalett *n.et* toilet
tobakk *n.en* tobacco
tog *n.et* railway train;
   procession
toleranse *n.en* tolerance
tolk *n.en* interpreter
tolke *v.* to interpret
toll *n.en* customs
tollangivelse *n.en* customs
   declaration
tollavgift *n.en* customs duty
tollbetjent *n.en* customs
   officer
tollbu *n.en* customs house
tollfri *adj.* duty free
tolv *num.* twelve
tom *adj.* empty
tomat *n.en* tomato
tomme *n.en* inch; thumb
tomt *n.en* yard
tone *n.en* sound
tonefall *n.et* accent; intonation
topografisk *adj.* topographical
topp *n.en* top, summit
torden *n.en* thunder
tordenvær *n.et* thunderstorm

tore *v.* to dare
torg *n.et* marketplace
torn *n.en* thorn
torsday *n.* Thursday
torsk *n.en* cod
tort *n.en* injury
tortur *n.en* torture
toskeskap *n.en* foolishness
total *adj.* total
tradisjonell *adj.* traditional
trafikant *n.en* traveler;
   trafficker
trafikk *n.en* traffic; trade
traffikere *v.* to trade, traffic in
tragedie *n.en* tragedy
trampe *v.* to tramp; trample
tran *n.en* codliver oil
trang *n.en* need; want;
trang *adj.* narrow
transitt *n.en* transit
transport *n.en* transportation;
   shipment
transportere *v.* to transport
trapp *n.en* staircase
trappetrin *n.et* step
travel *adj.* busy
tre *num.* three; *n.et* tree, wood
treff *n.et* chance, coincidence;
   hit
treffe *v.* to meet; hit
trekant *n.en* triangle
trekk *n.et* pull; facial feature;
   migration; draft of air;
   v. to drag; draw
trekke seg *v.* to pull oneself
   out, withdraw
trelast *n.en* timber
trene *v.* to train, practice
trenge *v.* to force, press; need,
   require
tresko *n.en* wooden shoe
tresnitt *n.et* woodcut
trett *adj.* tired
tretten *num.* thirteen
tretti *num.* thirty
trikk *n.en* streetcar, trolley;
   subway
trille *v.* to roll, wheel
trin *n.et* step; rung

tripp *n.en* short trip
trist *adj.* sad
triumf *n.en* triumph
trivelig *adj.* plump; cosy;
   healthy
trives *v.* to thrive
trofast *adj.* faithful
troll *n.et* ogre
trollskap *n.en* witchcraft
tromme *n.en* drum; *v.* to beat
   a drum
trompet *n.en* trumpet
trone *n.en* throne
tronarving *n.en* heir to the
   throne
tropene *n.pl.* the tropics
tropisk *adj.* tropical
tropp *n.en* troop
troskap *n.en* fidelity
tross *prep.* in spite of
trossig *adj.* stubborn
trost *n.en* thrush
troverdig *adj.* trustworthy
true *v.* to threaten
trusel *n.en* threat
trygd *n.en* insurance; security
trygg *adj.* safe
trygghet *n.en* safety
trykk *n.en* pressure; print
trykkende *adj.* oppressive
trykkeri *n.et* printing house
trykkfeil *n.en* misprint
trylle *v.* to enchant
trylleri *n.et* magic
trøste *v.* to comfort
tråd *n.en* thread
tsar *n.en* czar
Tsjekkisk Republikk *Pln.*
   Czech Republic
tsjekker *n.en* Czech
tsjekkisk *adj.* Czech
tube *n.en* tube
tukt *n.en* discipline; propriety
tulipan *n.en* tulip
tulle *n.en* nonsense
tumle *v.* to tumble
tummel *n.en* turmoil
tung *adj.* heavy; dull
tunge *n.en* tongue

tunnel *n.en* tunnel
tur *n.en* trip
turbillett *n.en* one-way ticket
turbin *n.en* turbine
turist *n.en* tourist
turnips *n.en* turnip
tusen *num.* thousand
tusj *n.en* ink
tvang *n.en* coercion
tverr *adj.* grumpy; stubborn
tverrsnitt *n.et* cross section
tvertimot *adv.* on the contrary
tvil *n.en* doubt
tvile *v.* to doubt
tvilsom *adj.* doubtful
tvilling *n.en* twin
tvinge *v.* to force
tyde *v.* to interpret
tydelig *adj.* clear, obvious
tygge *v.* to chew
tykk *adj.* thick; fat
tykkelse *n.en* thickness
tynn *adj.* thin
type *n.en* type
typisk *adj.* typical
tyrani *n.et* tyranny
tyrk *n.en* Turk
Tyrkia *Pln.* Turkey
tyrkisk *adj.* Turkish
tysk *adj.* German
tysker *n.en* German
Tyskland *Pln.* Germany
tyst *adj.* silent
tyttebær *n.et* lingonberry
tyv *n.en* thief
tyve *num.* twenty
tyveri *n.et* theft
tæring *n.en* tuberculosis
tøffel *n.en* slipper
tøffelhelt *n.en* henpecked
   husband
tømme *v.* to empty
tømmer *n.et* timber
tømmerhugger *n.en*
   lumberjack
tønne *n.en* barrel
tørke *v.* to dry
tørkle *n.et* handkerchief
tørr *adj.* dry

tørre *v.* to dry
tørst *n.en* thirst; *adj.* thirsty
tøy *n.et* material, stuff; fabric;
  clothes
tå *n.en* toe
tåke *n.en* fog
tåket *adj.* foggy
tåle *v.* to endure, bear
tålmodig *adj.* patient
tåpelig *adj.* foolish
tåre *n.en* teardrop
tårn *n.et* tower; steeple

U

ualminnelig *adj.* uncommon
uavbrutt *adj.* uninterrupted
uavhengig *adj.* independent
ubegrenset *adj.* unbounded
ubegripelig *adj.*
  incomprehensible
ubehagelig *adj.* disagreeable
ubeskrivelig *adj.* indescribable
ubestemt *adj.* indefinite;
  undetermined
ubevisst *adj.* unconscious,
  subconscious
ubrukbar *adj.* useless
udannet *adj.* uncultivated
udødelig *adj.* immortal
uenig *adj.* in disagreement
uendelig *adj.* endless
uerfaren *adj.* inexperienced
uff da, huff da *interj.* oh dear!
  ugh!
uforståelig *adj.* unintelligible
uforsvarlig *adj.* indefensible
ufrivillig *adj.* involuntary;
  unintentional
ugle *n.en* owl
ugyldig *adj.* invalid
uheldig *adj.* unfortunate
uhyre *n.et* monster; *adj.* huge;
  adv. extremely
ulik *adj.* unlike
ulike *adj.* unequal
ull *n.en* wool
ullen *adj.* woollen
ullteppe *n.et* blanket
ulovlig *adj.* illegal

ulv *n.en* wolf
ulvinne *n.en* she-wolf
ulydig *adj.* disobedient
ulykke *n.en* accident;
  misfortune
umiddelbar *adj.* immediate,
  firsthand
umoralsk *adj.* immoral
umulig *adj.* impossible
umøblert *adj.* unfurnished
under *n.et* wonder, marvel;
  adj.; prep. under, below,
  beneath; during
underbevisshet *n.en*
  subconsciousness
undergang *n.en* ruin
underholdende *adj.*
  entertaining
underholdning *n.en*
  entertainment
underlig *adj.* strange
underliv *n.et* abdomen
underretning *n.en*
  information
underskrift *n.en* signature
underskrive *v.* to sign
underskudd *n.et* deficit
underst *adj.* lowest
understreke *v.* to emphasize
undersøke *v.* to examine
undersøkelse *n.en*
  examination
undertøy *n.et* underwear
underveis *adv.* on the way
underverden *n.en* underworld
undervise *v.* to teach
undervisning *n.en* instruction
undervurdere *v.* to undervalue
ung *adj.* young (*de unge* =
  young people)
Ungarn *Pln.* Hungary
ungarer *n.en* Hungarian
ungarsk *adj.* Hungarian
ungdom *n.en* youth
ungkar *n.en* bachelor
uniform *n.en* uniform
universell *adj.* universal
universitet *n.et* university

unnskylde *v.* to excuse
(*unnskyld* = *I beg your
pardon*)
unyttig *adj.* useless
unødig *adj.* unnecessary
unødvendig *adj.* unnecessary
uorden *n.en* disorder
upopulær *adj.* unpopular
upratisk *adj.* impractical
ur *n.et* watch, clock
urmaker *n.en* watchmaker
uren *adj.* impure
urett *n.en* injustice; *adj.* wrong
uriktig *adj.* incorrect
urimelig *adj.* unreasonable,
excessive; *adv.*
unreasonably
urin *n.en* urine
uro *n.en* disturbance
urolig *adj.* troubled; noisy
usann *adj.* untrue
usedelig *adj.* immoral
uselskapelig *adj.* unsociable
uskikk *n.en* bad custom
uskikkelig *adj.* naughty
ustanselig *adj.* incessant
ustell *n.et* disorder
usynlig *adj.* invisible
utbrudd *n.et* outbreak
utbryte *v.* to break out; cry out
utdannelse *n.en* education
utdele *v.* to distribute
ute *adv.* out
uten *prep.*; *conj.* without
utenkelig *adj.* unimaginable
utenfor *prep.* outside
utenlands *adj.* abroad
utfordre *v.* to challenge
utfordring *n.en* challenge
utføre *v.* to carry out
utgang *n.en* exit; departure
utgave *n.en* edition
utgift *n.en* expense
utgivelse *n.en* publication
utholde *v.* to bear, endure
utklipp *n.et* newspaper
clipping
utlegg *n.et* expenses
utmerket *adj.* outstanding

utruste *v.* to outfit
utrydde *v.* to root out
utsalg *n.et* sale
utside *adj.* outside
utslitt *adj.* worn out
utsolgt *adj.* sold out
utstyr *n.et* outfit; decor
utta *v.* to select
uttale *n.en* pronunciation;
v. to pronounce
uttrykk *n.et* expression
utvalg *n.et* selection
utvalgt *adj.* selected; select
utvandre *v.* to emigrate
utvide *v.* expand
utvidelse *n.en* expansion
utvikling *n.en* development
utålmodig *adj.* impatient
uventet *adj.* unexpected
uvilkårlig *adj.* involuntary;
adv. involuntarily
uvær *n.et* bad weather

V

vakker *adj.* attractive,
handsome; good,
commendable
vakt *n.en* guard, watch
valg *n.et* choice
vals *n.en* waltz
vandre *v.* to wander, roam
vane *n.en* custom
vanilje *n.en* vanilla
vann *n.et* water
vannrett *adj.* level
vannstoff *n.et* hydrogen
vanskelig *adj.* difficult
vant *adj.* accustomed
vantro *n.en* unbelief
vanvittig *adj.* insane
vare *n.en* goods; *v.* to last
variabel *adj.* variable
varm *adj.* warm
varme *n.en* warmth, heat;
v. to heat up
varsel *n.et* warning
vask *n.en* wash; laundry; sink.
vaske *v.* to wash
vaske opp *v.* to do the dishes

ved *adv.* near by; *prep.* at,
    by, near
vedde *v.* to bet
vedlagt *adj.* enclosed,
    accompanying
vedlegge *v.* to enclose
vekk *adv.* away
vekk! *interj.* go away!
vekke *v.* to awaken
vekt *n.en* weight; scales
vel *adj.* well, lucky; *adv.*
    happily; of course; rather
veldig *adj.* mighty, enormous;
    adv. very
velge *v.* to choose
velkledd *adj.* well-dressed
velkommen *adj.* welcome
    (*Velkommen! = Welcome!*
    You are welcome)
vellykket *adj.* successful
veloppdragen *adj.* well
    brought up
velsigne *v.* to bless
velskapt *adj.* well formed
velstand *n.en* prosperity
vemmelig *adj.* disgusting
vemod *n.et* sadness
vende *v.* to turn
venn *n.en* friend
venninne *n.en* female friend
vennlig *adj.* friendly
vennligst *adj.* if you please
vennskap *n.et* friendship
venstre *adj.* left
vente *v.* to wait, expect
veps *n.en* wasp
veranda *n.en* veranda
verbum *n.et* verb
verd *n.et* worth; *adj.*
    worthwhile; worthy
verden *n.en* world
verdi *n.en* value
verdifull *adj.* valuable
verksted *n.et* workplace
vern *n.et* defence
verne *v.* to protect
vers *n.et* verse
vert *n.en* landlord; host
vertikal *adj.* vertical

vertinne *n.en* landlady;
    hostess
vesen *n.et* being
vesentlig *adj.* essential;
    adv. chiefly, mainly
veske *n.en* handbag
vestlig *adj.* western
veteran *n.en* veteran
veto *n.et* veto
veve *v.* to weave
vid *adj.* wide
videre *adj.; adv.* farther
vidunderlig *adj.* wonderful
vie *v.* to dedicate; marry
vifte *v.* to fan
vigør *n.en* vigor
vik *n.en* creek; bay
viktig *adj.* important
viktigst *adj.* most important
vilje *n.en* will; determination
vill *adj.* wild
villa *n.en* private home; villa
ville *v.* to want, would like
vin *n.en* wine
vind *n.en* wind
vindu *n.et* window
vinge *n.en* wing
vinglass *n.et* wine glass
vinkaraffel *n.en* wine carafe
vinkart *n.et* wine list
vinke *v.* to wave
vinne *v.* to win
vinter *n.en* winter
virke *v.* to influence; bring
    about
virkelig *adj.* real; *adv.* really
virkelighet *n.en* reality
virkning *n.en* effect
virksom *adj.* effective; active
virksomhet *n.en* activity;
    operations
vis *adj.* wise
visdom *n.en* wisdom
vise *v.* to show, indicate
visitere *v.* to inspect
visitt *n.en* visit
visjon *n.en* vision
visne *v.* to fade

viss *adj.* certain
visst *adv.* certainly
vitamin *n.et* vitamin
vite *v.* to know
vitenskap *n.en* knowledge
vitenskapelig *adj.* scientific
vitne *n.et* witness
vits *n.en* joke
vittig *adj.* witty
vogn *n.en* wagon; vehicle;
  railway car; streetcar;
  vehicle
vokabular *n.et* vocabulary
voks *n.et* wax
vokse *v.* to grow
voksen *adj.* adult
vold *n.en* force, power;
  violence
voldsom *adj.* violent
voldtekt *n.en* rape; violent
  assault
volum *n.et* volume
vond *adj.* difficult; painful;
  evil; bad
votere *v.* to vote
vrak *n.et* wreckage
vred *adj.* angry
vri *v.* to wring
vugge *n.en* cradle; *v.* to rock
vulgær *adj.* vulgar
vurdere *v.* to value
væpne seg *v.* to arm oneself
vær *n.et* weather
være *n.et* existence; *v.* to be
værforandring *n.en* weather
  change
værgud *n.en* weather-god
værhane *n.en* weather vane
værmelding *n.en* weather
  forecast
værvarsel *n.et* weather
  forecast
væte *n.en* humidity; rain;
  v. to wet
vørterøl *n.et* near-beer,
  alcohol-free beer
våge *v.* to dare
våge seg *v.* to venture

vågsom *adj.* daring; dangerous
våke *v.* to wake
våken *adj.* awake
våkne *v.* to wake
våpen *n.et* weapon
vår *n.en* springtime
vår *pron.* our, ours
vårlig *adj.* vernal
våt *adj.* wet
våtvær *n.et* wet weather

W

weekend *n.en* weekend trip
whiskey *n.en* Scotch whiskey
wienerbrød *n.et* Danish pastry

X

x-stråle *n.en* X-ray

Y

ydmyk *adj.* humble
yndelig *adj.* charming
yngling *n.en* youth
yngere *adj.* younger
ypperlig *adj.* excellent
yrke *n.et* work, trade,
  occupation

Z

zoologi *n.en* zoology

Æ

ærbarhet *n.en* repect,
  deference
ære *n.en* honor, praise
ærend *n.et.* errand
ærlig *adj.* honest; honestly
  (*ærlig talt* = *honestly
  speaking*)
ærlighet *n.en* honesty

Ø

øde *n.et* wasteland; *adj.*
  deserted; bare, empty
ødelegge *v.* to destroy
ødeleggelse *n.en* ruin
ødsel *adj.* wasteful
ødslig *adj.* lonely, deserted

øke *v.* to increase
økning *n.en* increase
økonom *n.en* economist
økonomi *n.en* economy
økonomisk *adj.* economical
øks *n.en* ax
øl *n.et* ale, beer
øm *adj.* tender, sore;
    affectionate; sensitive
ønske *v.* to desire, wish
øre *n.et* ear
ørken *n.en* desert
ørn *n.en* eagle
ørret *n.en* trout
øst *adv.* east
Østen *Pln.* the East
østenfor *prep.* east of
østerlandsk *adj.* oriental
Østerrike *Pln.* Austria
østerriksk *adj.* Austrian
østers *n.en* oysters
Østersjøen *Pln.* the Baltic Sea
Østlandet *Pln.* southeastern
    part of Norway
østlig *adj.* eastern
øve *v.* to practice
øvelse *n.en* practice
øverst *adj.* uppermost
Øverstkommanderende *n.en*
    Commander-in-chief
øy *n.en* island

øyeblikk *n.et* moment (*et
    øyeblikk!* = *one moment!*)
øyebryn *n.et* eyebrow
øyensynlig *adj.* evident,
    obvious; *adv.* evidently
øyesyn *n.et* eyesight

Å

åker *n.en* field
åkerbruk *n.et* agriculture
ål *n.en* eel
ånd *n.en* spirit; phantom;
    genius, intelligence
ånde *n.en* breath; *v.* to breathe
åndeløs *adj.* breathless
åpen *adj.* open; frank
åpenbar *adj.* evident
åpne *v.* to open
åpning *n.en* opening
år *n.et* year
åre *n.en* artery, vein; oar
årelang *adj.* for years
årgang *n.en* annual
    publication
århundre *n.et* century
årlig *adj.* annual; *adv.* annually
årsak *n.en* cause, reason
årstall *n.et* year, date
årstid *n.en* season
åtte *num.* eight
åtti *num* eighty

English-Norwegian Dictionary

A

abdomen *n.* underliv *et*

able *v.* kan, kunne (*be able to*); *adj.* dyktig, flink

about *prep.* om, omkring, omtrent

above *prep.* over

abroad *adj.* til utlandet, utenlands

absent *adj.* fraværerende, ikke til stede

accept *v.* akseptere, godkjenne, få imot

accident *n.* tilfeldighet *en*, ulykke *en*

accommodation *n.* hotellplass *en*, overnattingsmulighet *en*

accompany *v.* følge

accustomed (to) *adj.* vant til

account *n.* konto *en* (*bank*); *v.* regne for, forklare

across *adv.; prep.* over

action *n.* handling *en*

active *adj.* virksom

actor, actress *n.* skuespiller *en*, skuespillerinne *en*

actually *adv.* egentlig, faktisk

add *v.* legge sammen

address *n.* adresse *en; v.* adressere

admire *v.* beundre

admission *n.* adgang *en*; adgang forbudt (*no admittance*)

adult *n.; adj.* voksen *en*

advantage *n.* fordel *en*

adventure *n.* eventyr *et*

advertisement *n.* reklame *en*, avertissement *et*

advice *n.* rad *en*

advise *v.* råde; advisere

afraid *adj.* redd

after *adv.; prep.; conj.* etter

afternoon *n.* ettermiddag *en*

afterwards *adv.* etterpå

again *adv.* igjen

against *prep.* mot

age *n.* alder *en; v.* å bli gammel

agree on *v.* avtale, bli enig om

agreement *n.* avtale *en*

agriculture *n.* landbruk *et*

AIDS *abbrev.* AIDS

aim *n.* sikte *et*

air *n.* luft *en*

air conditioning *n.* airconditioning *en*, luftkondisjonering *en*

airmail *n.* luftpost *en*; med luftpøst (*by airmail*)

airplane *n.* fly *et*

airport *n.* flyplass *en*

alarm clock *n.* vekkerklokke *en*

alcohol *n.* alkohol *en*, sprit *en*

alive *adj.* i live, levende

all *adj.* all, alt, alle

allergic *adj.* allergisk

allow *v.* tillate, la

almost *adv.* nesten

alone *adv.* alene

along *prep.* langs

already *adv.* allerede

also *adv.* også

although *conj.* skjønt

altitude sickness *n.* høyde sykdom *en*

always *adv.* alltid

a.m. *abbrev.* om formidagen

ambulance *n.* ambulanse *en*

America *Pln.* Amerika

American *n.* amerikaner *en*; *adj.* amerikansk

April *n.* april

amount *n.* beløp *et*, størrelse *en*

amusing *adv.* morsom

and *conj.* og

anesthetic *n.* bedøvelsesmiddel *et*

angry *adj.* sint

ankle *n.* ankel *en*

animal *n.* dyr *et*

anniversary *n.* årsdag *en;*
  bryllupsdag *en (wedding*
  anniversary)
announce *v.* bekjentgjøre,
  melde, annonsere
another *pron.* en annen;
  hverandre *(each other)*
answer *n.* svar *et; v.* svare
antibiotic *n.* antibiotikum *et*
antiquarian bookshop *n.*
  antikvariat *et*
antique *n.* antikvitet *en;*
  adj. antikk
antiseptic *adj.* antiseptisk
any, anybody *pron.* noen
apartment *n.* leilighet *en*
appendicitis *n.*
  blindtarmsbetennelse *en*
appetizer *n.* appetittvekker *en*
applaud *v.* klappe
apple *n.* eple *et*
appointment *n.* ansettelse *en,*
  stilling *en (position);* avtale
  en (date,hour)
architect *n.* arkitekt *en*
architecture *n.* arkitektur *en*
area *n.* område *et*
area code *n.* fylkeskode *en*
arise *v.* stige
arm *n.* arm *en*
army *n.* armé *et,* hær *en*
around *adv.; prep.* rundt, rundt
  omkring
arouse *v.* vekke
arrest *n.* arrestasjon *en;*
  v. arrestere
arrival *n.* ankomst *en*
arrive *v.* ankomme, komme
  frem
art *n.* kunst *en*
art gallery *n.* kunstgalleri *et*
artist *n.* kunstner *en*
as *adv.; conj.* som
as far as *adv.* helt til
as if *conj.* som om
ashamed *adj.* skamfull
ashtray *n.* askebeger *et*
ask *v.* spørre

aspirin *n.* aspirin *en,* globoid *en*
associate *v.* forbinde, assosiere
association *n.* forening *en*
assortment *n.* assortiment *et;*
  utvalg *et (choice)*
asthma *n.* astma *en*
at *prep.* ved
at last *adv.* endelig, til sist
at once *adv.* med en gang
attack *n.* angrep *et; v.* angripe
attempt *n.* forsøk *et; v.* forsøke
attractive *adj.* tiltrekkenke
audience *n.* publikum *et;*
  tilhørere *pl.,* audiens *en*
August *n.* august
aunt *n.* tante *en*
author *n.* forfatter *en*
automatic *adj.* automatisk
avalanche *n.* snøskred *et*
average *adj.* gjennomsnittlig
awake *v.* våkne; *adj.* våken
away *adv.* bort, borte, vekk
awful *adj.* fryktelig
axe *n.* øks *en*

B

baby *n.* spedbarn *et,* spebarn *et*
babysitter *n.* barnevakt *en*
back *n.* rygg *en; adv.* tilbake
backache *n.* ryggsmerter *pl.*
backpack *n.* ryggsekk *en*
backward *adj.* baklengs
bacon *n.* bacon *et*
bad *adj.* dårlig; ond *(evil);* slem
  (naughty)
bag *n.* sekk *en,* pose *en;*
  papirpose *en (paperbag);*
  sovepose *en (sleeping bag);*
  veske *en (handbag);*
  shopping veske *en*
  (shopping bag)
bait *n.* lokkemat *en;* sluk *en*
  (spoon or spinning lure)
bake *v.* bake
bakery *n.* bakeri *et*
balance *n.* balanse *en,* likevekt
  en; v. balansere
balcony *n.* balkong *en;* altan *en*
  (balcony, porch)
bald *adj.* skallet

ball *n.* ball *en*; kule *en* (*golfball*; *cannonball*); bolle *en* (*meatball*; *bun*, *roll*); ball *et* (*dance*)
ballet *n.* ballett *en*
banana *n.* banan *en*
bandage *n.* bandasje *en*; brokkbind *et* (*truss*)
bank *n.* bank *en*; *v.* sette i banken
bank draft *n.* bankremisse *en*
banknote *n.* pengeseddel *en*
bankrupt *adj.* fallitt gå konkurs (*go bankrupt*)
baptism *n.* dåp *en*
bar *n.* stang *en*; jernstang *en* (*iron bar*); fengselsgitter *pl.* (*prison bars*); gullbarre *en* (*gold bar*); svingstenger *pl.* (*parallel bars in gym*); sandbanke *en* (*offshore bar*); vertshus *et* (*pub*)
barber *n.* herrefrisør *en*
barbershop *n.* herrefrisørsalong *en*
barely *adv.* knapt
barn *n.* låve *en*
barracks *n.* kaserne *en*
barrel *n.* tønne *en* (*container*)
basil *n.* basilikum *et*
basin *n.* balje *en* (*wash tub*)
basket *n.* kurv *en*
bath *n.* bad *et*; badekar *et* (*bathtub*)
bathe *v.* bade
bathing suit *n.* badedrakt *en*
bathroom *n.* bad *et*, badeværelse *et*; toalett *et*, W.C. *et*
battery *n.* batteri *et*
battle *n.* slag *et*, kamp *en*; *v.* kjempe
battlefield *n.* slagmark *en*
bay *n.* bukt *en*
be *v.* være; bli
beach *n.* strand *en*
bean *n.* bønne *en*
bear *n.* bjørn *en*; *v.* tåle (*endure*)

beard *n.* skjegg *et*
beautiful *adj.* vakker, meget pen
beauty *n.* skjønnhet *en*
beauty salon *n.* skjønnhetssalong *en*
because *conj.* fordi, siden
because of *prep.* på grunn av
become *v.* bli; kle (*suit, flatter*)
bed *n.* seng *en*; blomsterbed *et* (*bed of flowers*)
(go to) bed *v.* legge seg, gå til sengs
bed and breakfast *n.* værelse med frokost *et*
bedroom *n.* soveværelse *et*
bee *n.* bie *en*
beef, beefsteak *n.* okekjøtt *et*
beer *n.* øl *et*
before *prep.* tidligere, før (*earlier*); foran (*in front of*)
begin *v.* begynne
beginner *n.* nybeggynner *en*
behave *v.* oppføre seg
behavior *n.* oppførsel *en*
behind *prep.*; *adv.*; *n.* bak *en*; rumpe *en* (*buttocks*)
believe *v.* tro
bell *n.* klokke *en*
below *adv.*; *prep.* under
belt *n.* belte *et*
bench *n.* benk *en*; arbeidsbenk *en* (*workbench*); *en* benk i parken (*park bench*)
bend *n.* veisving *en*, kurve i veien *en* (*curve in the road*); *v.* bøye
best *adj.* best
better *adj.* bedre
between *prep.* mellom
bicycle *n.* sykkel *en*; *v.* sykle
big *adj.* stor
bill *n.* regning *en* (*account*)
binoculars *n.* kikkert *en*
biography *n.* biografi *en*
biology *n.* biologi *en*
biopsy *n.* biopsi *en*
biplane *n.* todekker *en*
bird *n.* fugl *en*

birth *n.* fødsel *en*
birth control *n.*
    prevensjonsmiddel *et*
birthday *n.* fødseldag *en*
birthplace *n.* fødested *et*
biscuit *n.* kjeks *en*
bit *n.* lite stykke *et* (*small
    piece*); *adv.* litt (*a little*)
bitter *adj.* bitter
black *adj.* svart
blackboard *n.* veggtavle *en*
blade *n.* blad *et*
blame *n.* skyld *en; v.* kritisere
blanket *n.* teppe *et*
bleed *v.* blø
blind *adj.* blind
blister *n.* blemme *en,* vable *en*
blizzard *n.* snøstorm *et*
block *n.* blokk *en* (*of wood,
    stone*); veisperring *en* (*road
    block*); *v.* spere, blokkere
blood *n.* blod *et*
blood poisoning *n.*
    blodforgiftning *en*
blood pressure *n.* blodtrykk *et*
blood transfusion *n.*
    blodtransfusjon *en,*
    blodoverføring *en*
blouse *n.* bluse *en*
blue *adj.* blå
boarding house *n.* pensjonat *et*
boarding pass *n.* boarding card,
    ombordstigningskort *et*
boat *n.* båt *en*
body *n.* kropp *en;* lik *et* (*corpse*)
bog *n.* myr *en*
boil *n.* byll *en* (*medical term*);
    v. koke
bone *n.* ben *et*
book *n.* bok *en; v.* bestille
bookstore *n.* bokhandel *en*
boot *n.* støvel *en* (*footwear*);
    bagasjerom *et* (*UK: trunk
    of car*)
border *n.* kant *en;* rand *en*
    (*edge*); grense *en* (*between
    countries*)
boring *adj.* kjedelig
born *adj.* født
boss *n.* sjef *en*

botanical *adj.* botanisk
both *adj.; pron.* begge; *conj.*
    både ... og (*both ... and*)
bottle *n.* flaske *en*
bottle-opener *n.* flaskeåpner *en*
bottom *n.* bunn *en;* havbunn
    en (*bottom of the sea*);
    adj. lavest, nederst
boundary *n.* grense *en*
bouquet *n.* bukett *en* (*of
    flowers*)
bourgeois *n.* spissborger *en;*
    adj. spissborgerlig
bowels *n.* tarm *en*
bowel movement *n.* avføring *en*
bowl *n.* bolle *en,* skål *en;*
    sukerskål *en* (*sugar bowl*)
box *n.* kasse *en;* postkasse *en*
    (*letter box*); eske *en*
    (*cardboard box*);
    konfekteske *en* (*a box of
    chocolates*)
box office *n.* billettkontor *en*
boy *n.* gutt *en*
boyfriend *n.* venn *en*
bracelet *n.* armbånd *net*
brain *n.* hjerne *en*
brake *v.* bremse
brakes *n.* brems *en*
branch *n.* gren *en*
branch office *n.* filialkontor *et*
brand *n.* merke *et* (*as in brand
    of tea*); *v.* svimerke
brass *n.* messing *en*
brassiere, bra *n.* bysteholder
    en; behå *en*
brave *adj.* modig, tapper
bread *n.* brød *et;* loff *en* (*white
    bread*)
break *v.* brekke, knekke, gå i
    stykker
broken *adj.* i stykker
breakdown *n.* motorstopp *en*
    (*machine*); nervøst
    sammenbrudd *et* (*nervous
    breakdown*)
breakfast *n.* frokost *en*
breast *n.* bryst *et*
breath *n.* pusten, ånde *en*
breathe *v.* puste, ånde

breeze *n.* bris *en*
bride *n.* brud *en*
bridegroom *n.* brudgom *en*
bridge *n.* bru *en*
brief *v.* briefe, orientere; *adj.* kort
bring *v.* bringe, komme med; hente (*fetch*); resultere (*result in*); komme tilbake med (*bring back, return*); oppdra (*bring up, raise*)
Britain *Pln.* Storbritannia
British *adj.* britisk
broad *adj.* bred
broken *adj.* i stukker
bronze *n.* bronse *en*
broom *n.* kost *en*
brother *n.* bror *en*
brother-in-law *n.* svoger *en*
brown *adj.* brun
bruise *n.* blått merke *et* (*on body*); flekk *en* (*on fruit*)
brush *n.* børste *en*, tannbørste *en* (*toothbrush*); malerpensel *en* (*artist's brush*)
bucket *n.* bøtte *en*
build *v.* bygge, bygge opp (*to build up*)
building *n.* bygning *en*
bulb *n.* blomsterløk *en* (*flowerbulb*); lyspær *en* (*lightbulb*)
bull *n.* okse *en*
burn *n.* brannsår *et*, forbrenning *en*; *v.* brenne
bus *n.* buss *en*
bus stop *n.* bussholdepass *en*
business *n.* forretning *en* (*commercial enterprise*); sak *en* (*matter*)
busy *adj.* opptat, travel
but *conj.* men
butcher *n.* slakter *en*
butter *n.* smør *et*
butterfly *n.* sommerfugl *en*
buttocks *n.* rumpe *en*
button *n.* knapp *en*
button up *v.* kneppe
buy *v.* kjøpe

C

cabbage *n.* kål *en*
cab, taxi *n.* drosje *en*, taxi *en*
cabin *n.* lugar *en* (*shipboard*); hytte *en* (*log cabin*)
cable *n.* kabel *en* (*telegram*); *v.* telegrafere
café *n.* kafé *en*
caffeine *n.* koffein *et*
caffeine-free *adj.* uten koffein, koffeinfri
cake *n.* kake *en*
calculator *n.* regnemaskin *en*
calendar *n.* kalender *en*
call *n.* rop *et*, skrik *et* (*shriek*), besøke *et* (*visit*); samtale *en* (*telephone call*); *v.* rope; avlyse (*call off, cancel*); besøke (*visit*)
calm *n.* stillhet *en*, ro *en*; *v.* berolige; *adj.* rolig
camera *n.* kamera *et*, fotoapparat *et*
camp *n.* leir *en*; *v.* slå leir, ligge i leir
camper, trailer *n.* campingbil *en*
campsite *n.* campingplass *et*
can *n.* kanne *en*; en boks øl *en* (*a can of beer*); *v.* kan (*be able*)
Canada *Pln.* Canada
Canadian *adj.* kanadier
can opener, tin opener *n.* bokseåpner *en*
cancel *v.* avlyse (*call off*); stryke over, stryke ut (*crossout*)
cancer *n.* kreft *en*
candle *n.* lys *et*
canoe *n.* kano *en*
cap *n.* lue *en*
capable *adj.* dyktig, flink
capital *n.* hovedstad *en* (*capital city*); stor bokstav *en* (*capital letter*), kapital *en* (*funds*); *adj.* som straffes med døden (*capital offense*); flott, utmerket (*excellent*)

car *n.* bil *en;* spisevogn *en*
(*dining car*); sovevogn *en*
(*sleeping car*); bagasjevogn
en (*baggage car*)
card *n.* kort *et,* postkort *et*
(*postcard*); en kortstokk *en*
(*a pack of cards*)
care *n.* forsiktighet *en*
(*caution*); bekymring *en*
(*worry*); *v.* bry seg om
careful *adj.* forsiktig
carrot *n.* gulrot *en*
carry *v.* bære
cash *n.* kontanter *pl.*
cashier *n.* kasserer *en*
cassette *n.* kassett *en*
cat *n.* katt *en*
catalogue *n.* katalog *en*
cathedral *n.* domkirke *en*
Catholic *n.* katolikk *en;*
adj. katolsk
cattle *n.* kveg *et*
cauliflower *n.* blomkål *en*
cause *n.* årsak *en,* grunn *en;*
v. foråsake
caution *n.* forsiktighet *en;*
v. advare
cave *n.* hule *en*
CD *n.* CD *et*
CD player *n.* CD spiller *en*
ceiling *n.* tak *et*
celery *n.* selleri *en*
cemetery *n.* gravlund *en*
center *n.* sentrum *et,*
midpunkt *et*
centimeter *n.* centimeter *en*
century *n.* århundre *et*
ceramics *n.* keramikk *en*
cereal *n.* kornslag *et*
ceremony *n.* seremoni *en*
certificate *n.* attest *en*
chain *n.* kjede *en*
chair *n.* stol *en*
championship *n.* mesterskap *et*
chance *n.* sjanse *en*
(*possibility*); anledning *en*
(*opportunity*); *adv.*
tilfeldigvis (*by chance*)

change *n.* forandring *en* (*til det*
bedre = for the better); (*til*
det verre = for the worse); et
skift *et* (*a change of clothes*);
småpenger *pl.* (*money*);
v. forandre, bil forandret;
bytte (*exchange*)
chart, map *n.* kart *et*
cheap *adj.* billig
cheaper *adj.* billigere
check *n.* regning *en* (*restaurant*
bill); sjekkemerke *et*
(*baggage check*);
garderobemerke *et*
(*cloakroom ticket*);
v. sjekke, kontrollere; levere
(*check your coat or hat*);
sjekke inn (*check in a*
hotel); sjekkeut, reise
(*checkout*)
checkbook *n.* sjekkhefte *et*
cheers! *n.* skål *en* (*a toast*)
cheese *n.* ost *en*
chef *n.* kjøkkensjef *en*
cherry *n.* kirsebær *et*
chess *n.* sjakk *en;* *v.* spille sjakk
(*play chess*)
chestnut *n.* kastanje *en*
chew *v.* tygge
chicken *n.* høne *en;* kylling *en*
(*as food*)
chief *n.* sjef *en;* sjefredaktør *en*
(*editor in chief*); *adj.*
viktigst; hoved
child, children *n.* barn *et;*
småbarn *pl.* (*babies*)
China *Pln.* kina
Chinese *n.* kineser *en;*
adj. kinesisk
chocolate *n.* sjokolade *en*
choice *n.* valg *et,* utvalg *et*
choose *v.* velge
Christ *n.* Kristus
Christian *adj.* kristen
Christmas *n.* jul *en;* god jul
(*Merry Christmas*)
church *n.* kirke *en*
cider *n.* sider *en;* eplesaft *en*
(*apple juice*)

cigar *n.* sigar *en*
cigarette *n.* sigarett *en*
cinema *n.* kino *en*
cinnamon *n.* kanel *en*
circle *n.* sirkel *et;* krets *en*
  (*circle of friends*)
citizen *n.* borger *en;*
  statsborger *en*
city *n.* by *en*
clam *n.* spiselig musling *en*
class *n.* klasse *en*
clean *v.* gjøre rent; rense (*a
  chicken*); pusse (*windows*);
  adj. ren
clear *v.* klarne, rense rydde;
  adj. klar
clerk *n.* ekspeditør *en* (*shop
  assistant*); resepsjonist *en*
  (*reception clerk*)
clever *adj.* flink
cliff *n.* fjellskrent *en;* klippe *et*
climate *n.* klima *et*
climb *v.* klatre
cloakroom *n.* garderobe *en*
clock *n.* klokke *en*
close *v.* lukke, stenge; avslutte
  (*bring to a close*)
closed *adj.* stengt
clothes *n.* klær *pl.;* sengeklær
  pl. (*bedclothes*)
cloud *n.* sky *en*
cloudy *adj.* skyet, overskyet
coat *n.* frakk *en;* kåpe *en*
  (*woman's coat*); jakke *en*
  (*man's coat*)
cod *n.* torsk *en*
coffee *n.* kaffe *en*
coin *n.* mynt *en*
cold *adj.* kald; jeg fryser (*I am
  cold*)
color *n.* farge *en*
come *v.* komme; komme inn
  (*come in*); komme med
  (*come with*); komme til
  bevissthet (*regain
  consiousness*)
comedy *n.* komedie *en*,
  lystspill *et*

comfortable *adj.* komfortabel,
  behagelig
commerce *n.* handel *en*
commercial *n.* TV annonse *en*,
  reklame *en*
commission *n.* kommisjon *en;*
  v. bestille
common *adj.* alminnelig
communicate *v.* meddele
company *n.* selskap *et*, firma, *et*
compare *v.* sammenligne
compartment *n.* avdeling *en*
compass *n.* kompass *en*
compensation *n.* erstatning *en*
compete *v.* konkurrere
competitor *n.* konkurrent *en*
competence *n.* dyktighet *en*
complaint *n.* klage *en*
composer *n.* komponist *en*
computer *n.* computer,
  datamaskin *en*
concerned *adj.* bekymret
concerning *prep.* angående, om
concert *n.* konsert *en*
condom *n.* kondom *en*
conductor *n.* konduktør *en*
  (*railway*); dirigent *en*
  (*orchestra conductor*)
confidence *n.* tillit *en*,
  sikkerhet *en*
confident *adj.* sikker, trygg
confirm *v.* bekrefte
conflict *n.* kamp *en*, strid *en*,
  konflict *en*
confusion *n.* uorden *en*,
  forvirring *en*
congratulate *v.* gratulere
congress *n.* kongress *en*
connect *v.* forbinde
consequence *n.* følge *en*,
  konsekvens *en*
constipated *adj.* forstoppet
constitution *n.* konstitusjon *en*
construction *n.* bygging *en*,
  konstruksjon *en*
consultant *n.* konsulent *en*
contact *n.* kontakt *en;*
  v. kontakte

contact lenses *n.* kontaktlinse *en*
contact lens solution *n.*
    kontaktlinse solution *en*
contain *v.* inneholde, romme
contemporary *adj.* samtidig
content *adj.* tilfreds
continual *adj.* stadig
continue *v.* fortsette
contract *n.* kontrakt *en*
control *n.* kontroll *en*;
    v. kontrollere
controversial *adj.* omstridt,
    controversiell
convention *n.* kongress *en*
conventional *adj.* tradisjonell
cook *n.* kokk *en*; *v.* lage mat
cookie *n.* småkake *en*
cool *adj.* kjølig
copper *n.* kopper *et*
cork *n.* kork *en*
corkscrew *n.* korketrekker *en*
corner *n.* hjørne *et*
correction *n.* rettelse *en*
correspondence *n.*
    brevveksling *en*
cosmetic *adj.* kosmetisk
cost *n.* pris *en*; *v.* koste
cost of living *n.*
    leveomkostninger *pl.*
cozy *adj.* koselig
cot *n.* barneseng *en* (*crib*);
    feltseng *en* (*camp bed*)
cotton *n.* bomull *en*
cough *v.* hoste
count *v.* telle
counterfeit *adj.* forfalsket
country *n.* land *et*
countryside *n.* land *et*; på
    landet (*in the country*)
courthouse *n.* tinghus *et*
cousin *n.* fetter *en* (*male*);
    kusine *en* (*female*)
cover *v.* dekke
crab *n.* krabbe *en*
crack *n.* sprekk *en*; *v.* sprekke
cramp *n.* krampe *en* (*spasm*)
crazy *adj.* gal
cream *n.* fløte *en* (*dairy cream*);
    solkrem *en* (*suntan cream*)

credit *n.* kreditt *en*; på kredit
    (*on credit*)
credit card *n.* kredittkort *et*
criminal *adj.* kriminell
crisis *n.* krise *en*
cross *n.* kryss *et*, kors *et*;
    v. krysse
crossing *n.* gatekryss *et*;
    fotgjengerovergang *en*
    (*pedestrian crossing*)
crutches *n.* krykker *pl.*
cry *n.* skrik *et*; *v.* gråte (*weep*);
    rope om (*call for*)
crystal *n.* krystall *en*
cucumber *n.* slangeagurk *en*,
    agurk *en*
culture *n.* kultur *en*
cup *n.* kopp *en*
currency *n.* valuta *en*
current *n.* strøm *en*;
    adj. aktuell
curtains *n.* gardiner *en*
curve *n.* kurve *en*; sving *en*
    (*curve in the road*)
custom *n.* skikk *en*
customer *n.* kunde *en*
customs *n.* toll *en*
cut *n.* snitt *et*; *v.* hogge, skjære
cylinder *n.* sylinder *en*

D

dad *n.* pappa *en*
damage *n.* skade *en*; *v.* skade
damp, humid *adj.* fuktig
dance *n.* dans *en*; *v.* danse
Dane *n.* danske *en*
Danish *adj.* dansk
danger *n.* fare *en*
dangerous *adj.* farling
dare *v.* våge
daring *adj.* dristig
dark *adj.* mørke
darling *adj.* yndig
date *n.* dato *en*; fødselsdato *en*
    (*date of birth*)
daughter *n.* datter *en*
daughter-in-law *n.*
    svigerdatter *en*

dawn *n.* daggry *et;* ved daggry
  (*at dawn*)
day *n.* dag *en;* om dagen
  (*during the day*)
dead *adj.* død
deadline *n.* frist *en*
deaf *adj.* døv
deal *n.* del *en;* en god del
  (*a good deal*)
dear *adj.* kjær; *adj.* kjære
  (*kjære fru Olsen =*
  Dear Mrs. Olsen)
death *n.* død *en*
debt *n.* gjeld *en*
December *n.* desember
decide *v.* bestemme
decision *n.* avgjørelse *en*
decoration *n.* dekorasjon *en*
deep *adj.* dyp
defective *adj.* mangelfull
defend *v.* forsvare
delay *n.* forsinkelse *en;*
  v. forsinke
delicate *adj.* delikat
delicious *adj.* deilig
deliver *v.* levere
demand *n.* krav *et; v.* kreve,
  forlange
demolish *v.* rive ned
Denmark *Pln.* Danmark
dense *adj.* tett
dentist *n.* tannlege *en*
deodorant *n.* deodorant
depart *v.* dra
department *n.* avdeling *en*
department store *n.*
  varemagasin *et*
departure *n.* avreise *en,*
  avgang *en*
depend *v.* avheng
deposit *n.* innskudd *et;*
  v. sette inn
describe *v.* beskrive
dessert *n.* dessert *en*
desperate *adj.* fortviilet
despite *prep.* til tross for
destiny, fate *n.* skjebne *en*
destroy *v.* ødelegge
detergent *n.* vaskemiddel *et*

detour *n.* omvei *en*
develop *v.* utvikle
development *n.* utvikling *en*
devote *v.* vie
diabetes *n.* sukkersyke *en*
diabetic *adj.* diabetisk
diamond *n.* diamant *en*
diarrhea *n.* diaré *en*
diary *n.* dagbok *en*
dictionary *n.* ordbok *en*
die *v.* dø
diet *n.* diett *en; v.* sette på diett,
  slanke seg
difference *n.* forskjell *en*
difficult *adj.* vanskelig
difficulty *n.* vanskelighet *en*
digest *v.* fordøye
digital *adj.* digital
diligent *adj.* flittig
dine *v.* spise middag
dining room *n.* spisestue *en*
dinner *n.* middag *en*
dinner jacket *n.* smoking *en*
direct *v.* vise veien (*show the*
  way); dirigere (*conduct*
  an orchestra)
directory *n.* telefonkatalog *en*
direction *n.* retning *en*
director *n.* direktør *en;* registør
  en (*film director*)
dirt *n.* skitt *en*
dirty *adj.* skitten
disabled *adj.* arbeidsufør
disagree *v.* være uenig
disappear *v.* forsvinne
disappointed *adj.* skuffet
discover *v.* oppdage, finne ut
disease *n.* sykdom *en*
disgusting *adj.* vemmelig
dish *n.* fat *et* (*plate*); rett *en*
  (*course*)
dishonest *adj.* uærlig
disk, disc *n.* skive *en;*
  grammofonplate *en*
  (*record*)
dislike *v.* mislike, ikke like
disobedience *n.* ulydighet *en*
dissatisfied *adj.* misfornøyd
distance *n.* avstand *en*

district *n.* distrikt *et*, område *et*
disturb *v.* forstyrre
disturbance *n.* forstyrrelse *en*
dive *v.* dykke
divorce *n.* skilsmisse *en*
divorced *adj.* skilt
dizzy *adj.* svimmel
dock *n.* dokk *en*
doctor *n.* doktor en lege *en*
   (*physician*)
document *n.* dokument *et*;
   v. dokumentere
dog *n.* hund *en*
doll *n.* dukke *en*
dollar *n.* dollar *en*
donkey *n.* esel *en*
door *n.* dør *en*
dormitory *n.* sovesal *en*
double *adj.* dobbel, dobbelt
double bed *n.* doppeltseng *en*
double room *n.* værelse for
   to *et*
doubt *n.* tvil *en*; *v.* tvile på,
   betvile
dough *n.* deig *en*
doughnut *n.* smultring *en*
down *adv.* ned
downstairs *adv.* ned
downtown *adv.* ned i byen
dozen *n.* dusin *et*
draft *n.* utkast *et* (*sketch*);
   innkallelse *en* (*military
   draft*); *v.* kladde (*write a
   rough draft*); innkalle
   (*military*)
draw *v.* tegne
drawer tegner *en* (*draftsman*);
   skuff *en*; kommode *en*
   (*chest of drawers*)
dream *n.* drøm *en*; *v.* rømme
dress *n.* kjole *en*, selskapskjole
   en (*evening dress*); *v.* kle på;
   kle på seg (*dress oneself*);
   pynte på (*dress up*)
drink *n.* drikk *en*; drink *en*
   (*alcohol*); *v.* drikke
drive *n.* kjøretur *en*; *v.* kjøre,
   kjøre videre (*drive on*); kjør
   videre! (*drive on!*)

driver's license *en* førerkort *et*
drop *n.* dråpe *en*; *v.* falle, la falle
drown *v.* drukne
drug *n.* legemiddel *et*;
   narkotikum *et*
drug addict *n.* narkoman *en*
drug addiction *n.* narkomani *en*
drugstore *n.* apotek *et*
drum *n.* tromme *et*
drunk *adj.* full, beruset
dry *v.* tørke; *adj.* tørr
dry out *v.* bli tørr
dry-clean *v.* rense
duck *n.* and *en*; *v.* dukke
dull *adj.* sløv (*blunt*); kjedelig
   (*boring*)
during *prep.* under (*om dagen
   = during the day*)
dusk *n.* skumring *en*
dust *n.* støv *et*
Dutch *adj.* nederlandsk,
   hollandsk
duty *n.* plikt *en* (*obligation*);
   toll *en* (*customs*); aktiv
   tjeneste *en* (*active military
   duty*); *adj.* tollfri (*duty-free*)
dye *n.* farve / farge *en*; *v.* farve /
   farge

E

each *pron.* hver
eagle *n.* ørn *en*
ear *n.* øre *et*
early *adj.*; *adv.* tidlig
earn *v.* tjene
earth *n.* jord *en*
east *adj.* østlig
the East *Pln.* Østen
Easter *n.* Påske *en*
easy *adj.* lett
eat *v.* spise
economy *n.* økonomi *et*
edge *n.* kant *en*
education *n.* utdannelse *en*
effort *n.* anstrengelse *en*
egg *n.* egg *en*
eggplant *n.* eggplante *en*
eight *num.* åtte
eighteen *num.* atten

eighty *num.* åtti
elect *v.* velge
election *n.* valg *et*
electric *adj.* elektrisk
electricity *n.* elektrisitet *en*
electronic *adj.* elektronisk
elephant *n.* elefant *en*
elevator *n.* heis *en*
eleven *num.* elleve
elsewhere *adv.* annetsteds
e-mail *n.; v.* e-mail
e-mail address *n.* e-mail
    adresse *en*
embarrassed *adj.* flau
embassy *n.* ambassade *en*
embrace *v.* omfavne
emergency *n.* krise *en*
emergency exit *n.* nødutgang *en*
emigration *n.* emigrasjon *en*
emotion *n.* følelse *en*
empty *v.* tømme; *adj.* tom
end *n.* ende *en; v.* ende
endure *v.* tåle, holde ut
enemy *n.* fiende *en*
energetic *adj.* energisk
engaged *adj.* forlovet (*to be
    married*); opptatt (*busy*)
engagement *n.* forlovelse *en*
    (*wedding*); avtale *en*
    (*appointment*)
engineer *n.* ingeniør *en*
England *Pln.* England
English *adj.* engelsk
enjoy *v.* like, more seg (*enjoy
    oneself*)
enjoyable *adj.* hyggelig, koselig
enlarge *v.* forstørre
enough *adv.* nok
enrage *v.* gjøre rasende
ensure *v.* sørge for (*make sure*)
enter *v.* gå inn, komme inn
entertain *v.* more, underholde
enthusiastic *adj.* begeistret
entrance *n.* inngang *en*
entry *n.* adgang *en*
    (*admission*); postering *en*
    (*bookkeeping entry*)
entry card *n.* innkomstkort *et*
envelope *n.* konvolutt *en*

envy *n.* misunnelse *en;
    v.* misunne
epileptic *n.* epileptiker *en*
equally *adv.* likt
equipment *n.* utstyr *et*
eraser *n.* viskelær *et*
escape *v.* unnslippe, rømme
especially *adv.* særlig, spesielt
esteem *v.* respektere
eternity *n.* evighet *en*
Europe *Pln.* Europa
European *n.* europeer *en;
    adj.* europeisk
European Union *abbrev.* EU
even *adj.* jevn (*flat*), lik (*equal*);
    rolig (*even-tempered*); *adv.*
    enda (*e.g. still brighter*);
    conj. selv om (*even if, even
    though*)
evening *n.* kveld *en*
every *adj.* hver
everything *pron.* alt
everywhere *adj.* overalt
examination *n.* undesøkelse
    en (*close inspection*);
    eksamen *en* (*exam*)
example *n.* eksempel *et*
excellent *adj.* utmerket
except *prep.* unntatt, bortsett fra
exception *n.* unntagelse *en*
exceptional *adj.* uvanlig
exchange *n.* bytte *et; v.* veksle
exchange rate *n.* valutakurs *en*
excited *adj.* opphisset
export *n.* eksportvare *en;
    v.* eksportere
excursion *n.* ekskursjon *en*
excuse *n.* unnskyldning *en;
    v.* unnskylde; unnskyld!
    (*excuse me!*)
exercise *n.* mosjon *en;
    v.* mosjonere
exhausted *adj.* oppbrukt (*used
    up*); trett (*tired*)
exile *n.* eksil *et*
exit *n.* utgang *en;* nødutgang
    en (*emergency exit*)
expect *v.* vente
expenses *n.* utgift *en*

expensive *adj.* dyr, kostbar
experience *n.* erfaring *en*
expert *n.* ekspert *en;* fagmann
  en; adj. sakkyndig
explain *v.* forklare
express *n.* ekspresstog *et*
  (*train*); express *en* (*post,*
  train); *v.* uttrykke;
  adj. ekspress
extensive *adj.* stor, omfattende
exterminate *v.* tilintetgjøre,
  utryddelse
extinguish *v.* slukke
extra *adj.* ekstra
extract *v.* trekke ut
extreme *adj.* ytterst
eye *n.* øye *et*
eyebrow *n.* øyenbryn *et*
eyeglasses *n.* briller *en*
eyesight *n.* syn *et*

F
face *n.* ansikt *et*
factory *n.* fabrikk *en*
failure *n.* fiasko *en;* bankerott
  en (*bankruptcy*)
faint *v.* besvime
faith *n.* tro *en*
fall *n.* fall *et;* snøfall *et*
  (*snowfall*); prisfall *et* (*drop*
  in prices); høst *en*
  (*autumn*); foss *en*
  (*waterfall*); *v.* falle
false *adj.* usann, falsk
family *n.* familie *en*
famous *adj.* berømt
fanatic *n.* fanatiker *en*
fantastic *adj.* fantastisk
far *adj.* fjern, langt borte;
  adv. langt
fare *n.* billettpris *en* (*price*);
  kost *en* (*food*)
farm *n.* bondegård *en*
farmer *n.* bonde *en*
farming *n.* gårdsbruk *et*
fashion *n.* måte *en* (*manner*);
  mote *en* (*style of dress*)
fashion show *n.*
  moteoppvisning *en*

fat *n.* fett *et,* fettstoff *et; adj.* fet
  (*oily*); tykk (*thick*)
father *n.* far *en*
father-in-law *n.* svigerfar *en*
fault *n.* feil *en; v.* kritisere
  (*find fault*)
favor *n.* tjeneste *en* (*good*
  turn); *v.* favorisere (*show*
  preference); ligne (*look like*)
favorite *n.* ynding *en* (*person*);
  favoritt *en* (*e.g. food, sport*)
fax *n.* faks *en*
fax machine *n.* faks maskin *en*
fear *n.* frykt *en; v.* frykte, være
  redd for
feast *n.* fest *en*
February *n.* februar
fee *n.* honorar *et;* skolepenger
  pl. (*school fee*)
feel *v.* føle
feeling *n.* følelse *en*
female *adj.* kvinnelig
feminine *adj.* kvinnelig
feminist *n.* kvinnesakskvinne *en*
fence *n.* gjerde *et*
festival *n.* fest *en;* høytid *en*
  (*religious*); folkefest *en*
  (*folk festival*)
fever *n.* feber *en*
few *adj.* få
fiancé, fiancée *n.* forlovede *en*
fidelity *n.* trofasthet *en*
field *n.* jorde *et,* åker *en*
  (*cultivated field*);
  fotballbane *en*
  (*soccerfield*); slagmark *en*
  (*field of battle*);
  interesseområde *et* (*field*
  of interest)
fifteen *num.* femten
fifth *adj.* femte
fifty *num.* femti
fight *n.* kamp *en; v.* slåss
figure *n.* skikkelse *en* (*shape*);
  tall *et* (*number*); pris *en*
  (*price*)
file *v.* fylle
filing cabinet *n.* arkivskap *et*
film *n.* film *en; v.* filme

filter *n.* filter *et*
finally *adv.* endelig
financial *adj.* finansiell
find *v.* finne
fine *adj.* fin, pent
finger *n.* finger *en*
finish *n.* slutt *en; v.* avslutte, bli
    ferdig med
Finland *Pln.* Finland
Finn *n.* finne *en*
Finnish *adj.* finsk
fire *n.* ild *en*, brann *en*, bål *et*
    (*bonfire*); *v.* skyte (*shoot*);
    brenne (*fire a kiln*);
    oppildne (*inspire*)
firewood *n.* ved *en*
fire alarm *n.* brannalarm *en*
firm *n.* firma *et*
first *adj.* først
first class *adj.* første klasse
fish *n.* fisk *en; v.* fiske
fit *n.* anfall *et* (*attack*); *v.* passe;
    adj. frisk (*healthy*); skikket
    for (*suited for*)
five *num.* fem
fix *v.* feste (*fasten*); reparere
    (*repair*)
flag *n.* flagg *et*
flash *n.* blitzlampe *en* (for a
    camera)
flashlight *n.* lommelykt *en*
flat *n.* leilighet *en* (*apartment*);
    punktering *en* (*flat tire*);
    adj. flat
flatter *v.* smigre
flaw *n.* feil *en*
flight *n.* flukt *en*
flight number *n.* fly nummer *et*
floor *n.* gulv *et*; etasje *en* (*story*)
florist *n.* blomsterhandler *en*
flounder *n.* flyndre *en*
flour *n.* mel *et*
flower *n.* blomst *en*
flu *n.* influensa *en*
fly *n.* flue *en* (*housefly*);
    buksesmekk *en* (*zipper*);
    v. fly
fly-fish *v.* fiske med flue
fog *n.* tåke *en*

folk *n.* folk *et*
folk dancing *n.* folkedans *en*
folklore *n.* folklore *en*
folk music *n.* folkemusikk *en*
follow *v.* følge
food *n.* mat *en*
foot *n.* fot *en*
foothills *n.* høydedrag ved
    foten av fjellene *et*
for *prep.* for, til
forbid *v.* forby; Gud forby! (*God
    forbid!*)
forbidden *adj.* forbudt
force *n.* kraft *en; v.* tvinge
forehead *n.* panne *en*
foreign *adj.* utenlandsk
foreigner *n.* utlending *en*
forest *n.* skog *en*
forget *v.* glemme
forgive *v.* tilgi
fork *n.* gaffel *en*
form *n.* form *en*;
    søknadsskjema *et* (*appli-
    cation form*); *v.* danne
fortress *n.* festning *en*
fortunately *adv.* heldigvis
forty *num.* førti
forward *adj.* fremover
foundation *n.* grunnleggelse
    en; stiftelse *en*, fond *et*
    (*institution*)
fountain *n.* fontene *en*
four *num.* fire
fourteen *num.* fjorten
fourth *adj.* fjerde
fracture *n.* brudd *et*, fraktur *en*
fragile *adj.* skjør (*easily
    broken*); svak (*weak*)
France *Pln.* Frankrike
free *adj.* fri; *v.* sette fri
freedom *n.* frihet *en*
freight *n.* frakt *en*
French *adj.* fransk
fresh *adj.* frisk
Friday *n.* fredag
fridge *n.* kjøleskap *et*
fried *adj.* stekt
friend *n.* venn *en* (*male*);
    venninne *en* (female)

frog *n.* frosk *en*
from *prep.* fra
front *n.* forside *en*; fasade *en*;
   kamuflasje *en* (*cover*)
frost *n.* frost *en*
frostbite *n.* forfrysning *en*
frozen *adj.* frossen, frosset
fruit *n.* frukt *en*
fry *v.* steke
fuel *n.* brennstoff *et*
full *adj.* full
function *n.* funksjon *en*
funeral *n.* begravelse *en*
funny *adj.* morsom
fur *n.* pels *en*
furious *adj.* rasende
furniture *n.* møbler *et*
future *n.* fremtid *en*;
   adj. fremtidig

G

game *n.* lek *en*; selskapslek *en*
   (*parlor game*); fuglevilt *et*
   (*gamebird*); storvilt *et*
   (*big game*)
garage *n.* garasje *en* (*parking*);
   bilverksted *et* (*repairs*)
garbage *n.* søppel *et*
garden *n.* have *en*
garlic *n.* hvitløk *en*
gas *n.* gass *en*; tåregass *en*
   (*tear gas*)
gasoline *n.* bensin *en*
gastritis *n.* magekatarr *en*
gate *n.* port *en*; utgang *en*
   (*airport gate*)
gather *v.* samle
gathering *n.* sammenkomst *en*
gay *adj.* glad (*happy*);
   homoseksuell
gear *n.* utstyr *et*; automatisk gir
   et (*automatice drive*); i gir
   (*in gear*); i fri (*out of gear*)
general *adj.* generell,
   alminnelig
generosity *n.* gavmildhet *en*
gentleman *n.* herre *en*
genuine *adj.* ekte
German *adj.*; *n.* tysker *en*

Germany *Pln.* Tyskland
get *v.* få, hente (*fetch*)
gift *n.* gave *en*, presang *en*
girl *n.* jente *en*, pike *en*
girlfriend *n.* venninne *en*
give *v.* gi
glad *adj.* glad, gledelig (*joyous*)
glass *n.* glass *et*
glasses *n.* briller *pl.*
globe *n.* globus *en*
gloomy *adj.* mørk, dyster
glove *n.* hanske *en*
go *v.* gå, kjøre (*drive*); reise
   (*travel*); dra (*leave*)
goal *n.* mål *et*
goat *n.* geit *en*
God *n.* gud *en*
gold *n.* gull *et*
golf *n.* golf *en*
good *adj.* god, bra
good-bye *n.* adjø *et*; *interj.*
   morn så lenge, ha det!
goods *n.* varer *pl.*
goose *n.* gås *en*
gooseberry *n.* stikkelsbær *et*
gossip *n.* sladder *en*
government *n.* regjeringen *en*
grain *n.* korn *et* (*food*); tekstur
   en (*texture*)
gram *n.* gram *et*
granddaughter *n.* barnebarn
   et; sønndatter *en* (*son's
   daughter*), datterdatter *en*
   (*daughter's daughter*)
grandfather *n.* bestefar *en*;
   morfar *en* (*mother's
   father*), farfar *en* (*father's
   father*)
grandmother *n.* bestemor *en*;
   mormor *en* (*mother's
   mother*); farmor *en*
   (*father's mother*)
grandson *n.* barnebarn *et*;
   sønnesønn *en* (*son's son*);
   dattersønn *en*
   (*daughter's son*)
grape *n.* drue *en*
grass *n.* gress *et*
gravy *n.* saus *en*

grease *n.* fett *en; v.* smøre
Great Britain *Pln.*
 Storbritannia
Greece *Pln.* Hellas
Greek *n.* greker *en (person);*
 Greek *adj.* gresk
green *n.* grønt *et (color); adj.*
 grønn
greetings *n.* hilsen *en*
grey *n.* grått *et; adj.* grå
grief *n.* sorg *en*
group *n.* gruppe *en*
grow *v.* vokse, vokse opp
 (grow up)
guarantee *n.* garanti *en;*
 v. garantere
guest *n.* gjest *en*
guest bedroom *n.*
 gjesteværelse *et*
guesthouse *n.* pensjonat *et*
 (small hotel)
guide *n.* guide *en; v.* lede
guidebook *n.* guide *en*
gymnastics *n.* gymnastikk *en*
gynecologist *n.* gynekolog *en*
gypsy *n.* sigøyner *en*

H

habit *n.* vane *en*
hair *n.* hår *et*
haircut *n.* hårklipp *et;* få
 klippet håret *(get a haircut)*
hairbrush *n.* hårbørste *en*
hairdresser *n.* damefrisør *en*
 (ladies), herrefrisør *en (men)*
half *n.* halvpart *en; adv.* halv,
 halvt
hall *n.* hall *en*
ham *n.* skinke *en*
hammer *n.* hammer *en;*
 v. hamre
hand *n.* hånd *en; v.* henge
handbag *n.* håndveske *en*
 (handbag), veske *en*
handkerchief *n.* lommetørkle *et*
handle *n.* håndtak *et*
handmade *adj.* håndlaget
handsome *adj.* pen, kjekk
happen *v.* hende, skje

happiness *n.* lykke *en*
happy *adj.* glad, lykkelig
harbor *n.* havn *en*
hard *adj.* hard
harm *n.* skade *en; v.* skade
harvest *n.* innhøstning *en;*
 v. høste
hat *n.* hatt *en*
hate *n.* hat *et; v.* hate
have *v.* ha
he *pron.* han
head *n.* hode *et*
headache *n.* hodepine *en*
headlights *n.* frontlys *et*
heal *v.* helbrede
health *n.* sunnhet *en,* helse *en*
healthy *adj.* sunn, frisk
hear *v.* høre
heart *n.* hjerte *et*
heart attack *n.* hjerteanfall *et*
heat *n.* varme *en; v.* varme
heaven *n.* himmel *en*
heavy *adj.* tung
heel *n.* hæl *en*
height *n.* høyde *en*
helicopter *n.* helikopter *et*
hell *n.* helvete *et*
hello *interj.* goddag
help *n.* hjelp *en; v.* hjelpe
her *pron.* henne; *adj.* hennes
herbs *n.* krydder *et*
here *adv.* her
heritage *n.* arv *en*
herring *n.* sild *en*
hi! *interj.* hei! morn!
hide *v.* gjemme
high *adj.* høy
hill *n.* bakke *en,* ås *en,* høyde *en*
hip *n.* hofte *en*
hire *v.* til leie *(for hire);* ansette
 (employ); leie *(rent)*
historical *adj.* historisk
history *n.* historie *en*
hit *v.* treffe, slå, ramme
hitchhike *v.* haike
hold *v.* holde
hole *n.* hull *et*
holiday *n.* fridag *en,* ferie *en*

Holland *Pln.* Holland,
Nederland
home *n.* hjem *et*
honest *adj.* ærlig
honey *n.* honning *en*
honeymoon *n.* bryllupsreise *en*
honor *n.* ære *en*
hook *n.* krok *en*
hope *n.* håpe *et*
horror *n.* redsel *en*
horse *n.* hest *en*
(to go) horseback riding
v. ri *en* hest
hospital *n.* sykehus *et*
host *n.* vert *en*
hostel *n.* herberge *et*
hostess *n.* vertinne *en*
hostage *n.* gissel *en*
hot *adj.* varm
hotel *n.* hotell *et*
hotel manager *n.*
hotelldirektør *en*
hot-water bottle *n.*
varmeflaske *en*
hour *n.* time *en*
how *adv.* hvordan
however *v.* hvordan; *conj.* men
hug *n.* klem *en*; *v.* klemme
huge *adj.* kjempestor
human *adj.* menneskelig
humid *adj.* fuktig
humor *n.* humor *en*
humorous *adj.* komisk
hundred *num.* hundre
Hungarian *n.* ungarer *en*
(*person*); *adj.* ungarsk
Hungary *Pln.* Ungarn
hunger *n.* sult *en*
hungry *adj.* sulten
hunt *v.* jakte
hunter *n.* jeger *en*
hurricane *n.* orkan *en*
hurry *n.* hast *en*; *v.* skynde seg
hurt *v.* skade, gjøre vondt
husband *n.* ektemann *en*

I

I *pron.* jeg
ice *n.* is *en*

ice cream *n.* iskrem *en*, is *en*
idea *n.* ide *en*, tanke *en*
identification (ID) *n.*
identifikasjon *en*
identity *n.* identitet *en*
if *conj.* hvis, om
ignition *n.* tenning *en*
ignition key *n.*
tenningsnøkkel *en*
ill *adj.* syk
illegal *adj.* ulovlig
illness *n.* sykdom *en*
image *n.* bilde *et*
imagine *v.* tenke seg
immediately *adv.* straks, med
en gang
immigrant *n.* immigrant *en*
immigration *n.* innvandring *en*
immoral *adj.* umoralsk
immortal *adj.* udødelighet
import *n.* import *en*;
v. importere
immunity *n.* immunitet *en*;
diplomatisk immunitet
(*diplomatic immunity*)
impatient *adj.* utålmodig
important *adj.* viktig
impossible *adj.* umulig
impression *n.* inntrykk *et*
improper *adj.* upassende
improve *v.* forbedre, bedre
in *prep.* inne, i byen (*in town*),
på landet (*in the
countryside*), på kontoret
(*in the office*)
incapable *adj.* hjelpeløs
incident *n.* hendelse *en*
include *v.* inkludere
income *n.* inntekt *en*
incomprehensible *adj.*
uforståelig
increase *n.* stigning *en*; *v.* tilta,
stige, vokse
incredible *adj.* utrolig
independence *n.*
uavhengighet *en*
independent *adj.* uavhengig,
selvstendig

indigestion *n.* dårlig
    fordøyelse *en*
industry *n.* industri *en*
inexpensive *adj.* billig
infant *n.* spebarn *et*
infect *v.* smitte
infected *adj.* infisert
infection *n.* infeksjon *en*,
    smitte *en*
inflammable *adj.*
    lettantennelig
influenza *n.* influensa *en*
information *n.* informasjon *en*
inherit *v.* arve
inheritance *n.* arv *en*
injection *n.* innsprøytning *en*,
    injeksjon *en*
injured *adj.* skadet
injury *n.* skade *en*
ink *n.* blekk *et*
innocent *adj.* uskyldig
inquire *v.* spørre
insane *adj.* sinnssyk
insect *n.* insekt *et*
inside *adj.* inne; innvendig
    (*internal*)
instead *adv.* istedenfor
instead of *prep.* istedenfor
institute *n.* institutt *et*
instrument *n.* instrument *et*
insult *n.* fornærmelse *en*;
    v. fornærme
insurance *n.* forsikring *et*
interest *n.* interesse *en*; rente
    en (*rate of interest*);
    v. interessere
interested *adj.* interessert
interesting *adj.* interessant
intermission *n.* pause *en*
international *adj.*
    internasjonal
interpret *v.* tolke
interpreter *n.* tolker *en*
interrogation *n.* avhør *et*,
    forhør *et*
intersection, crossroads *n.*
    veikryss *et*
intestines *n.* tarm *en*
into *prep.* inne in

introduce *v.* ta i bruk (*begin to
    use*); introdusere
    (*introduce a speaker*),
    presentere (*introduce
    someone to someone else*)
introduction *n.* innledning *en*
    (*to a book*); presentasjon
    en (*of one person to
    another*)
invalid *adj.* ugyldig
invest *v.* investere (*money*)
investigate *v.* etteforske,
    undersøke
investigation *n.* etterforskning
    en, undersøkelse *en*
investment *n.* investering *en*
invitation *n.* invitasjon *en*,
    innbydelse *en*
invite *v.* invitere, innby
invoice *n.* faktura *en*
iodine *n.* jod *en*
Ireland *Pln.* Irland
Irish *n.* irlender *en*; *adj.* irsk
iron *n.* jern *et*; *v.* strykke
irregular *adj.* unregelmessig,
    ujevn
irresponsible *adj.* uansvarlig
irritate *v.* irriteri
island *n.* øy *en*
Israel *Pln.* Israel
Israeli *n.* israeler *en*;
    adj. israelsk
Italian *n.* italiensk *en*
Italy *Pln.* Italia
itch *v.* klø
ivory *n.* elfenbein *et*

J

jacket *n.* jakke *en* (*coat*);
    omslag *et* (*book jacket*)
jail *n.* fengsel *et*
jam *n.* syltetøy *et*
January *n.* januar
Japan *Pln.* Japan
Japanese *n.* japaner *en*
    (*Japanese person*);
    adj. japansk
jaw *n.* kjeve *en*
jealous *adj.* sjalu
jealousy *n.* sjalusi *en*

jelly *n.* gelé *en*
Jew *n.* jøde *en*
jewel *n.* juvel *en*
jewelry *n.* smykke *et*
Jewish *adj.* jødisk
joke *n.* vits *en; v.* spøke
journey *n.* reise *en; v.* reise
judge *n.* dømmer *en; v.* dømme
jug *n.* mugge *en*
juice *n.* saft *en*
July *n.* juli
jump *n.* sprang *et;* hopp *et;*
    v. hoppe
June *n.* juni
just *adj.* rettferdig;
    adv. nettopp
justice *n.* rettferdighet *en*

K

keep *v.* holde
kettle *n.* kjele *en*
key *n.* nøkkel *en*
kidney *n.* nyre *en*
kill *v.* drepe
kilogram *n.* kilo *en*
kilometer *n.* kilometer *en*
kind *adj.* snill
kindness *n.* vennlighet *en*
king *n.* konge *en*
kiosk *n.* kiosk *en*
kiss *n.* kyss *et; v.* kysse
kitchen *n.* kjøkken *et*
knee *n.* kne *et*
knife *n.* kniv *en*
knit *v.* strikke
knitting *v.* strikning *en*
knitting needle *v.*
    strikkepinne *en*
knock *n.* slag *et; v.* slå
know *v.* vite (*to know*
    something); kjenne (*to*
    know someone, to be
    familiar with)
known *adj.* kjent
kudos *n.* ros *en*

L

label *n.* merkelapp *en*
lady *n.* dame *en*

lake *n.* innsjø *en*
lamb *n.* lam *et;* lammestek *en*
    (*roast lamb*)
lamp *n.* lampe *en*
land *n.* land *et*
landscape *n.* landskap *et*
language *n.* språk *et*
large *adj.* stor
last *v.* vare; *adj.* sist
late *adj.* sen
later *adv.* senere
laugh *v.* le av (*laugh at*)
laundry *n.* vaskeri *et*
lavatory *n.* W.C. *et*
law *n.* lov *en*
lawyer *n.* jurist *en,* advokat *en*
laxative *n.* avførende middel *et*
lazy *adj.* doven
lead *n.* bly *et* (*metal*); ledelse *en*
    (*a lead in sports*); *v.* lede
leader *n.* leder *en*
leaf *n.* blad *et*
learn *v.* lære
leather *n.* lær *et,* skinn *et*
leave *v.* reise, gå, dra (*depart*);
    etterlate (*leave behind*)
leftovers *n.* matrest *en*
leg *n.* ben *et*
lemon *n.* sitron *en*
lend *v.* låne
length *n.* lengde *en*
lens *n.* linse *en;* kameralinse *en*
less *adj.* mindre
lesson *n.* lekse *en*
let *v.* la
letter *n.* brev *et* (*post*); bokstav
    en (*of alphabet*)
lettuce *n.* salat *en*
liar *n.* løgner *en*
liberation *n.* frigivelse *en*
library *n.* bibliotek *et*
lie *n.* løgn *en; v.* ligge (*lie down;*
    be situated)
life *n.* liv *et*
lift *v.* løfte
light *n.* lys *et; v.* lyse; tenne på
    (*ignite*); *adj.* lett (*not*
    heavy); lys (*not dark*)
lightning *n.* lyn *et*

like *v.* like; *prep.* like, sliksom
line *n.* snor *en*, fiskesnøre *et*
    (*fishing line*); linje *en*
    (*mark, railway*)
linen *n.* lintøy *et* (*linen*);
    sengetøy *et* (*bed linen*);
    dekketøy *et* (*tablecloth*)
lion *n.* løve *en*
lip *n.* leppe *en*
lipstick *n.* leppestift *en*
liqueur *n.* likør *en*
liquid *n.* veske *en*
listen *v.* lytte; høre på (*listen to*)
literature *n.* litteratur *en*
liter *n.* liter *en*
little *adj.* liten, små
live *v.* leve, overleve (*survive*)
liver *n.* lever *en*
lobster *n.* hummer *en*
local *adj.* stedlig
locate *v.* finne
lock *n.* las *en; v.* låse
locksmith *n.* låsesmed *en*
lonely *adj.* ensom
long *adj.* lang
look *n.* blink *et; v.* se
lose *v.* miste
loss *n.* tap *et*
lost *adj.* tapt
a lot of *adj.* mange (*many*),
    mye (*much*)
lottery *n.* lotteri *et*
loud *adj.* høy
love *n.* kjælighet *en; v.* elske
lovely *adj.* vakker, deilig
lover *n.* elsker *en* (*male*);
    elskerinne *en* (*female*)
low *adj.* lav
luck *n.* lykke *en*
lucky *adj.* heldig
luggage *n.* bagasje *en*
lump *n.* klump *en; kul en*
    (*swelling*)
lunch *n.* lunsj *en; v.* spise lunsj
lungs *n.* lunge *en*

M

machine *n.* maskin *en*
mackerel *n.* makrell *en*

mad *adj.* gal (*insane*);
    sint (*angry*)
magazine *n.* magasin *et*,
    ukeblad *et* (*weekly*)
magnificent *adj.* praktfull
mail *n.* post *en*
mailbox *n.* postkasse *en*
main *adj.* hoved
mountain *n.* fjell *et*
majority *n.* flertall *et*
make *v.* lage (*produce*); skape
    (*create*); gjøre (*do*);
    fortjene (*earn*)
makeup *n.* sminke *en*
man *n.* mann *en*
manage *v.* bestyre (*be in charge
    of*); greie; klare (*negotiate*)
manager *n.* leder *en*, sjef *en*,
    bestyrer *en*
manual *n.* håndbok *en;*
    adj. manuell
many *adj.* mange
map *n.* kart *et*
March *n.* mars
margarine *n.* margarin *en*
marinated *adj.*marinert
market *n.* marked *en*
marmalade *n.*
    appelsinmarmelade *en*
marriage *n.* ekteskap *et*
married *adj.* gift
marry *v.* gifte seg
match *n.* fyrstikk *en* (*light*);
    match *en*, kamp *en* (*sport*)
material *n.* materiale *et*, stoff
    et; adj. materiell
mathematics *n.* matematikk *en*
mattress *n.* madrass *en*
May *n.* mai
maybe *adj.* kanskje
meal *n.* måltid *en*
mean *v.* bety (*signify*); mene
    (*intend*); *adj.* lumpen
meaning *n.* betydning *en*
means *n.* midler *et*, penger *pl.*
    (*money*); middel *et* (*way,
    instrument*)
meanwhile *adv.* imens
measles *n.* meslinger *pl.*

measure *v.* måle
measurement *n.* mål *et*
meat *n.* kjøtt *et*
mechanic *n.* mekaniker *en*
medicine *n.* medisin *en*
meet *v.* møte
meeting *n.* møte *et*
melon *n.* melon *en*
member *n.* medlem *et*
membership *n.* medlemskap *et*
memory *n.* hukommelse *en*;
    minne *et* (*recollection*;
    memorial)
menu *n.* meny *en*, spisekart *et*
mercy *n.* barmhjertighet *en*
merry *adj.* livlig, munter, glad
mess *n.* rot *et*; spisesal *en*
    (*dining room*); messe *en*
    (*meal in the military*)
message *n.* beskjed *en*
messy *adj.* rotet
meter *n.* meter *en*
middle *adj.* midt, mellom
midnight *n.* midnatt *en*
midwife *n.* jordmor *en*
mileage *n.* antall *et* (*number*);
    avstand *en* (*distance*)
milk *n.* melk *en*
million *num.* million *en*
mind *n.* sinn *et*
mineral *n.* mineral *et*;
    adj. mineralsk
minor *n.* mindreåring *en*
    (*underage*); *adj.* mindre;
    mindre viktig (*less
    important*)
minute *n.* minutt *et*
mirror *n.* speil *et*
miserable *adj.* ulykuelig,
    elendig
Miss *n.* frøken *title*
    (*abbrev. frk.*)
miss *v.* bomme, ikke treffe (*not
    hit, not meet*); savne (*long
    to see*)
mistake *n.* feil *en*
misunderstand *v.* misforstå
misunderstanding *n.*
    misforståelse *en*

mix *v.* blande
mobile phone, cell phone *n.*
    mobil telefon *en*
modern *adj.* moderne
modesty *n.* beskjedenhet *en*
moist *adj.* fuktig
moment *n.* øyeblikk *et*
monarch *n.* monark *en*
Monday *n.* mandag
money *n.* penger *pl.*
monkey *n.* apekatt *en*
month *n.* måned *en*
monument *n.* monument *et*,
    minnesmerke *et*
mood *n.* humør *et*
moon *n.* måne *en*
moral *n.* moral *en*;
    adj. moralsk
more *adj.* mer, flere
morning *n.* morgan *en*
mosquito *n.* moskito *en*,
    mygg *en*
most *adj.* flest *en*
mother *n.* mor *en*
mother-in-law *n.* svigermor *en*
motion *n.* bevegelse *en*
motorbike, motorcycle *n.*
    motorsykkel *en*
mountain *n.* fjell *et*
mouse *n.* mus *en*
moustache *n.* bart *en*
mouth *n.* munn *en*
move *v.* flytte, bevege
movies *n.* film *en*
Mr. *n.* herr (*abbrev. hr.*)
Mrs. *n.* fru (*abbrev. fr.*)
Ms. *n.* frøken (*abbrev. frk.*)
much *adj.* meget, mye
muddy *v.* søle; *adj.* sølet
mug *n.* krus *et*
multiplication *n.*
    multiplikasjon *en*
murder *n.* mord *et*; *v.* myrde
murderer *n.* morder *en*
muscle *n.* muskel *en*
museum *n.* museum *et*
mushroom *n.* sopp *en*
music *n.* musikk *en*

must *v.* må
mustard *n.* sennep *en*
mute *adj.* stum
mutual *adj.* felles
my *pron.* min, mitt
mystery *n.* mysterium *et*

N

nail *n.* negl *en* (*fingernail*);
spiker *en*; *v.* spikre
naked *adj.* naken
name *n.* navn *et*; *v.* oppnevne,
kalle
napkin *n.* serviett *en*
narrow *adj.* smal
nation *n.* nasjon *en*
national *adj.* nasjonal
nationality *n.* nasjonalitet *en*
native *adj.* innfødt
nature *n.* natur *en*
nausea *n.* kvalme *en*
near *adj.*; *prep.* nær
necessary *adj.* nødvendig
necessity *n.* nøvendighet *en*
neck *n.* hals *en*
necklace *n.* halsbånd *et*
necktie *n.* slips *et*
need *n.* behov *et*; *v.* behøve
needle *n.* nål *en*
negative *adj.* negativ
neglect *v.* forsømme
neighbor *n.* nabo *en*
neighborhood *n.* nabolag *et*
neither ... nor *conj.* hverken ...
eller
nephew *n.* nevø *en*
nerve *n.* nerve *en*
nervous *adj.* nervøs
neurotic *adj.* neurotisk
never *adv.* aldri
new *adj.* ny
news *n.* nyhet *en*
newspaper *n.* blad *en*, avis *en*
newsstand *n.* aviskiosk *en*
New Year's Eve *n.*
nyttårsaften
next *adj.* neste
nice *adj.* hyggelig
nickname *n.* oppnavn *et*

niece *n.* niese *en*
night *n.* natt *en*
nightclub *n.* nattklubb *en*
nine *num.* ni
nineteen *num.* nitten
ninety *num.* nitti
no *adj.*; *interj.* nei
nobody *pron.* ingen
noise *n.* lyd *en*
noisy *adj.* bråkende
non-alcoholic *adj.* alkoholfri
none *pron.* ingen
nonsense *n.* tøys *et*, tull *et*
normal *adj.* normal, vannlig
north *n.* nord *en*; *adv.* nord
northern *adj.* nordlig
nose *n.* nese *en*
not *adv.* ikke
notebook *n.* notisbok *en*
nothing *n.* ingenting *et*
notice *n.* notis *en*; *v.* legge
merke til
nourish *v.* føde, nære
nourishing *adj.* næringsrik
novel *n.* roman *en*
novelist *n.* romanforfatter *en*
November *n.* November
now *adv.* nå
nowhere *adv.* ingensteds
number *n.* nummer *et*
nurse *n.* sykepleier *en* (*male*);
sykepleieske *en* (*female*);
v. pleie
nut *n.* nøtt *en*

O

oak *n.* eik *en*
oar *n.* åre *en*
obedient *adj.* lydig
object *n.* gjenstand *en*;
v. innvende
obligation *n.* forpliktelse *en*
obnoxious *adj.* ubehagelig
obtain *v.* få
obvious *adj.* tydelig, klar
occasion *n.* anledning *en*
occasionally *adv.* av og til
occupation *n.* yrke *et*
occupied *adj.* opptatt

occupy *v.* bo; oppta
ocean *n.* verdenshav *et*
October *n.* oktober
odd *adj.* odde
of *prep.* av
of course *adv.* selvfølgelig
off *adv.* bort
offence *n.* fornærmelse *en*
offend *v.* fornærme
offer *n.* tilbud *et*; *v.* tilby
office *n.* kontor *et*
often *adv.* ofte
oil *n.* olje *en*
oil tanker *n.* oljetanker *en*
oil well *n.* oljekilde *en*
old *adj.* gammel
omelet *n.* omelett *en*
on *prep.* på
once *prep.* en gang
one *adj.* en, et
one-way street *n.*
    enveiskjøring *en*
one-way ticket *n.* enkeltbillett *en*
onion *n.* løk *en*
only *adj.*eneste; *adv.* bare
open *adj.* åpne, lukke opp
opera *n.* opera *en*
operation *n.* operasjon *en*
operator *n.* operatør *en*
opinion *n.* mening *en*
opportunity *n.* anledning *en*,
    sjanse *en*
opposite *adj.* motsatt
oral *adj.* muntlig
orange *n.* appelsin *en*
order *n.* ordre *en* (*command*);
    orden *en* (*classification*;
    orderliness); *v.* bestille;
    beordre (*command*)
ordinance *n.* forordning *en*
organ *n.* organ *et*
organic *adj.* organisk
organize *v.* organisere, ordne
origin *n.* opprinelse *en*
original *adj.* original
ornament *n.* ornament *et*;
    v. ornamentere
orphan *n.* foreldreløst barn *et*
orthodox *adj.* ortodoks

other *pron.*; *adj.* annen, annet,
    andre
otherwise *adv.* ellers
ought *v.* bør, burde
our, ours *pron.* vår, vårt, våre
out *adj.* ut, ute
outboard *adj.* utenbords
outdated *adj.* gammeldags
outdoor *adj.* utendørs
outfit *n.* utstyr *et*
outlaw *adj.* fredløs
outline *n.* omriss *et*, skisse *en*;
    v. skissere
outlook *n.* utsikt *en*
out of the way *adj.* avsides
out of work *adj.* arbeidsløs
output *n.* produksjon *en*
outrageous *adj.* skandaløs
outside *adj.* utvendig
outsider *n.* fremmed *en*
outskirts *n.* utkant *en*
outstanding *adj.* fremragende
outward *adj.* ytre
over *adv.*; *prep.* over
overall *adj.* samlet; *adv.* i alt
overbook *v.* overbooke
overcast *adj.* overskyet
overcharge *v.* ta for høy pris
overcrowded *adj.* overfylt
overdraw *v.* overtrekke
overdue *adj.* forsinket
overgrown *adj.* overgrodd
overheat *v.* overopphete
overload *n.* for tungt lass *et*;
    v. lesse for tungt
overnight *adv.* natten over
overseas *adv.* utenlands
oversee *v.* ha oppsyn med
overtax *v.* beskatte for høyt
overvalue *v.* overvurdere
overwork *v.* arbeide for hardt
overworked *adj.* overarbeidet
owe *v.* skylde
owl *n.* ugle
own *v.* eie; *adj.* egen, eget, egne
owner *n.* eier
ox *n.* okse
oxygen *n.* oksygen *et*, surstoff *et*

oxygen mask *n.*
 surstoffmaske *en*
oyster *n.* østers *en*
ozone *n.* ozon *en*

P

pain *n.* smerte *en*
paper *n.* papir *et*
parents *n.* foreldre *pl.*
park *n.* park *en; v.* parkere
passenger *n.* passasjer *en*
passport *n.* pass *et*
payment *n.* betaling *en*
pen *n.* penn *en* (*writing
 instrument*); *n.* kve *en* (*pen
 for livestock*); *n.* lekegrind
 en (*playpen*)
pencil *n.* blyant *en*
phone *n.* telefon *en*
please *adv.* vær så snill;
 v. behage
police *n.* politi *et*
pool *n.* svømmebasseng *et*
population *n.* befolkning *en*
postcard *n.* kort *et*
post office *n.* postkontor *et*
precaution *n.*
 forsiktighetsregel *en*
precious *adj.* kjær (*dear*); edel
 (*edelmetall = precious
 metal*)
precise *adj.* nøyaktig
pregnant *adj.* gravid
prehistoric *adj.* forhistorisk
prepare *v.* forberede
prescribe *v.* foreskrive
prescription *n.* resept *en*
present *n.* gave *en* (*gift*); nåtid
 en (*time*); *v.* presentere;
 adj. til stede (*here*)
pressure *n.* trykk *et*
pretend *v.* foregi, pretendere
pretty *adj.* pen
price *n.* pris *en*
pride *n.* stolthet *en*
priest *n.* prest *en*
prince *n.* fyrste *en,* prins *en*
princess *n.* prinsesse *en*
problem *n.* problem *et*

R

radio *n.* radio *en*
railway *n.* jernbane *en*
railway station *n.*
 jernbanestasjon *en*
rain *n.* regn *et; v.* regne
raise *v.* heve (*lift*); øke
 (*increase*)
raisin *n.* rosin *en*
rare *adj.* sjelden (*seldom*);
 rødstekt, lite stekt
 (*undercooked*)
raspberry *n.* bringebær *et*
rat *n.* rotte *en*
rather *adv.* nokså
raw *adj.* rå (*uncooked*); fersk
 (*untrained*); råkald (*cold
 and raw weather*)
razor *n.* barberkniv *en*
 (*straight*)
read *v.* lese
ready *adj.* ferdig
real *adj.* virkelig
rear *n.* bakside *en; v.* oppdra
reason *n.* fornuft *en* (*intellect*);
 grunn *en* (*cause*)
receipt *n.* kvittering *en*
receive *v.* motta; få
receiver *n.* rør *et* (*earphone*)
reception *n.* mottagelse *en;*
 resepsjon *en* (*reception
 desk*)
receptionist *n.* resepsjonist *en*
recipe *n.* oppskrift *en*
recognize *v.* gjenkjenne
recommend *v.* anbefale
recommendation *n.*
 anbefaling *en*
recover *v.* komme seg (*from
 illness*); få tak i igjen
 (*get back*)
recovery *n.* bedring *en*
red *adj.* rød
reduction *n.* reduksjon *en*
reflect *v.* reflektere (*mirror*);
 tenke (*consider*)
reflection *n.* speilbilde *et*
 (*picture*); tanker *pl.*
 (*thoughts*)

refresh *v.* kvikke opp
refreshment *n.* forfriskning *en*
refrigerator *n.* kjøleskap *et*
refugee *n.* flyktning *en*
refund *n.* tilbakebetaling *en;*
   v. refundere, betale tilbake
refusal *n.* avslag *et*
refuse *n.* avslag *et; v.* nekte
regarding *prep.* angående
regards, greetings *n.*
   hilsninger *pl.*
region *n.* distrikt *et,* område *et*
register *n.* register *et;*
   v. registrere
registration *n.* registrering *en*
regularly *adj.* regelmessig
rejoice *v.* glede seg
relationship *n.* forbindelse *en*
relative *n.* slektning *en*
relax *v.* slappe av
relief *n.* lettelse *en*
religion *n.* religion *en*
religious *adj.* religiøs
reluctant *adj.* motvillig
remember *v.* huske
rent *n.* husleie *en; v.* leie
repair *v.* reparere
repeat *v.* gjenta
report *n.* nyhetsmelding *en*
   (news); årsberetning *en*
   (annual report); v. melde
   (announce); rapportere
representative *n.*
   representant *en*
rescue *n.* redning *en; v.* redde
research *n.* forskning *en;*
   v. forske
resemblance *n.* likhet *en*
reservation *n* bestilling *en*
   (booking)
reservation desk *n.*
   bookingkontor *et*
reserve *v.* reservere
reside *v.* bo
residence *n.* bosted *et*
respect *n.* respekt *en;*
   v. respektere
respectable *adj.* respektabel
responsibility *n.* ansvar *et*

responsible *adj.* ansvarlig
rest *n.* hvile *en; v.* hvile
restaurant *n.* restaurant *en*
restroom *n.* toalett *et*
return *v.* komme tilbake *(come*
   back); gi tilbake *(give back)*
return ticket *n.* returbillett *en*
   (round ticket)
revenge *n.* hevn *en*
reverse *v.* reversere;
   adj. omvendt
rheumatism *n.* reumatisme *en*
rib *n.* ribben *et*
ribbon *n.* bånd *et*
rice *n.* ris *en*
rich *adj.* rik
ride *v.* ri
ridiculous *adj.* latterlig
right *n.* rett *en; adj.* riktig
ring *n.* ring *en (circle);* klang
   en (sound); v. ringe; klinge
   (sound)
rival *n.* konkurrent *en*
river *n.* elv *en*
road *n.* vei *en*
road sign *n.* veiskilt *et*
rob *v.* plyndre, røve
robber *n.* ransmann *en*
robe *n.* kappe *en*
rock *n.* stein *en;* skjær *et*
   (skerry); v. vukke
roof *n.* tak *et*
room *n.* rom *et,* værelse *et;*
   dagligstue *en (sitting*
   room); plass *en (space)*
room number *n.*
   værelsesnummer *et*
room service *n.*
   værelsesbetjening *en*
rose *n.* rose *en*
rotten *adj.* råtten
round *adj.* rund
route *n.* rute *en,* vei *en*
row *n.* rekke *(row of seats,*
   houses); v. ro
rubber *n.* gummi *en*
rug *n.* teppe *et*
ruin *n.* ruin *en; v.* ruinere
ruined *adj.* ruinert

run *n.* tur *en; v.* løpe (*run a race*); renne (*water*); gå (*motor*); vare (*to last*)
Russia *Pln.* Russland
Russian *n.* russer *en* (*person*); *adj.* russisk
rust *n.* rust *en*
rust *v.* ruste
rye *n.* rug *en* (*grain*)

S

sacred *adj.* hellig
sad *adj.* trist
sadly *adv.* trist
safe *adj.* sikker, trygg; *n.* pengeskap *et* (*for keeping valuables*)
safety *n.* sikkerhet *en*, trygghet *en*
sail *n.* seil *et; v.* seile
saint *n.* helgen *en*
salad *n.* salat *en*
salary *n.* gasje *en*
salmon *n.* laks *en*
salt *n.* salt *et; v.* salte
same *pron.* samme
sand *n.* sand *en*
sandal *n.* sandal *en*
sandwich *n.* samdwich *en*
sanitary napkin *n.* damebind *et*, sanitetsbind *et*
sardine *n.* sardin *en*
satisfied *adj.* tilfreds, fornøyd
saturate *v.* gjennomvæte
Saturday *n.* lørdag
sauce *n.* saus *en*
saucepan *n.* kasserolle *en*
saucer *n.* skål *en*
sausage *n.* pølse *en*
save *v.* redde
say *v.* si
scale *n.* skjell *en* (*fish scale*); vektskål *en* (*weighing scales*); *v.* skrape skjell av
scallop *n.* kammusling *en*
scarf *n.* skjerf *et*
schedule *n.* tidsramme *en*, programm *et*, plan *en*

scholarship *n.* stipend *et*
school *n.* skole *en*
science *n.* vitenskap *en*
scientist *n.* vitenskapsmann *en*
scissors *n.* saks *en*
Scot *n.* skotte *en*
Scotland *Pln.* Skottland
Scottish *adj.* skotsk
scream *n.* skrik *et; v.* skrike
sculptor *n.* billedhugger *en*
sculpture *n.* skulptur *en*
sea *n.* hav *en.,* sjø *en*
seafood *n.* fiskemat *en*
search *n.* leting *en*
search *v.* lete, søke
season *n.* arstid *en,* sesong *en; v.* krydre
seat *n.* plasse *en; v.* plassere
seatbelt *n.* sikkerhetsbelte *et*
second *n.* sekund *et* (*time*); *adj.* nummer to (*number*)
second-hand *adj.* brukt
secret *n.* hemmelighet *en; adj.* hemmelig
secretly *adv.* hemmelig
security *n.* sikkerhet *en*
see *v.* se
seem *v.* synes
seldom *adj.; adv.* sjelden
self *pron.* seg selv
self-esteem *n.* selvrespekt *en*
sell *v.* selge
send *v.* sende
senior *adj.; n.* senior *en*
sense *n.* sans *en* (*one of the five senses*); fornuft *en* (*reason*)
sensitive *adj.* følsom
sentence *n.* setning *en* (*linguistic unit*); dom *en* (*judgment*)
separate *v.* skilles; *adj.* separat
separation *n.* atskillelse *en;* separasjon *en* (*legal separation*)
September *n.* September
serious *adj.* alvorlig
serve *n.* serve *en* (*tennis*); *v.* tjene, severe

service *n.* tjeneste *en*
(*assistance*); gudstjeneste
en (*church service*)
session *n.* sesjon *en,* møte *et*
(*meeting*)
seven *num.* syv, sju
seventeen *num.* sytten
seventy *num.* sytti
several *adj.* noen, flere
sew *v.* sy
sex *n.* kjønn *et* (*male or
female*); erotikk *en*
(*eroticism*)
shadow *n.* skygge *en*
shake *v.* riste; skjelve (*quiver*);
sjokkere (*shock*)
shallow *adj.* grunn (*creek*);
flat (*bowl*)
shame *n.* skam *en*
shampoo *n.* sjampo *en*
share *n.* del *en; v.* dele
shark *n.* hai *en*
sharp *adj.* skarp
sharpen *v.* skjerpe
shave *v.* barbere seg
shaving cream *n.* barberkrem *en*
she *pron.* hun
sheep *n.* sau *en*
sheet *n.* ark *et* (*paper*); plate *en*
(*metal, ice*)
shelf *n.* hylle *en*
shell *n.* skall *et*
shine *n.* glans *en; v.* skinne
shirt *n.* skjorte *en*
shoe *n.* sko *en*
shoot *v.* skyte; ta opp (*film*)
shop *n.* butikk *en; v.* handle
shopkeeper *n.* kjøpmann *en*
shore *n.* kyst *en*
short *adj.* kort
shortage *n.* mangel *en*
shorten *v.* forkorte
shoulder *n.* skulder *en*
shout *v.* rope
show *n.* utstilling *en; v.* vise
shower *n.* dusj *en* (*shower,
bath*); *v.* dusje
shrimp *n.* reke *en*

sick *adj.* syk
sickness *n.* sykdom *en*
side *n.* side *en*
sidewalk *n.* fortau *et*
sigh *n.* sukke *en; v.* sukke
sight *n.* syn *et*
sightseeing *n.* sightseeing *en*
sign *n.* tegn *et; v.* undertegne
(*signature*)
signature *n.* underskrift *en*
silence *n.* stillhett *en*
silk *n.* silke *en*
silver *n.* sølv *et*
similar *adj.* lik
simple *adj.* lett, enkel
simplify *v.* enkelt
sin *n.* synd *en; v.* synde
since *adv.; conj.* siden
sincere *adj.* oppriktig
sincerity *n.* oppriktighet *en*
sing *v.* synge
single *adj.* enkelt; *adj.* ugift
(*unmarried*)
single bed *n.* enkeltseng *en*
singer *n.* sanger *en* (*male*);
sangerinne *en* (*female*)
sink *n.* oppvaskkum *en; v.* synke
sister *n.* søster *en*
sister-in-law *n.* svigerinne *en*
sit *v.* sitte
situation *n.* situasjon *en*
six *num.* seks
sixteen *num.* seksten
sixty *num.* seksti
size *n.* størrelse *en*
skates *n.* skøyte *en*
ski *n.* ski *en; v.* gå på ski
ski slope *n.* skibakke *en*
skill *n.* dyktighet *en*
skilled *adj.* dyktig
skin *n.* hud *en; v.* flå
skirt *n.* skjørt *en*
sky *n.* himmel *en*
sleep *v.* sove
sleeping accommodations *n.*
soveplass *en*
sleeping bag *n.* sovepose *en*
sleeping car *n.* sovevogn *en*
sleepless *adj.* søvnløs

sleeve *n.* erme *et*
sleigh *n.* slede *en*
slide *n.* glid *en; v.* gli
slim *v.* slanke seg (*diet*);
   adj. slank
slow *v.* sakne farten;
   adj. langsom
small *adj.* liten, små
smart *adj.* smart; flink (clever)
smell *n.* lukt *en; v.* lukte
smelly *adj.* illeluktende
smile *n.* smil *en; v.* smile
smoked salmon *n.* røykelaks *en*
smoke *v.* røyke
smoker *n.* røyker *en*
smooth *adj.* glatt, jeve
snake *n.* slange *en*
sneeze *v.* nyse
snore *v.* snorke
snow *n.* sne *en;* snø *en; v.* snø
so *adv.; conj.* så
soap *n.* såpe *en*
soccer *n.* fotball *en*
soccer match *n.* fotballkamp *en*
social *adj.* sosial
society *n.* samfunn *et*
socks *n.* trømper *pl.*
soft *adj.* bløt, myk
solitude *n.* ensomhet *en*
some *pron.; adj.* noen
someone *pron.* noen
something *pron.* noe
sometime *adv.* engang
sometimes *adv.* av og til
somewhere *adv.* et eller
   annet sted
son *n.* sønn *en*
song *n.* sang *en*
son-in-law *n.* svigersønn *en*
soon *adv.* snart
sorrow *n.* sorg *en*
sorry! *interj.* unnskyld!
soul *n.* sjel *en*
soup *n.* suppe *en*
sour *adj.* sur
south *n.* syd *en; adv.* syd, sør
southern *adj.* sørlig, sydlig
souvenir *n.* suvenir *en*
spa *n.* kurbad *et*

Spain *Pln.* Spania
Spaniard *n.* spanjol *en;*
   spanjolene (*the Spanish*)
Spanish *adj.* spansk
spare tire *n.* reservehjul *et*
spark *n.* gnist *en; v.* gnistre
sparrow *n.* spurv *en*
speak *v.* snakke
special *adj.* spesiell
speech *n.* tale *en;* holde en tale
   (*make a speech*)
speed *n.* fart *en* (*på farten = on*
   the go); *v.* kjøre fort
speed limit *n.* fartsgrense *en*
spell *n.* trolldom *en; v.* stave
spend *v.* bruke
spice *n.* krydder *et*
spinach *n.* spinat *en*
spiritual *adj.* åndelig, sjelelig
splendid *adj.* strålende, flott
splendor *n.* glans *en,* prakt *en*
spoil *v.* ødelegge
spoiled *adj.* ødelagt
spoon *n.* skje *en*
sports *n.* idrett *en*
spot *n.* flekk *en*
spring *n.* kilde *en* (*source of*
   water); vår *en* (*season*);
   spring *v.* springe
spy *n.* spion *en; v.* spionere
square *n.* kvadrat *et;* firkant *en;*
   plass *en* (*city square*); *adj.*
   kvadratisk, firkantet
stadium *n.* stadion *et*
stamp *n.* frimerke *et* (*postage*
   stamp)
stain *n.* flekk *en*
stain remover *n.* flekkefjerner *en*
staircase *n.* trapp *en*
stand *n.* posisjon *en; v.* stå
star *n.* stjerne *en*
start *v.* starte; dra (*leave*)
state *n.* tilstand *en* (*condition*);
   stat *en* (*nation*); De forente
   stater (*USA*); *v.* si
station *n.* stasjon *en;*
   jernbanestasjon *en*
   (*railway station*)
statue *n.* statue *en*

stay *v.* oppholde seg
steak *n.* biff *en*
steal *v.* stjele
steel *n.* stål *et*
steering wheel *n.* ratt *et*
step *v.* trå, gå
stew *n.* lapskaus *en*
stiff *adj.* stiv
still *adj.* rolig, stille
sting *n.* stikk *et; v.* stikke
stink *v.* stinke
stir *v.* røre om
stomach *n.* mage *en*
stomach ache *adj.* vondt i
    magen
stone *n.* stein *en*
stop *n.* stopp *en;*
    busholdeplass *en (bus
    stop); v.* stoppe
store *n.* forretning *en (shop);*
    v. lagre
storeroom *n.* lagerrom *et*
storm *n.* uvær *et*
story *n.* historie *en (narrative);*
    etasje *en (of a building)*
storybook *n.* eventyrbok *en*
stove *n.* ovn *en*
straight *adj.* rett
straighten *v.* rette
strange *adj.* fremmed
straw *n.* strå *en*
strawberry *n.* jordbær *et*
stream *n.* bekk *en*
street *n.* gate *en*
stress *n.* spenning *en,* stress *en;*
    v. betone
strict *adj.* streng
strike *n.* streik *en (workers'
    strike);* angre *en (attack);*
    v. slå, ramme
strong *adj.* sterk, kraftig
student *n.* student *en;* elev *en*
    (pupil)
study *n.* arbeidsværelse *et*
    (den); v. studere
stupid *adj.* dum
subject *n.* fag *et (school
    course);* emne *et,* tema *et*
    (theme); statsborger *en*
    (citizen)

suburbs *n.* forsteder *pl.*
subway *n.* undergrunn *en*
succeed *v.* lykkes
success *n.* suksess *en*
sudden *adj.* plutselig
suddenly *adv.* plutselig
suffer *v.* lide
sugar *n.* sukkar *en*
suicide *n.* selvmord *et*
suit (men's) *n.* dress *en*
suitable *adj.* passende
suitcase *n.* koffert *en*
summer *n.* sommer *en*
sun *n.* sol *en; v.* sole seg
sunbathe *v.* ta solbad; sole seg
sun block *n.* solskjerm *en*
Sunday *n.* søndag
sunglasses *n.* solbriller *pl.*
sunny *adj.* strålende
sunrise *n.* soloppgang *en*
sunset *n.* solnedgang *en*
supermarket *n.* kolonial *en*
supper *n.* aftens *en*
support *n.* støtte *en; v.* støtte
sure *adj.* sikke
surely *adv.* sikker
surface *n.* flate *en,* overflate *en;*
    v. komme til overflaten
surgeon *n.* kirurg *en*
surgery *n.* kirurgi *en*
surname *n.* etternavn *et*
surprise *n.* overraskelse *en;*
    v. overraske
suspicious *adj.* mistenksom
swallow *n.* slurk *en (drink);*
    svale *en (bird); v.* svelge
swear *v.* sverge
sweat *n.* svette *en; v.* svette
sweater *n.* genser *en*
sweet *adj.* søt
sweets *n.* sukkertøy *et*
swim *v.* svømme
swimming pool *n.*
    svømmebasseng *et*
swimsuit *n.* badedrakt *en*
Swiss *n.* sveitser *en;* sveitserne
    pl. (the Swiss)
Swiss *adj.* sveitsisk
Switzerland *Pln.* Sveits

symphony *n.* symfoni *en*
synthetic *adj.* syntetisk
system *n.* system *et*

T

table *n.* bord *et*
tablecloth *n.* duk *en*
taboo *n.* tabu *et*
tablet *n.* tablett *en*
tactical *adj.* taktisk
tactics *n.* taktikk *en*
tag *n.* merkelapp *en*; *v.* sette
    merkelapp på
tail *n.* hale *en*
tailor *n.* skredder *en*
take *v.* ta
takeover *n.* overtagelse *en*
tale *n.* historie *en* (*story*); løgn
    en (*lie*)
talent *n.* talent *et*
talk *n.* snakk *et* (*conversation*;
    gossip); prat *en* (*chat*);
    foredrag *et* (*lecture*,
    address); sladder *en*
    (*gossip*); *v.* snakke
tampon *n.* tampong *en*
take *v.* ta
tape *n.* bånd *et*
taste n. smak *en*; *v.* smake
tasty *adj.* meget god
tax *n.* skatt *en*; *v.* beskatte
tea *n.* te *en*
teach *v.* undervise
teacher *n.* lærer *en* (*male*),
    lærerinne *en* (*female*)
tear *n.* rift *en*; *v.* rive
teaspoon *n.* teskje *en*
tedious *adj.* kjedelig
telegram *n.* telegram *et*
telephone *n.* telefon *en*; *v.* ringe
telephone call *n.*
    telefonsamtale *en*
television *n.* fjernsyn *et*
tell *v.* fortelle, si
temperature *n.* temperatur *en*
temporary *adj.* midlertidig
ten *num.* ti
tender *adj.* mør (*mørt kjøtt =
    tender meat*); øm (*sore*)

tent *n.* telt *et*
tenth *adj.* tiende (*number in
    line*); tidel (*one-tenth*)
terrace *n.* terrasse *en*
terrible *adj.* forferdelig,
    fryktelig
territory *n.* område *et*
terror *n.* terror *en*, skrekk *en*
testify *v.* vitne for (*for*), vitne
    mot (*against*)
testimony *n.* vitneutsagn *et*
tetanus *n.* stivkrampe *en*
than *adv.*; *conj.* enn
thank *v.* takke
thank you *v.* takk (*nei takk = no
    thank you*)
that *pron.* den, det; som; *conj.* at
theater *n.* teater *et*
theft *n.* tyveri *et*
then *adv.* den gangen (*at that
    time*); etterpå (*afterwards*)
there *adv.* der
therefore *adv.* derfor
thermometer *n.* termometer *et*
they *pron.* de
thick *adj.* tykk
thief *n.* tyv *en*
thigh *n.* lår *et*
thin *adj.* tynn
thing *n.* ting *en*
think *v.* tenke, tenke på (*think
    about*)
thinking, way of thinking *n.*
    tenkning *en*
third *adj.* tredje (*number*);
    tredje (*third in a row*);
    tredjedel (*one-third*)
thirst *n.* tørst *en*; *v.* tørste
thirsty *adj.* tørst
thirteen *num.* tretten
thirty *num.* tretti
thousand *num.* tusen
thread *n.* tråd *en*
threat *n.* trusel *en*
threaten *v.* true
three *num.* tre
throat *n.* hals *en*
through *prep.* gjennom
throw *v.* kaste

thunder *n.* torden *en*
Thursday *n.* torsdag
thyme *n.* timian *en*
ticket *n.* billett *en*
tide *n.* tidevann *et*, høyvann *et*
(*high tide*); lavvann *et*
(*low tide*)
tie *n.* slips *et* (*necktie*); *v.* knytte
tight *adj.* tett
tighten *v.* stramme
time *n.* tid *en*; *v.* ta tiden på
time exposure *n.*
tidseksponering *en*
timely *adj.* i rettetid
tip *n.* topp *en*, spiss *en* (*tiptop*);
drikkepenger *pl.* (*tips,*
gratuity); tips *et* (*hint*);
v. tippe, gi drikkepenger
(*leave a gratuity*)
tissues *n.* papirlommetørkler
pl.; *n.* toalettpapir *et* (toilet
paper)
toast *n.* skål *en* (*drink*)
tobacconist's shop *n.*
tobakkforretning *en*
today *adv.* i dag
toe *n.* tå *en*
together *adv.* sammen
toilet *n.* toalett *et* (*gå på do = go*
to the toilet)
toilet paper *n.* toalettpapir *et*
tolerant *adj.* tolerant
tomato *n.* tomat *en*
tomb *n.* grav *en*
tomorrow *adv.* i morgen
tongue *n.* tunge *en*
tonight *adv.* i natt; i kveld (*this*
evening)
tonsils *n.* mandeler *pl.*
too *adv.* for, altfor mye (*all too*
much); osgå (*also*)
tooth *n.* tann *en*
toothache *n.* tannpine *en*; *v.* ha
tannpine (*have a toothache*)
toothbrush *n.* tannbørste *en*
toothpaste *n.* tannpaste *en*
toothpick *n.* tannpirker *en*
top *n.* topp *en*
torrent *n.* strøm *en*

torture *n.* tortur *en*;
v. torturere; plage (*trouble*)
touch *n.* berøring *en*; *v.* røre,
berøre
tough *adj.* seig (*tough meat*);
vanskelig (*difficult*); synd
(*det var synd = that was*
tough luck)
tour *n.* rundtur *en*; omvisning
en (*guided tour*); *v.* reise
rundt
tourist *n.* turist *en*
tourist office *n.* turistbyrå *et*
tow *n.* slep *et*; *v.* slepe
toward(s) *prep.* mot
towel *n.* håndkle *et*
tower *n.* tårn *et*
town *n.* by *et*; i byen (*in town*);
v. dra til byen (*go to town*)
toy *n.* leketøy *et*
track *n.* spor *et*; *v.* følge
trade *n.* handel *en*; *v.* handel
(*shop*)
tradition *n.* tradisjon *en*
traditional *adj.* tradisjonell
traffic *n.* trafikk *en*
traffic circle *n.* rundkjøring *en*
(*roundabout*)
traffic lights *n.* trafikklys *et*
train *n.* tog *et*; *v.* trene (*train for*
a race); utdanne (*educate*)
train station *n.*
jernbanestasjon *en*
trait *n.* trekk *et*
traitor *n.* forræder *en*
tranquilizer *n.* beroligende
middel *et*
transfer *v.* overføre
translate *v.* oversette
translation *n.* oversettelse *en*
translator *n.* oversetter *en*
transport *v.* bringe
transportation *n.* transport *en*
travel *n.* reise en; *v.* reise
travel agency *n.* reisebyrå *et*
traveler *n.* reisende *en*
traveler's check *n.* reisesjekk *en*
treat *v.* behandle (*handle*);
spandere (*give a treat to*)

tree *n.* tre *et*
tremendous *adj.* enorm,
    kjempe
trick *n.* knep *et; v.* lure
trolley *n.* tralle *en (luggage*
    trolley); trikk *en (electric*
    city trolley, subway)
trousers *n.* bukser *pl.*
trout *n.* ørret *en*
true *adj.* sann, riktig
truly *adj.* virkelig
trumpet *n.* trompet *en*
trunk *n.* stamme *en (tree*
    trunk); bagasjerom *et*
    (trunk or boot of auto);
    koffert *en (suitcase,*
    footlocker)
trunks *n.* badebukse *en (man's*
    bathing suit)
truth *n.* sannhet *en*
try *v.* prøve, forsøke
Tuesday *n.* tirsdag
tumor *n.* svulst *en*
tuna *n.* tunfisk *en*
tunnel *n.* tunnel *en*
Turk *n.* tyrk *en*
Turkey *Pln.* Tyrkia
turkey *n.* kalkun *en*
Turkish *adj.* tyrkisk
turn *n.* sving *en (in the road)*;
    v. snu *(rotate)*; skru av
    (turn off; screw off)
turquoise *n.* turkis *en*
twelve *num.* tolv
twenty *num.* tyve, tjue
twice *adv.* to ganger
twin *n.* tvilling *en*
twins *n.* tvillinger *pl.*
two *num.* to
type *n.* type *en (print)*; type *en*,
    sorte *en (type); v.* skrive
    på maskin *(write on*
    a machine)
typewriter *n.* skrivemaskin *en*

U

ugly *adj.* stygg
ulcer *n.* sår *et;* magesår *et*
    (stomach ulcer)

umbrella *n.* paraply *en*
unbelievable *adj.* utrolig
uncertain *adj.* usikker
uncle *n.* onkel *en*
uncomfortable *adj.* ubekvem
unconscious *adj.* bevisstløs
under *adv.; prep.* under
understand *v.* forstå, skjønne
understanding *n.* forståelse *en*
undertaking *n.* oppgave *en*
underwear *n.* undertøy *et*
undress *v.* kle av
undressed *adj.* upåkledd
unemployed *adj.* arbeidsløs
unfit *adj.* ikke i form
unfold *v.* brette ut *(open up)*
unfortunately *adv.* dessverre
unhappy *adj.* ulykkelig;
    uheldig *(unlucky)*
unhealthy *adj.* usunn
uninterested *adj.* uinteressert
union *n.* union *en,* forening *en*;
    fagforening *en (trade*
    union); ekteskap *et*
    (marriage)
unite *v.* forene seg
United States, USA *Pln.* De
    forente stater
universe *n.* univers *et*
university *n.* universitet *et*
unjust *adj.* urettferdig
unkind *adj.* uvennlig
unknown *adj.* ukjent
unlawful *adj.* ulovlig
unnecessary *adj.* unødvendig
unofficial *adj.* uoffisiell
unpack *v.* pakke ut
unpleasant *adj.* ubehagelig
unpopular *adj.* upopulær
unqualified *adj.* ukvalifisert
unreal *adj.* uvirkelig
unreasonable *adj.* ufornuftig
unreliable *adj.* upålitelig
unrest *n.* uro *en*
unsafe *adj.* utrygg, usikker,
    farlig
unstable *adj.* ustabil
until *prep.; conj.* til
untrue *adj.* usann, uriktig

unusual *adj.* ualminnelig, usedvanlig
up *adv.* oppe
upbringing *n.* oppdragelse *en*
upper *adj.; adv.* øvre
upset *v.* velte; *adj.* oppbrakt
upstairs *adv.* ovenpå
up-to-date *adj.* moderne
urban *adj.* i byen
urgent *adj.* presserende
urgently *adv.* inntrengende
urinate *v.* urinere; gå på do (*go to the bathroom*)
urine *n.* urin *en*
use *n.* bruk *et; v.* bruke
used *adj.* brukt (*second-hand*)
useful *adj.* nyttig
useless *adj.* unyttig
usher *n.* plassanviser *en*
usual *adj.* vanlig
usually *adv.* vanligvis
utensils *n.* kjøkkentøy *et* (*kitchen utensils*)
utmost *adj.* ytterst
U-turn *n.* U-sving *en*

V

vacancy *n.* ledig stilling *en*, ledig værelse *et* (*vacant room*)
vacant *adj.* ledig
vacation *n.* ferie *en*
vaccinate *v.* vaksinere
vacuum cleaner *n.* støvsuger *en*
vaginal *adj.* vaginal
vague *adj.* uklar
vain *adj.* forfengelig
valet service *n.* tjener *en*
valid *adj.* gyldig
valley *n.* dal *en*
value *n.* verdi *en; v.* verdsette
vandalism *n.* vandalisme *en*
vandalize *v.* vandalisere
vanilla *n.* vanilje *en*
variable *adj.* ustadig
variety *n.* variasjon *en*
various *adj.* forskjellige
vase *n.* vase *en*

veal *n.* kalvekotelett *en*; kalvekjøtt *et*
vegetables *n.* grønnsaker *pl.*
vehicle *n.* motorvogn *en* (*motor vehicle*)
veil *n.* slør *et*
vein *n.* vene *en*
verb *n.* verbum *et*
verdict *n.* kjennelse *en*, dom *en*
verse *n.* vers *et*
version *n.* versjon *en*
very *adv.* meget, veldig
veterinarian *n.* dyrlege *en*
victim *n.* offer *et*
victory *n.* seier *en*
view *n.* utsikt *en* (*sight*); mening *en* (*opinion*); *v.* se
village *n.* landsby *en*
villain *n.* skurk *en*
vinegar *n.* eddik *en*
violate *v.* krenke; voldta (*rape*)
violence *n.* voldsomhet *en*
violent *adj.* voldsom
violin *n.* fiolinist *en*
virtue *n.* dyd *en*
visa *n.* visum *et*
visible *adj.* synlig
vision *n.* syn *et*
visit *n.* visitt *en; v.* besøke
visitor *n.* gjest *en*
vitamin *n.* vitamin *et*
vocabulary *n.* vokabular *et*, ordliste *en*
voice *n.* stemme *en*
voltage *n.* spenning *en*
volume *n.* bind *et* (*book*); rominnhold *et* (*capacity*); volum *et* (*sound*)
volunteer *n.* frivillig *en; v.* tilby seg; *adj.* frivillig
vomit *n.* oppkast *et; v.* kaste opp
vote *n.* avstemning *en*; *v.* stemme
voucher *n.* kupong *en*; matkupong *en* (*meal voucher*)
vowel *n.* vokal *en*
voyage *n.* sjøreene *en*

vulgar *adj.* vulgær
vulnerable *adj.* sårbar

W

wages *n.* lønn *en*
wagon *n.* vogn *en*
waist *n.* liv *et*
waistband *n.* linning *en*
wait *v.* vente på (*wait for*);
   varte opp (*wait on tables*)
waiter *n.* kelner *en*
waiting room *n.* venteværelse *et*
waitress *n.* serveringsdame *en*
wake *v.* våkne (*wake up*); vekke
   (*wake someone else up*)
walk *n.* spasertur *en*; *v.* gå
wall *n.* mur *en*
wallet *n.* lommebok *en*
walnut *n.* valnøtt *en*
wander *v.* vandre
want *n.* nød *en*, behov *et*; *v.*
   ville, ville ha; trenge (*need*)
war *n.* krig *en*
wardrobe *n.* garderobe *en*,
   garderobeskap *et*
warm *v.* varme; *adj.* varm
wash *n.* vask *en*; *v.* vaske
waste *n.* avfall *et*; *v.* sløse
wastepaper basket *n.*
   papirkurv *en*
watch *n.* vakt *en*, vaktmann *en*
   (*watchman*); ur *et*
   (*timepiece*); *v.* betrakte
watchmaker *n.* urmaker *en*
water *n.* vann *et*; *v.* vanne
watercolor *n.* akvarell *en*
waterfall *n.* foss *en*
water power *n.* vannkraft *en*
   (*hydroelectric power*)
waterside café *n.* kafé ved
   vannet *en*
waterski *n.* vannski *en*; *v.* stå på
   vannski
wave *n.* bølge *en* (*water*); vinke
   et (*signal*); *v.* bølge; vinke
way *n.* vei *en* (*road*); måte *en*
   (*method*)
we *pron.* vi

weak *adj.* svak
weakness *n.* svakhet *en*
wealth *n.* rikdom *en*
weapon *n.* våpen *et*
wear *v.* ha på seg (*attire*); slite
   ut (*wear out*)
weather *n.* vær *et*
wed *v.* gifte seg
wedding *n.* bryllup *et*
Wednesday *n.* onsdag
week *n.* uke *en*
weekend cottage *n.* hytte *en*
weigh *v.* veie
weight *n.* vekt *en*
welcome *n.* velkommen *en*
well *n.* brønn *en*; *adj.* frisk;
   adv. godt
well-done *adj.* gjennomstekt
   (*cooked*)
well-earned *adj.* velfortjent
well-to-do *adj.* velstående
west *adv.* vest
the West *Pln.* Vesten
western *adj.* vestlig
wet *adv.* våt
whale *n.* hval *en*
what *pron.* hva; *adj.* hvilken,
   hvilket (*which*)
whatever *pron.* alt hva; hva
   som helst (*anything at all*)
wheel *n.* hjul *et*
when *adv.* når; *conj.* da
whenever *adv.* når; når som
   helst (*at any time*)
where *adv.; conj.* hvor
wherever *adv.* hvor; hvor som
   helst (*in any place*)
whether ... or *conj.* enten ...
   eller
which *pron.* hvilken, hvilket,
   som
while *conj.* mens
whisper *v.* hviske
whistle *n.* fløyte *en*
   (*instrument*); *v.* plystre
white *adj.* hvit; *n.* eggehvite *en*
   (*eggwhite*)
white sauce *n.* hvit saus *en*

who, whom *pron.* hvem, som
whole *adj.* hel
whose *pron.* hvis
why *adv.* hvorfor
wide *adj.* bred
widow *n.* enke *en*
widower *n.* enkemann *en*
width *n.* bredde *en*
wife *n.* hustru *en* (*politer term*);
  kone *en*
wild *adj.* vill
will *n.* vilje *en* (*wish*);
  viljestyrke *en* (*will power*);
  testament *et* (*legacy*)
win *v.* vinne
wind *n.* vind *en; v.* trekke opp
  (*wind up a clock*)
windscreen, windshield *n.*
  frontglas *et;* knust frontglas
  (*broken windshield*)
windshield wipers *n.*
  vindupusser *pl.*
windy *adj.* det blåser (*it's windy*)
wine *n.* vin *en*
wineglass *n.* vinglass *et*
wine merchant *n.* vinhandler *en*
winter *n.* vinter *en*
winter resort *n.*
  vintersportssted *et*
winter sports *n.* vintersport *en*
wipe *v.* tørke
wise *adj.* klok, vis
wish *n.* ønske *et; v.* ønske
wit *n.* vidd *et*
with *prep.* med
withdraw *v.* trekke tilbake (*pull
  back*); ta ut (*take money
  out of an account*)
within *adv.; prep.* inni
without *adv; prep.* uten
witness *n.* vitne *et; v.* være
  vitne til
wolf *n.* ulv *en*
woman *n.* kvinne *en*
women's liberation *n.*
  kvinnesak *en*
wonder *v.* undres

wonderful *adj.* praktfull,
  vidunderlig
wood *n.* tre *et;* ved *en*
  (*firewood*); skog *en*
  (*woods*); trekølle *en* (*golf*)
wood carving *n.* treskurd *en*
wood carver *n.* treskærer *en*
woodcutter *n.* tømmerhugger
  en (*lumberjack*)
wooded *adj.* skogkledd
wooden *adj.* av tre
woodwork *n.* treverk *et*
  (*furniture*); snekkerarbeid
  et (*carpentry*)
wool *n.* ull *en*
woolens *n.* ullstoff *et*
word *n.* ord *et*
work *n.* arbeid *et; v.* arbeide
worker *n.* arbeider *en*
working day *n.* arbeidsdag *en*
  (*work day*)
workload *n.*
  arbeidsbelastning *en*
workout *n.* trening *en*
worry *n.* bekymring *en;*
  v. bekymre seg
worse *adj.* verre
worsen *v.* bli verre (*become
  worse*); gjøre verre
  (*make worse*)
worship *v.* tilbe
worst *adj.* verst
wound *n.* sår *et; v.* såre
wounded *adj.* såret
wrap *v.* pakke inn (*wrap a
  package*)
wrapping paper *n.*
  innpakningspapir *et*
wreck *n.* vrak *et; v.* ødelegge
wrench *n.* nøkkel *en;*
  skiftenøkkel *en* (*adjustable
  wrench*)
write *v.* skrive
writer *n.* forfatter *en*
writing paper *n.* skrivepapir *et*
wrong *n.* urett *en; adj.* gal;
  adv. galt

X

xenophobia *n.* fremmedhat *et*
X-ray *n.* røntgenstråle *en;*
røntgenbilde *et*
(*X-ray picture*);
v. røngenfotografere

Y

yacht *n.* yacht *en*
yard *n.* gård *en* (*garden*);
verft *et* (*shipyard*);
jernbenetomt *en* (*railway yard*)
yarn *n.* garn *et* (*wool*); skrøne
en, skipperskrøne *en*
(*tall tale*)
yawn *n.* gjesp *et; v.* gjespe
year *n.* år *et*
yearbook *n.* årbok *en*
yearly *adv.* årlig
yearn *v.* lengte
yeast *n.* gjær *en*
yell *v.* hyle, skrike
yellow *n.* gult *et; adj.* gul
yes *adv.* ja, jo
yesterday *adv.* i går
yesterday morning *adv.* i går morges
yet *conj.* enda

yolk *n.* eggeplomme *en*
you *pron.* du, deg (*singular informal*); De, Dem
(*singular formal*)
you *pron.* dere (*plural informal*); De, Dere (*plural formal*)
young *adj.* ung
your *pron.* din, ditt (*informal*);
Deres (*formal*)
yourself, oneself *pron.* deg selv
(*informal*)
youth *n.* ungdom *en*
youth hostel *n.*
ungdomsherberge *et*

Z

zeal *n.* iver *en*
zealous *adj.* ivrig
zero *n.* null *en*
zest *n.* iver *en*
zinc *n.* sink *en*
zipper *n.* glidelås *en*
zionist *n.* sionist *en*
zone *n.* sone *en*
zoo *n.* dyrehage *en*
zoological *adj.* zoologisk
zoologist *n.* zoolog *en*
zoology *n.* zoologi *en*

Phrasebook Contents

BASICS
Everyday Words & Expressions

Yes	Ja
No	Nei
Please	Vær så snill
Thank you	Takk
Thank you very much	Tusen takk
You're welcome	Ikke noe å takke for
Excuse me	Om forlatelse
Pardon me	Unnskyld
I'm sorry	Om forlatelse
I am really very sorry	Jeg er virkelig lei meg

I am here ...
  on vacation
  visiting family/friends
  on business

Jeg er her ...
  på ferie
  på familiebesøk
  på grund av
    forretninger

I am ...
  American
  Canadian
  British
  Australian

Jeg er ...
  amerikaner
  kanadier
  britisk
  australier

How old are you?	Hvor gammel er du?
I'm ... years old	Jeg er ... år gammel

Greetings

Hello	Morn
Good morning, good afternoon	God dag
Good night	God natt
Good-bye	Ha det
Good-bye, take care of yourself	Ha det bra
How are you?	Hvordan står det til?
How are you?	Hvordan har du det?
Fine, thanks	Bare bra takk

BASICS

Good	**Godt**
Bad	**Dårlig**

My name is ...	**Jeg heter ...**
What's your name?	**Hva heter du?**
Good to meet you	**Hyggelig å hilse på deg**

Common Questions

Who?	**Hvem?**
Who is that?	**Hvem er det?**
Where?	**Hvor?**
Where is it?	**Hvor er det?**
Where are you going?	**Hvor skal du hen?**
When?	**Når?**
When are we going?	**Når skal vi gå?**
Why?	**Hvorfor?**
Why has the bus stopped?	**Hvorfor stopper bussen?**
What?	**Hva?**
What has happened?	**Hva skjedd?**
How?	**Hvordan?**
How's it going?	**Hvordan står det til?**
How much?	**Hvor mye?**
How much longer is it?	**Hvor mye lengere er det?**
Is it far from here?	**Er det langt borte herfra?**
How much does it cost?	**Hvor mye koster det?**
What time is it?	**Hvor mange er klokken?**

Asking for Directions

Can you help me?
Kan du hjelpe meg?

Can you tell me ...?
Kan du si meg ...?

Please show me the way to ...
Var så snill å vise meg veien til ...

the railway station	**jernbanestasjonen**
the bus station	**bussstasjonen**
the bus stop	**bussholdeplass**
the hotel	**hotellet**
the hostel	**herberget**

the post office	**postkontoret**
the tram,	**trikk**
the underground	
the underground	**T-bane**

Can you show me on the map, please?
Kan du vise meg på kartet, er du snill?

I am lost.
Jeg har gått meg vill.
Jeg har gått meg bort.

Where is the restroom?
Hvor er W. C.?
Hvor er toalettet?

Where is the ladies' room?
Hvor er dametoalettet?

Can you tell me the way to the ferry to Bygdøy?
Kan du si meg veien til ferjen til Bygdøy?

Is it far?
Er det langt borte?

Is this the way to the Vigland Park?
Er dette veien til Vigelandsparken?

How do we get there?
Hvordan kommer man dit?

Please show me on the map.
Vis meg på kartet, er du snill.

Do we go to the left or the right?
Går vi til venstre eller til høyre?

Go right at the corner.
Gå til høyre ved hjørnet.

Go left.
Gå til venstre.

Where should we turn off?
Hvor skal vi ta av?

Can we go straight ahead?
Kan vi gå rett frem?

Does the trolley/underground go there?
Går trikken dit?

Is this the right way to the National Gallery?
Er dette den riktige retningen til Nasjonalgalleriet?

You have to turn around.
Du må snu rundt.

Communicating

May I please ask you a question?
Kan jeg få lov å spørre deg et spørsmål, er du snill?

I don't speak Norwegian.
Jeg snakker ikke norsk.

I speak only a little Norwegian.
Jeg snakker litt norsk.

Do you speak English?
Snakker du engelsk?

Could you show me in this guidebook?
Kan du vise meg det i reiseboken?

I don't understand.
Jeg forstår ikke.

Could you write that down for me please?
Kan du skrive det ned for meg, er du snill?

Could you translate this for me please?
Kan du oversette det for meg, er du snill?

How do you say this in Norwegian?
Hvordan sies det på norsk?

Is it possible to speak more slowly?
Er det mulig å snakke litt langsommere?

Can you speak a little slower?
Kan du snakke langsommere?

Please say that one more time, please.
Si det en gang til, er du snill.

Thank you very much for your help.
Tusen takk for hjelpen.

TRAVEL & TRANSPORTATION

At the Airport (På Flyplassen)

Departure (Avgang)

Does the train go to the airport?
Går toget til flyplassen?

Does the bus go to the airport?
Går det buss til flyplassen?

Can we order the limousine to go to the airport?
Kan vi bestille det limousin til flyplassen?

When will it pick us up?
Når vil det hente oss?

We have a lot of luggage. Where can I find a trolley?
Vi har mye bagasje. Hvor kan jeg finne en tralle?

Does it cost anything?
Koster det noe?

When is there a flight to Bergen?
Når går det et fly til Bergen?

Can I have a round trip ticket to Tromsø?
Kan jeg få en returbillett til Tromsø?

Can I have a one-way ticket to Vardø?
Kan jeg få en enkeltbillett til Vardø?

Do we have to change planes?
Må vi bytte fly?

I already have my tickets. Where can I check my suitcase?
Jeg har min billett. Hvor kan jeg levere inn min koffert?

How many kilos may I have?
Hvor mange kilo kan jeg ta med?

This is hand luggage (carry-on).
Dette er håndbagasje.

May I have a seat by the window?
Kan jeg få vinduplass?

When is flight departure?
Når går flyet?

Which gate does my flight leave from?
Hvilken utgang går mitt fly fra?

Is the flight delayed?
Er flyet forsinket?

How long will it be delayed?
Hvor lenge skal det være forsinket?

Now the flight is boarding.
Nå er flyet klart til avgang.

Arrival (Ankomst)

We have just arrived from London. One bag is missing.
Vi har nettopp ankommet fra London. Vi mangler en koffert.

Let's check Left-Luggage. Was your name on the bag?
La oss sjekke bagasjeoppbevaring. Var ditt navn på kofferten?

Yes, my name, address and flight number.
Ja, mitt navn, adresse og flyturnummer.

If it stayed in London, it will be sent on the next plane. We'll send it to your hotel. Don't worry!
Hvis den er fremdeles i London, kommer den med det neste flyet. Vi skal sende det til hotellett ditt. Ta det med ro!

At the Railway Station (På Jernbanestasjon)

When does the train leave for Bergen?
Når går toget til Bergen?

Can I buy a one-way ticket?
Kan jeg få en turbillett / enkeltbillett?

Can I buy a roundtrip (return) ticket?
Kan jeg få en returbillett?

Must I change trains?
Må jeg bytte tog?

Do children get a discount?
Får barn en rabatt?

Where do I buy a ticket?
Hvor kjøpe man en billett?

Does this train go to Bergen?
Går dette toget til Bergen?

May I have a timetable?
Kan jeg få en time-tabell?

What is the price of a ticket to Tonsberg?
Hvor mye koster en billett til Tønsberg?

Is there an express train to Stavanger?
Er det hurtigtog til Stavanger?

I want to reserve a seat please.
Kan jeg få bestille plass?

Where is the right platform for the train to Lillehammer?
Hvor er den riktige plattformen for toget til Lillehammer?

Is this the train for Lillehammer?
Er dette toget tik Lillehammer?

Is the train late?
Er toget forsinket?

Would you help me with my bags?
Kan du hjelpe meg med bagasjen?

Is there a non-smoking compartment?
Finnes det en ikke-røkekupé?

Is this seat empty?
Er denne plassen ledig?

Is this seat taken?
Er plassen opptatt?

Is there a dining car on the train?
Er det spisevogn på toget?

Does the train stop at Finse?
Stopper toget på Finse?

Traveling Around Town

By Taxi

A taxi costs NKr 24 (NKr 30 after seven in the evening) plus NKr 12 per kilometer. It is common to tip the driver, usually by rounding the figure upwards to the nearest mark. For example, if it's 65 kroner, give the driver 70 kroner, and so on. Taxi's are not hard to find in Oslo and are usually parked at taxi stands outside hotels and at shopping centers. You can also telephone for a taxi. The number for Oslo is 22 38 80 90.

How much does a taxi cost?
Hvor mye koster en drosje?

Where can I find a taxi?
Hvor kan jeg få tak i en drosje/taxi?

Please take me to the SAS Hotel.
Ta meg til SAS Hotellet, er du snill.

By Public Transportation

It is not difficult to get around by public transportation in Oslo. There is the *trikk*, which is short for "electric" and can mean both tram and subway. The *T-bane*, subway, is easily accessible throughout the city. In addition, bus and ferry service is available. A day card (NKr 40), weekly card (NKr 140), and a monthly card (NKr 540) can be used for any of these forms of transportation. A *flexikort* (NKr 110) is good for eight trips, and, within an hour from the time the card is stamped, can be used to transfer from one service to another. You can buy these cards at kiosks, post offices and at major subway stations.

Where is the bus stop?
Hvor er bussholdeplassen?

Which bus takes me downtown?
Hvilken buss går til byen?

Which bus goes to the airport?
Hvilken buss går til lufthavnen?

Can you please tell me which train/subway goes to the Holmenkollen ski jump?
Kan du være så snill å si meg hvilken trikk går til Holmenkollen?

How frequently does the bus come?
Hvor ofte kommer bussen?

When is the last bus back to Oslo?
Når kommer den siste bussen til Oslo?

How much does a ticket cost?
Hvor mye koster en billett?

I have to get off at the National Theater.
Jeg må gå av på Nasjonalteateret.

I want to go to the Vigeland.
Jeg vil dra til Vigelandsparken.

Which trolley/subway goes to the Munch Museum?
Hvilken trikk går til Munchmuseet?

Can you please tell me where to get off?
Kan du være så snill å si ifra hvor jeg må gå av?

Renting a Car (Bilutleie)

We have found that lining up a rental car before you leave home is less expensive and more convenient. Try to reserve a car with a car rental chain which has offices in Norway before leaving the US.

If you are arriving at Gardermoen International Airport north of Oslo you will find that all of the major car rental companies have counters to assist you. Check the Yellow Pages under *Bilutleie* if you arrive without having a rental car pre-arranged. Cars are *personbiler*, vans *varebiler*, minibuses *minibusser*, and trucks *lastebiler*. To rent a car with a driver look up *limousineutleie* or *privatsjåfør* in the Yellow Pages.

Can I rent a car here?
Kan jeg få leie en bil her?

I would like to rent a car, please.
Jeg vil gjerne leie en bil.

Do I need to leave a deposit for the vehicle?
Må jeg gi deg et depositum for bilen?

Is accident insurance included in the price?
Er ulykkesforsikring inkludert i prisen?

I want to be fully covered.
Jeg vil bli fullt dekket.

Isn't that rather low coverage?
Er det ikke svært lav forsikring?

What should I do if I have an accident?
Hva burde jeg gjøre hvis jeg har en bilulykke?

I don't want insurance, thank you.
Jeg trenger ikke assuranse.

How much is the charge per day?
Hva koster bilen per dag?

How much is the charge per mile?
Hvor mye koster det per kilometer?

Do you have ...	**Har du ...**
a less expensive car?	**noe billigere?**
a larger car?	**en større bil?**
a smaller car?	**en bil som er nokså lit?**

a car with automatic drive?	**en bil med automatisk kjøring?**
a car with four-wheel drive?	**en bil med firehjulstrekk?**
a van with four-wheel drive?	**en vogn med firehjulstrekk?**
a truck with four-wheel drive?	**en lastebil med firehjulstrekk?**

Can we return the car in Bergen?
Er det mulig å levere bilen i Bergen?

Or must we bring it back here?
Eller må vi kjøre tilbake hit?

Here is my driver's license.
Her er mitt sertifikat.

Here's a credit card.
Her er mitt kredittkort.

Useful Information

In the mountains emergency telephones can be found along the road.

The Norge Automobil Forbund (NAF) provides 24-hours service from June 16th to August 14th (tel. 22 34 16 00). Other rescue services: Viking Redningtjenesten ("Viking Rescue Service") tel. 800 32 900 (toll-free) or 22 08 60 00; Falken Redningskorps ("Falcon Rescue Corps") tel. 800 30 050 (toll-free) or 22 95 00 00.

Driving/Highway information service (**vegmeldingssentralen**): tel. 22 65 40 40.

Drivers License: foreign driver's license good for one year.

Things to remember:

Alcohol: Until recently there has been a one-drink limit; new laws permit even less. It is important to take a taxi or to have a designated driver who drinks no alcohol. If arrested you may be jailed immediately.

Safety belts must be worn in front and back seats.

Children under four must sit in a car seat.

Speed limits: Highways 80–90 k.p.h. as posted
Trailers 60 k.p.h.

Drive on the right side of the road.

Right of way: At junctions the vehicle on the right has the right of way.

Vehicles on the "yellow diamond road" have the right of way.

Trams have the right of way; trams should be passed on the right unless you are on a one-way street.

Vehicles going down hill have the right of way; vehicles going up hill must yield and turn into the *møteplass* (passing area).

Headlights: Use headlights at all times when driving.

Road Signs

kjør sakte	drive slow
møteplass	passing lane
enveiskjøring	one-way traffic
parkering	parking
veiarbeid	roadwork
under veiarbeidet	road under construction
omvei	detour
omkjøring	detour
ferist	cattle grating
rasteplass	rest stop
svake kanter	soft shoulder
sentrum	downtown
rundkjøring	roundabout
gågate	pedestrian street
bomvei	toll road
fare	danger
farlig sving	dangerous curve
veikryss	junction

The Gas Station

Fuel: Unleaded gasoline is **blyfri bensin** (95 octane).
It is illegal to use diesel fuel from the red pump, which is only for farmers, taxis and buses.

Gas (filling) stations are usually open 7:00 A.M.–10:00 P.M. M-F and often closed on weekends except in cities.

Hello. Can you please tell where I can find a gas (filling) station?
Goddag. Kan du være så snill å si meg hvor jeg kan finne en bensinstasjon?

The tank is nearly empty.
Tanken er nesten tom.

We have to fill it up.
Vi må fylle bensin.

Fill the tank, please.
Fyll bensintanken, er du snill.

What grade (octane) gas is this?
Hva slags oktantall er det?

Thanks for your help.
Takk for hjelpen.

How much do I owe you?
Hvor meget skylder jeg deg?

Problems on the Road

Can you send a tow truck?
Kan du hente en kranbil?

I have a flat (tire).
Jeg har en punktering.

I have locked myself out of the car.
Jeg har låst meg selv ut av bilen.

The battery is dead.
Batteriet er dødt.

The car won't start.
Bilen vil ikke starte.

There is a problem with the car.
Det er et problem med bilen.

Is there a mechanic nearby?
Finnes det et bilverksted i nærheten?

How long will it take to repair?
Hvor lang tid vil det ta før bilen blir ferdig?

How much will it cost?
Hvor mye koster det?

I only have a credit card.
Jeg har bare et kredittikort.

Is there a telephone nearby?
Finnes det en telefon i nærheten?

There has been an accident.
Det har vært en bilulykke.

Here is my driver's license.
Her er mitt sertifikat.

brakes	**brems**
to brake, put on the brakes	**å bremse**
windshield wipers	**vindusvisker**
gearbox/ transmission	**girkasse**
fan belts	**viftereim**
clutch	**clutch, kløtsjpedal**
tire	**dekk, hjul**
flat tire	**punktert dekk (hjul)**
light bulb	**lyspære**
spark plugs	**tennplugg**
steering	**styring**
steering wheel	**ratt**

ACCOMMODATIONS

Staying at a Hotel

Hotell, turisthotell, and *høyfjellshotell* (high-mountain hotel) all provide lodging of good quality for a price. *Pensjonat, vertshus* and *gjestgiveri* all indicate boarding houses of varying ranges of quality and price; some serve breakfast and dinner, some only breakfast. *Turisthytte* is a tourist cabin in the mountains. *Rom* is a room in a private home. Ask for special rates if staying for several days. Tipping is not necessary.

Hello. Do you have any vacancies?
God dag. Har du et ledig værelse?

Hello. I have reservation for two persons for one night / two nights.
God dag. Jeg har reservert / bestilt et værelse for to personer for en natt / to netter.

Hello! Do you have a room for two?
Goddag! Har du et rom for to?

We'd like a room with two single beds with a toilet and bath / shower.
Vi vil gjerne ha et rom med to enkelsenger med toilett og bad / dusj.

How much is it per night?
Hva koster det per natt?

Would you like to look at the room?
Vil du se på rommet?

Can we have bed and breakfast here?
Kan vi få overnatting med frokost her?

Unfortunately we have no vacancies.
Dessverre vi har ikke plass.
Dessverre vi har ikke ledig rom.

Is breakfast included in the price?
Blir frokost inkludert?

When is breakfast / dinner served?
Når blir frokost / dinner serveret?

May we see the room?
Får vi lov å se på rommet?

Do you have a room with …	**Har du et rom med …**
a bath?	**bad?**
a view of Oslo and the Oslofjord?	**utsikt over Oslo og Oslofjorden?**
twin beds?	**to enkeltsenger?**
a double bed?	**dobbeltseng?**

The room suits us fine. We'll take it.
Rommet passer godt. Vi tar det.

We would like to change rooms.
Vi vil gjerne bytte værelser

When do we need to check-out?
Når trenger vi å sjekke ut?

We'll be staying until Sunday.
Vi skal bli til søndag.

We'll be staying two nights.
Vi skal bli to netter.

We are checking out now.
Vi skal sjekke ut nå.

May I have this laundry washed?
Kan jeg få dette tøyet vasket?

May we have a little more …?	**Kan vi få litt mer …?**
coffee	**kaffe**
tea	**te**
milk	**melk**
water	**vann**
bread	**brød**
butter	**smør**
jam	**syltetøy**
goat cheese	**geitost**

Is it possible to order a soft-boiled egg?
Er det possible å få et bløtkokt egg?

May we get two more woolen blankets?
Kan vi få to ulltepper til?

Do you have soap? another glass? towels?
Har du såpe? et glass til? håndklær?

bed	**seng**
double bed	**dobbeltseng**
single bed	**enkeltseng**
king-sized bed	**ekstrastor seng**
mattress	**madrass**
spring mattress	**springmadrass**
exercise bicycle	**ergometersykkel**
exercise equipment	**mosjonsapparat**
swimming pool	**svømmebasseng**
vending machine	**salgsautomat**
ice	**is**
breakfast	**frokost**
dining room	**spisestue**
room service	**romservice**
wake-up call	**vekk-opp telefonoppringning**
hotel reservation	**hotellbestilling**
fire escape	**brannstige**
lobby	**vestibyle**
room with a view	**rom med utsikt**
check-in	**innsjekking**
check-out	**utsjekking**

Camping *(Campliv)*

The Norway camping map, which is available at the Norwegian Tourist Board, gives campground and other information important to campers and caravaners. Campsite fees are NK. 80-150 per night.; in some camps cabins are available (NK. 200-600). The helpful Norwegian Camping Card (**Norsk campingkort**) can be bought at campgrounds (NK. 60). "Free camping" is allowed if your tent is pitched at least 150 meters from the nearest residence. Caravans with motorhomes can get information from the Norsk Caravan Club, Solheimveien 18, N-1473 Skårer. tel./ 67 97 49 20, fax 67 90 13 13.

Can you please help me?
Kan du vær så snill å hjelpe meg?

Is there a campground near here?
Er det en campingplass i nærheten?

Is there a campsite nearby?
Er det campering i nærheten?

Can we pitch our tent here?
Kan vi sette opp teltet her?

May I take a look at your map?
Kan jeg få se på kartet ditt?

Thanks. Here we are right now and here is the campground! Just go straight ahead and turn to the left a little farther up where you see the road.
Takk. Her er vi akkurat nu. Og her er campingplassen! Bare kjør rett frem, og ta til venstre litt lengere oppe hvor du ser veien.

Up the hill over there?
Opp bakken der borte?

Right. There should be some kind of sign there.
Akkurat. Det skulle være et skilt der.

Thanks very much.
Hjertlig takk.

Hello. Is there a place here we can camp for a couple of nights?
Goddag. Har du plass her for et par netter?

Room enough. Where are you from? You speak Norwegian like Americans.
Plass nok. Hvor er dere fra? Du snakke norske som enamerikaner.

Correct. But do you speak English?
Riktig. Men snakker du engelsk?

Yes, a little. But it is fun to hear you speak Norwegian.
Ja, litt. Med det er morsomt å høre deg snakke norsk.

Do both of you have fishing licenses?
Har dere begge fiskelisens?

What is the fee (per night)?
Hvor mye koster det?

Is there a store nearby?
Er det en forretning i nærheten?

Where is fresh drinking water?
Hvor kan jeg få tak i drikkevann?

Where can I take a shower?
Hvor kan jeg dusje?

firewood	**ved**
flashlight	**lommelykt**
tarp	**presenning**
lantern	**lanterne**
matches	**fyrstikker**
tent	**telt**
tent peg	**teltplugg**
tent pole	**teltstang**
tent poles	**teltstenger**

SERVICES & PROCEDURES
Dry Cleaning (Kjemisk rensing)

We have some clothes that have to be cleaned. Do you
know a place we can take them?
**Vi har noen klær som må renses. Vet du om et sted hvor
vi kan ta klærne våre?**

Just take the telephone directory and look up "dry cleaners."
But it's expensive!
**Bare ta telefonboken og slå opp på "renserier." Men det
er dyrt!**

Wait a minute! You can just ask about "kilorens" [bulk dry
cleaning]. That's not so bad.
**Vent litt! Du kan bare spørre om "kilorens." Det er ikke
så verst.**

Don't you use dry cleaning in Norway very often?
Bruker man ikke rensing så ofte i Norge?

Not so often. We usually air out clothes on the balcony. We
use a stain remover too.
**Ikke så ofte. Vi pleier å lufte klærne på balkongen. Vi
bruker flekkfjerner også.**

Hair Care (Hårpleie)

I would like to make an appointment at the ladies' hairdresser.
Jeg vil gjerne få bestille time hos damefrisøren.

Can I have a shampoo and set?
Kan jeg få vask og legg?

How would you like it cut?
Hvordan vil du ha det klippet?

Please do not take too much off.
Ikke klipp for mye, er du snill.

Is this about right?
Passer det?

Useful Words

barber	**herrefrisør, barber**
barbershop	**barbersalong**
brush	**børste**
to brush	**å børste**
color rinse	**fargeskylling**
curlers	**krøllruller**
curling iron	**krølltang**
dark	**mørkt**
hair	**hår**
haircut	**hårklipp**
hairdo, hairstyle	**frisyre**
hairdresser's assistant	**ryddepike**
hairdryer	**hårtørrer**
highlights	**striper**
ladies' hairdresser / beauty parlor	**damefrisør**
light	**lys**
long	**langt**
perm	**permanent**
shampoo	**sjampo**
shampoo and set	**vask og legg**
short	**kort**

The Post Office

Excuse me. Where is the post office?
Unnskyld! Hvor er post kontoret?

I want to send two letters and three post cards.
Jeg vil sende to brever og tre kort.

What is the postage for a letter to the U. S.?
Hva er portoen på brev til Amerika?

I want to buy ten stamps for postcards to the U. S.
Jeg vil kjøpe ti frimerker for postkort til Amerika.

Where is the postbox?
Hvor er postkassen?

I want to send this letter express mail.
Jeg vil sende dette brev ekspress.

address	**adresse**
airmail	**luftpost**
envelope	**konvolutt**
fax	**telefaks**
international	**internasjonal**
money order	**postanvisning**
letter	**brev**
money order	**postanvisning**
picture postcard	**prospektkort**
postage	**porto**
postbox	**postkasse**
postcard	**post kort**
registered letter	**rekommandert brev**
stamp	**frimerke**
surface mail	**vanlig post**
zip code, postal code	**postnummer**

Making a Phone Call

Please tell me where I can find a telephone.
Vær så snill å si meg hvor jeg kan finne en telefon.

I would like to get an Oslo number.
Jeg skal ha et nummer i Oslo.

I would like to reverse the charges.
Jeg vil gjerne ha noteringsoverføring.

Hello, I would like to speak to Bjørn?
Hallo, kan jeg få snakke med Bjørn?

Bjørn is not here.
Bjørn er ikke til stede.

Please tell him that Kjersti called.
Si ham at Kjersti ringte, er du snill.

He'll be home soon.
Han kommer hjem snart.

Please ask him to give me a ring.
Vaer så snill å be ham ringe meg.

Is Siri there?
Er Siri til stede?

Can you give her a message?
Kan du gi henne en beskjed?

telephone	**telefon**
receiver	**røret**
telephone number	**telefonnummer**
extension	**linje**
telephone directory	**telefonkatalog**
to call	**å ringe**
telephone call	**telefonsamtale**
busy	**opptatt**
wrong number	**feil nummer**
pay telephone	**telefon automat,**
	offentlig telefon
reverse the charges	**noteringsoverføring**
local call	**lokalsamtale**
long-distance call	**rikstelefon**
domestic long-distance call	**innenlandssamtale**
international call	**internasjonal/utenlands**
	samtale

FOOD & DRINK
Breakfast (Frokost)

Is breakfast ready?
Er frokosten ferdig?

Not yet.
Ikke enda.

Ready right away!
Snart ferdig!

Do you drink tea or coffee?
Drikker du te eller kaffe?

Which do you prefer?
Hva foretrekker du?

I prefer coffee/tea, thanks.
Jeg foretrekker kaffe/te, takk.

Will you take sugar and cream?
Vil du ha sukker og fløte?

Just cream, thanks.
Bare fløte, takk.

Here are toast and rolls, butter and jam.
Her er ristet brød, rundstykker, smør og syltetøy.

A glass of orange juice?
Et glass appelsinsaft?

Many thanks. It tastes very good.
Tusen takk. Det smakte godt.

Dinner (Middag)

Middag (dinner), which is served around 5 P.M., is the only hot meal of the day. It includes national dishes like *kjøttkaker* (meatballs), *får i kål* (lamb in cabbage), and *lapskaus* (stew). A light snack before bed is *aftens*, which has been described as whatever is in the house. It is tasty, filling and often includes fish. The *koldtbord* (cold table) held deep in Norwegian tradition combines all three meals; the table is laden with meats, cheeses, and other delicious sandwich spreads along with breads. It can be prepared for special occasions or just for whoever might stop by.

Norway is also famous for its drink, in particular a form of spirits called *akevitt* (aquavit) or *dram*, which was originally sold as a medicine. Oldtimers still swear by its health benefits, and many enjoy a small shot before bedtime. Distilled from potatoes and made with caraway seeds, anise, fennel, coriander, sherry, sugar, and salt, *akevitt* has improved considerably in taste since its creation. Credit for this improvement is said to go to a shipowner who sent a barrel of *akevitt* to South America for trade. No one was interested in it. After the barrel had been shipped back to Norway the shipowner discovered that the long journey had improved the taste of the drink considerably. From that day on the production of *Linie Akevitt* has not been thought complete until the liquor has been shipped in casks on a two-month round-trip. Its name refers to the fact that it crosses the Equator, the "Linie". *Akevitt* chased with *øl* (beer) accompanies *lutefisk, får i kål,* and salted and smoked dishes.

Around the table few lift a glass alone. Raise first *akevitt glasset*, meet the eyes of the person you are toasting, say *skål*, take a sip, return the glass to the table, pick up *øl glasset*, meet eyes again, have a drink of beer and return the glass to the table. You may toast a couple, a couple may toast a couple, or with "*hele rundt*" (everybody around the table) join in a full-table toast.

When do we have dinner today?
Når skal vi spise middag idag?

We dine at six.
Vi skal spise klokken seks.

Do you have an appetite?
Er du sulten?

I am very hungry.
Jeg er veldig sulten.

Eat well!
Spis godt!

What do you think of this dish?
Hva syns du om denne retten?

Excellent!
Utmerket!

Please give me a slice of the cheese.
Gi meg et lite stykke ost, er du snill.

Have another piece.
Ta et stykke til.

Will you have a glass of wine?
Vil du ha et glass vin?

Would you like a glass of beer?
Har du lyst på et glass øl?

Dining Out

Do you have a table available?
Har du et bord ledig?

I would like a table for ... people.
Jeg vil gjerne ha et bord til ... mennesker.

A menu, please.
En meny, vær så snill.

What would you recommend?
Hva vil du anbefale?

What is this called?
Hva heter denne retten?

What is in this dish?
Hva er i denne retten?

How much is this?
Hvor mye koster det?

I would like ...
Jeg vil gjerne ha ...

I am vegetarian.
Jeg er vegetarianer.

I don't eat meat.
Jeg spiser ikke kjøtt.

I don't drink alcohol.
Jeg drikker ikke brennevin.

I'm allergic to ...   **Jeg er allergisk mot ...**
  dairy foods   **meieriprodukter**
  wheat   **hvete**
  nuts   **nøtter**
  shellfish   **skalldyr**
  MSG   **MSG**

That is all, thank you.
Det er alt, takk.

The check please.
Kan jeg få regningen?

There is a problem with the bill.
Det er et problem med regningen.

You charged us twice for this.
Regningen er dobbelt så stor.

Is it correct?
Er det riktig?

Do you take credit cards?
Kan jeg bruke et kredittkort?

Do you take a traveler's check?
Kan jeg bruke en reisesjekk?

Is service (gratuity) included?
Er tippen inkludert?

MONEY & SHOPPING

Exchanging Money

money	**penger**
crowns	**kroner**
	(Kr. 10 = ten crowns)
change	**småpenger, vekslepenger**
cash	**kontant; kontanter**
coins	**mynter**

Where can I change money?
Hvor kan jeg veksle penger?

Can I change money here?
Kan jeg veksle penger her?

I want to buy Norwegian crowns.
Jeg vil kjøpe norske kroner.

What is the exchange rate?
Hva er valutakursen?

Do you accept traveler's checks?
Aksepterer du reisesjekker?

Do you accept a credit card?
Aksepterer du et kredittkort?

Do I have to show you my passport?
Må jeg vise deg mitt pass?

Do you have change for 100 crowns?
Har du småpenger for hundre kroner?

Shopping for Food

Supermarkets (**Supermarked**). The largest self-serve supermarket chains are Rimi, ICA and Rema 1000.

Health food (**Helsekost**). The best known health food shops are Helios, Vitamina Helse & Velvære ("Vitamin Health and Well-Being"), and Sunkost ("Healthy Fare").

Ethnic food markets (**utenlands matvarebutikker**) are found in Oslo and other major cities with immigrant populations.

I have to go grocery shopping today.
Jeg må kjøpe mat idag.

Is there a grocery store in the immediate neighborhood?
Finnes det en kolonial (kolonialforretning) i nærheten?

Yes, just across the street from the tram station.
Ja, rett over gaten fra trikkestasjonen.

Hello. Can you please tell me where I can find the vegetables?
God dag. Kan du være så snill å si meg hvor grønnsakene er?

Where can I find ...?
Hvor kan jeg finne ...?

Against the wall back there.
Mot bakkveggen der borte.

Could you show me please ...?
Kan du vise meg, er du snill ...?

I'd like to get ...
Jeg vil gjerne kjøpe ...

> a kilo of potatoes too.
> **en kilo poteter også.**

> one cauliflower.
> **et blomkål.**

> some carrots.
> **noen gulrøtter.**

> a head of lettuce.
> **et salat hode.**

> a can of peas.
> **en boks erter.**

> one kilo of coffee.
> **en kilo kaffe.**

a dozen eggs.
et dusin egg.

a carton of orange juice.
en kartong med appelsinsaft / appelsinjus.

a loaf of white bread.
en loff.

six beers.
seks øl.

What kind of meat do you have?
hva slags kjøtt har du?

We just have packaged meats. We do not have anything in
the way of fresh meat.
**Vi har bare pakket kjøtt. Vi har ikke freskt kjøtt i det hel
tatt.**

You'll have to shop at the butcher's if you want a special cut.
Du må handle hos en slakter hvis du vil ha noe spesielt.

Do you have anything ...?	Har du noe ...?
cheaper	**billigere**
better	**bedre**
large	**større**
smaller	**mindre**

How much does this cost?
Hvor mye koster dette?

Do you take credit cards?
Kan jeg bruke et kredittkort?

Can I use traveler's checks?
Kan jeg bruke en reisesjekk?

Can you write down the price please?
Kan du skrive opp prisen, er du snill?

Can I return this?
Kan jeg returnere dette?

Can I exchange this?
Kan jeg bytte dette?

I would like a receipt please.
Kan jeg få en kvittering, er du snill?

Thank you for waiting on me.
Takk for hjelpen.

for sale	til salgs
on sale	på salg
to wrap	å pakke inn
wrapping paper	innpakningspapir

Groceries

apples	epler
asparagus	asparges
bananas	bananer
baby food	spedbarnmat
bacon	bacon
baking powder	bakepulver
beans	bønner
beef	oksekjøtt
beer	øl
beets	rødbeter
biscuits	kjeks
blueberries	blåbær
bottle	flaske
bread	brød
butcher	slakter
butter	smør
cabbage	kål
candle	lys
candy	sukkertøy
canned goods	hermetisk mat, mat på box
cart	tralle
cashier	kasserer
cauliflower	blomkål
celery	selleri
change, coins	småpenger
cheese	ost
cherries	kirsebær
chops	koteletter
coconut	kokosnøtt
coffee	kaffe
coffee pot	kafekanne, kafekjele
cord	hyssing

corn	maiskolbe
corn flakes	cornflakes
cucumbers	agurker
customer	kunde
detergent	vaskemiddel
eggs	egg
fish	fisk
flour	mel (white, **hvetemel**; wholewheat, **grovt mel**)
fork	gaffel
frankfurters	pølser
fruit	frukt
glassware	glassvarer
grapefruit	grapefrukt
grapes	druer
green pepper	grønn paprika
ham	skinke
honey	honning
hot dogs	pølser
jam	syltetøy
knife	kniv
lamb	lammekjøtt
lemons	sitroner
lettuce	salat
matches	fyrstikk
meat	kjøtt
melons	meloner
milk	melk
money	penger
napkin	serviett
non-alcoholic beer	vørterøl
nutcracker	nøtteknekker
nuts	nøtter
oil	olje
onion	løk
orange juice	appelsinsaft, appelsinjus
oranges	appelsiner
pan	kasserolle
paper plate	papirtallerken
paper towel	papirhåndkle
peaches	ferskener
peanut butter	peanutsmør
pears	pærer
peas	erter
pepper	pepper
plate	tallerken

plums	plommer
popcorn	popcorn
pork	svinekjøtt
potatoes	poteter
potholder	gryteklut
raisins	rosiner
raspberries	bringebær
red pepper	rød paprika
salad dressing	salatdressing
salami	spekepølse, salami
salt	salt
scales	vekt
soft drink	brus
spaghetti	spagetti
spices	krydder
spinach	spinat
spoon	skje
strawberries	jordbær
sugar	sukker
tea	te
teapot	tekanne
tomatoes	tomater
turnips	turnips
vegetables	grønnsaker
watermelon	vannmelon
wine	vin
wrapping paper	innpakningspapir
yeast	gjær
yogurt	yoghurt, jogurt

Fish & Shellfish (Fisk og skalldyr)

cod	torsk
blue whiting	kolmule
burbot	lake
catfish	steinbit
clam	musling
crab	krabbe
crayfish	kreps
eel	ål
flounder	flyndre
haddock	kolje, hyse
hake	lysing
halibut	hellefisk, kveite
herring	sild

lobster	hummer
mackerel	makrell
monkfish	breiflabb
mussel	blåskjell
perch	abbor
pike	gjedde
plaice	rødspette
pollack	lyr
salmon	laks
sardine	sardin
scallop	kammusling
shrimp, prawn	reke
sole	sjøtunge
sprat	brisling
squid	akkar, blekksprut
trout	ørret
turbot	piggvar
whitefish	sik
whiting	hvitting

The Kitchen (Kjøkkenet)

baking mold	kakeform
baking sheet	bakeplate
broom	feiekost
cake server	kakespade
can opener	bokseåpner
coffee grinder	kaffekvern
coffee pot	kaffekjele
colander	dørslag
cookbook	kokebok
cupboard	skap
cutting board	fjel
dough	deig
dishwasher	oppvaskmaskin
dust pan	feiebrett
egg beater	hjulvisp
electric burner	kokeplate
flour bin	melboks
fork	gaffel
freezer	fryseboks
funnel	trakt
garbage can	søppelbøtte
hood with fan	damphette
kettle	kjele

kitchen table	kjøkkenbord
knife	kniv
ladle	øse
matches	fyrstikker
measuring cup	mål
measuring spoons	måleskjeer
meat grinder	kjøttkvern
mixer	mixmaster
mixing bowl	vispebolle
mop	mopp
mustard jar	sennepskrukke
napkin	serviett
oven	ovn
pan	kasserolle, panne
pepper mill	pepperkvern
refrigerator	kjøleskap
rolling pin	kjevle
saltshaker	saltbøsse
shelf	hylle
soap	såpe
socket/outlet	stikkontakt
soup spoon	suppeskje
stool	taburett
stove	komfyr
strainer	sil
teaspoon	teskje
toaster	brødrister

Clothing (Klær)

belt	belte
blouse	bluse
casual dress	klær til daglig bruk
	(clothes for daily use);
	daglig antrekk
evening dress	selskapskjole, aftenkjole
glasses, spectacles	briller
sunglasses	solbriller
gloves	hansker
hat	hatt
hem	fald
to hem up	å falde
knitted cap	strikkelue
to knit	å strikke

leather	skinn, lær
lengthen	legge ned
scarf	skjerf
shawl	sjal
shirt	skjorte
shoe	sko
a pair of shoes	et par sko
shoelaces	skolisser
shorten	legge opp
skirt	skjørt
sneakers	joggesko, turnsko
sock	sokk
a pair of socks	et par sokker
stocking	strømpe
a pair of stockings	et par strømper
sweater	genser, strikkejakke
tailor	skredder
tie, necktie	slips
bow tie	sløyfe
trousers (pants)	bukser
a pair of trousers	et par bukser
tuxedo (dinner jacket)	smoking
in full dress	i full gala
wallet	lommebok
wedding dress	brudekjole

Footwear (Skotøy)

Do you have this shoe in size 40?
Har du denne sko i størrelse førti?

Does this come in other colors?
Har du denne i andre farver?

Do you have something smaller / larger / narrower / wider?
Har du noe som er mindre / større / smalere / videre?

Does it fit?
Passer det?

Do you have ski boots?
Har du skistøvler?

Are these boots good for hiking?
Passer disse støvlene til fottur?

This shoe pinches.
Denne skoen klemmer.

Can I put in an insole?
Kan jeg legge inn en binnsåle?

Is this boot waterproof?
Er denne støvelen vanntett?

May I get a receipt?
Kan jeg få en kvittering?

boots	**støvler**
flip-flops	**strandssandaler**
galoshes	**kalosjer**
high heels	**høye heler**
insole for arch support	**binnsåle**
jogging shoes	**joggesko**
moccasins	**mokasiner**
sandals	**sandaler**
shoelaces	**skolisser**
shoemaker	**skomaker**
shoe polish	**skokrem**
shoe repair	**skoreparasjon**
shoeshine	**skopussing**
skiboots	**skistøvler**
slippers	**tøfler**
snowboot	**støvlett**
tennis shoes	**tennissko**
waterproof	**vanntett**
waterproofing	**impregnering**

Toys (Leker)

We would like to buy a soccer ball for our nephew.
Vi vil kjøpe en fotball for vår nevø.

Our friends have children four and six years old.
Våre venner har barn fire og seks år gamle.

airplane	**fly**
badge	**merke, skilt**
badminton set	**badmington sett**
ball	**ball**
balloons	**balonger**

blocks	klosser
boat	boat
book	bok
books	bøker
bracelet	armbånd
bubble blowing set	såpebobler
car	bil
children's book	barnebok
children's books	barnebøker
compass	kompass
crayons	farveblyanter, fargeblyanter
croquet set	krokket
doll	dukke
doll house	dukkehus
drawing pad	tegneblokk
drum	tromme
earrings	øreringer
electric train	elektrisk tog
fairy tale book	eventyrbok
flag	flagg
glider	glidefly
harmonica	harmonika, munnspill
hat	hatt
horn	horn
jigsaw puzzle	puslespill
jump rope	hoppetau
kite	drage
magnifying glass	forstørrelsesglass; lupe
map	kart
marbles	klinkekuler
mask	maske
model airplane	modellfly
model boat	modellbåt
modeling clay	modelleringsleire
necklace	halsbånd
party hat	selskapshatt
pencil	blyant
pennant	vimpel
playing cards	spillkort
pocket knife	lommekniv
soccer ball	fotball
tea service	teservise
teddy bear	teddybjørn
toy soldiers	tinnsoldater
tricycle	trehjulssykkel

truck	lastebil
video	videofilm
videocassette	videokassett
wristwatch	armbåndsur
yo-yo	jojo

Shops & Stores

Norway Tax-Free Shopping

In over 2000 stores in Norway a purchase of NKr 300 or more entitles you to a cash refund for the VAT paid (11%–18%). Be sure to ask for a voucher at the time of purchase. The purchase is labeled with a seal on the wrapped parcel which must not be opened before departure. When you leave the country present the receipt with your ticket and passport at the refund desk at the point of departure for the refund. For information about Norway Tax-Free Shopping telephone 67 14 99 01 and on line at http://www.globalrefund.com/norway.

Shopping Hours
(These are the general hours. Exceptions occur.)

Weekdays: 9 A.M.–5 P.M.; Thursday some stores stay open
    until 7 P.M.
Saturdays: 9 A.M.–2 P.M.
Kiosks 8 A.M.–10 P.M. seven days a week
Supermarkets 8 A.M.–8 P.M.
Gas stations 7 A.M.–11 P.M.
Shopping and entertainment centers like Aker brygge in
    Oslo stay open longer.

bakery	bakeri, bakerbutikk
butcher	slakter
confectioner/pastry shop	konditori
dairy shop	melkebutikk, melkeutsalg
delicatessen	delikatessforretning
fishmonger/fish shop	fiskehandler
goldsmith	gullsmed
greengrocer	grønnsakhandler, grønthandler
grocery store	dagligvareforretning, kolonialforretning
jeweler	juveler, gullsmed

jewelry	**smykker**
magazine	**ukeblad, magasin**
newspaper	**avis**
newsstand	**aviskiosk**
perfume	**parfyme**
perfumery	**parfymeri**
pharmacy	**apotek**
silversmith	**sølvsmed**
stationary	**skrivesaker**
stationer's	**papirhandler**
tobacco	**tobakk**
tobacconist	**tobakksforretning**
watchmaker	**urmaker**

SMALL TALK

The Weather

How's the weather?
Hvordan er været?

Beautiful day today.
Strålende dag idag.

It's warm.
Det er varmt.

It's cold.
Det er kaldt.

It's thundering.
Det tordner.

It's lightning.
Det lyner.

It's freezing.
Det er iskaldt.

It's going to snow.
Vi får sne / snø.

It's snowing.
Det snør.

The sidewalk is slippery.
Fortauet er glatt.

The highway / road is slick.
Veien er glatt.

Are you warm enough?
Er du varm nok?

There's a lot of fog.
Det er tåket.

It's going to rain today.
Det skal bli regnvær idag.

It's raining.
Det regner.

It's cloudy.
Det er skyet.

It's windy.
Det blåser.

The sun is coming out.
Solen kommer frem igjen.

Telling the Time

Do you know what time it is?
Vet du hva klokken er?

What time is it, please?
Vær så snill å si meg hva klokken er.

It's twelve.
Klokken er tolv.

It's about nine.
Det er ved ni tiden.

It's almost three.
Klokken er nesten tre.

It's a quarter after two.
Klokken er kvart over to.

It's twenty-five after.
Klokken er fem på halv. (Literally: The clock is five before the half hour.)

It's twenty-five till (the hour).
Klokken er fem over halv. (Literally: The clock is five over the half hour.)

Is your watch right?
Er klokken din riktig?

What day of the month is it?
Hvilken dag er det idag?

I believe it's the fifteenth.
Jeg tror det er den femtende.

today	**i dag**
this morning	**i morges**
yesterday	**i går**
yesterday morning	**i går morges**
yesterday evening	**i går kveld**
day before yesterday	**i forgårs**
tomorrow	**i morgen**
tomorrow morning	**i morgen tidlig**
tomorrow evening	**i morgen kveld**
the other day	**forleden dag**
daylong	**i hele dag**
by day	**om dagen**
during the day	**om dagen**
later in the day	**senere på dagen**
day by day	**dag for dag**
about a week	**omtrent en uke**
in a week	**om en uke**
in two weeks	**om to uker**
in a month	**om en måned**
last week	**siste uke**
next week	**neste uke**
during the week	**i uken**
every week	**hver uke**
twice a week	**to ganger i uken**
weekday	**hverday**
weekend	**helg / weekend**
over the weekend	**i helgen / i weekenden**
last year	**i fjor**
year before last	**i forfjor**
next year	**neste år**
in a year	**om et år**
late	**sen**
later	**senere**
early	**tidlig**
earlier	**tidligere**

A. M.	Om formiddagen
P. M.	Om ettermiddagen
noon	Klokken tolv
midnight	midnatt

Days of the Week (Ukedager)

Monday	mandag
Tuesday	tirsdag
Wednesday	onsdag
Thursday	torsdag
Friday	fredag
Saturday	lørdag
Sunday	søndag

Months of the Year (Måneder)

January	januar
February	februar
March	mars
April	april
May	mai
June	juni
July	juli
August	august
September	september
October	oktober
November	november
December	desember

Seasons (Årstidene)

Spring	vår
Summer	sommer
Fall	høst
Winter	vinter

OUTDOORS

Do you think it is safe to swim on this beach?
Tror du at det er trygt å bade på denne stranden?

How do we get to the beach?
Hvordan kommer man til stranden?

Is it legal to fish here?
Er det lovlig å fiske her?

Can I rent a boat nearby?
Kan jeg leie en båt i nærheten?

How much would it cost an hour?
Hvor mye koster det pr. time?

On Water

boat	**båt**
boat trip	**båttur**
canoe	**kano**
canoeing	**padling**
the coastal steamer	**Hurtigruten** (proper name)
ferry	**ferje**
kayak	**kajakk**
powerboat	**motorbåt**
rowboat	**robåt**
(to) row	**å ro**
sailboat	**seibåt**
ship	**skip**
yacht	**seilbåt, yacht, lystyacht**
passenger	**passasjer**
passage (trip)	**overfart**
cruise	**cruise, sjøreise**
seaport	**havneby**
cabin, berth	**lugar**
seasick	**sjøsyk**
dock	**dokk**
shipyard	**skipsverft**
to sail	**å seile**
sailing	**seiling**

sailing race	kappseilas, seilas, regatta
sailing ship	seilbåt
sailor	sjømann
sailor blouse	matrosbluse
sailor suit	matrosdress
anchor *n.*	anker
anchor *v.*	ankre
bridge	kommandobru
mast	mast
gangplank	landgang
sail *n.*	seil
rope, line	tau
buoy	bøye
oar	åre
paddle	padleåre
wake	kjølvann
bow	baug
stern	hekk
starboard	styrbord
port	(larboard) babord
seaman, sailor	sjømann
fishing line	fiskesnøre
fishing rod	fiskestang
fishing tackle	fiskeutstyr
fish *n.*	fisk
fish *v.*	fiske
fisherman	fisker
fishing *n.*	fiske
fish *v.* for trout	fiske ørret
beach	strand
lake	innsjø
sand	sand
sea	sjø
to swim	å svømme, å bade
swimmer	svømmer
swimming	svømming
swimming area	badeområde
swimming pool	svømmebasseng
swimming trunks	badebukse
swimsuit	badedrakt
wet suit	våtdrakt
goggles	svømmebriller

to waterski	å stå på vannski
waterskis	vannski
watersports	vannsport
to windsurf	å kjøre seilbrett

On Land

bicycle	sykkel
bike tour	sykkeltur
golf	golf
golf club	golfkølle, golfklubb
golf course	golfbane
golfer	golfspiller
to ride, a horse	å ri
rock climbing	fjellklatring
racket	racket, tennisracket
tennis court	tennisbane
tennis racket	tennisracket
to run	å løpe, å springe
runner	løper
to jog	jogge
walk	spasertur
walker	fotturist
walking in the mountains	gå tur i fjellet
walking stick	spaserstokk, stokk
soccer	fotball
stadium	stadion

Signs (Skilter)

no diving	ingen stuping
no fishing	ingen fisking
no swimming	ingen bading
beware avalanches	rasfare
forbidden	forbudt
restricted area	avgrenset område
footpath	gangsti

The Playground (Lekeplassen)

blowing bubbles	**blåse såpebobler**
bounce the ball	**sprette ballen**
hide-and-seek	**gjemsel**
hopscotch	**hoppe paradis**
jungle gym	**klatrestativ**
kite	**drage**
kite string	**dragesnor**
ladder	**stige**
leapfrog	**hoppe bukk**
marbles	**klinkekuler**
merry-go-round	**karusell**
ring-around-a-rosy	**runddans**
rings	**ringer**
roller skates	**rulleskøyter**
sandbox	**sandkasse**
seesaw	**dumphuske, vippe**
skip rope	**hoppe tau**
slide	**rutsjebane, sklie**
swing	**huske, slenghuske**
tag	**sisten**
top	**snurrebass**

Cycling (Sykkelferie)

bicycle path	**sykkelsti**
for rent	**til leie**
bicycle	**sykkel**
bike tour	**sykkeltur**

Will you take your bicycle to Norway this summer?
Skal du ta sykkelen din med til Norge i sommer?

Yes, it isn't hard to check bikes on the plane. My bike is my best friend.
Ja, det er ikke vanskelig å sjekke sykler på flyet. Sykkel er min beste venn.

I plan to rent a bike in Oslo. My brother and I have rented bikes before. Twenty-one speed bikes suit the mountain and country roads too.
Jeg planlegger å leie en sykkel i Oslo. Min bror og jeg har leiet sykler før. Det var ganske enkelt. Sykler med 21 gear passer i fjellet og på landveiene også.

What kind of map do you usually take?
Hva slags kart pleier du å ta med deg?

Cappelens maps are detailed and reliable. *Bicycle Vacation* in Norway gives a lot of Information, but the book is in Norwegian. You ought to become a member of the Cyclists National Federation. You can get the book from that club.
Cappelens er detaljerte og pålitelige. Sykkelferie i Norge gir mye informasjon, men boken er på norsk. Du bør bli medlem av Syklistenes Landsforening. Du kan få boken fra den klubben.

If you are very motivated, you can understand a lot. Especially on the road. If you have a travel guide in Norwegian and ask a Norwegian for help, he will certainly be eager to help.
Hvis man er meget motivert kan man forstå mye. Særlig på veien. Hvis du har en norsk reisehåndbok og spør en nordmann for hjelp, vil han sikkert gjerne hjelpe deg.

Tunnels longer than four kilometers may be closed to bicycles. You can just take local buses through longer tunnels.
Tunneler lengere enn fire kilometer, kan være stengt for sykler. Man kan bare ta lokalbusser gjennom lengre tunneler.

In the Winter

ski track	**løype**
ice hockey	**ishockey**
racing skis, cross-country skis	**langrennsski**
to skate	**å gå på skøtyer**
skates	**skøyter**
skating rink	**skøytebane**
ski	**ski**
ski bindings	**skibindinger**
ski boots	**skistøvler**
skiing	**skigåing**
downhill	**utforkjøing**
cross country	**langrenn**
slalom	**slalåmkjøring**
ski lift	**skiheis**

skiing country	**skiterreng**
ski pants	**skibukser**
ski pass (for ski-lift)	**skiheiskort**
ski pole	**staver**
skiing trip	**skitur**
ski-jump	**skihopp**
ski-jumper	**skihopper**
ski-tow	**skitrekk**
ski wax	**skismøring**

How are the ski conditions today?
Hvordan er skiføret i dag?

We skied a lot that time.
Vi gikk mye på ski den gangen.

She is eager to buy a pair of racing skis.
Hun vil gjerne kjøpe langrennsski.

He has a pair of touring skis you can borrow.
Han har langrensski som du kan få låne.

Let's go skiing.
La oss dra på skitur.

Our daughter is eager to try cross-country skiing.
Vår datter vil gjerne prøve langrenn.

How much is a weekend pass for the skilift?
Hvor mye koster et weekendkort til skiheisen?

HEALTH (Helse)

To find out about health care, consult *Helse* the Pink Pages in the telephone book. The Norwegian Board of Health (**Statens Helsetilsyn**) publishes a *Brief Introduction to Health Services in Norway* (Number IK-2563) (tel. 22 24 88 88, P. O. Box 8128 Dep, 0032 Oslo; http://www.helsetilsynet.no).

For dental work see *tannleger* (dentists) or *tannteknikere* (dental technicians) in the Yellow Pages. For emergencies look for *tannlegevakt.*

Alternative medicine in Norway can be explored at http://www.wrf.org.

For asthma and allergies consult **Norges Astma- og Allergiforbund** (NAAF) (Hegdehaugsveien 31, 0352. Oslo, tel. 22 93 37 30; e-mail naaaf@naaf.no; http://www.naaf.no).

For chiropractors look for *Kiropraktorer* in the Yellow pages (http://www.kiropraktikk.no).

For pharmacies (drug stores) look for *Apotek* in the Yellow Pages. For emergencies after hours look for *Apotekvakt* in the Yellow Pages. Keep in mind that the telephone book carries a list of "important telephone numbers" (**Viktige telefonnummer**) at the beginning of the Pink Pages.

At the Doctor's

I need to see a doctor.
Jeg må se en lege.

I need a doctor.
Jeg trenger en lege.

I don't feel good.
Jeg føler meg ikke bra.

I feel faint.
Jeg tror jeg besvimer.

It hurts right here.
Det gjør vondt akkurat her.

It's painful.
Det gjør vondt.

It stings.
Det svir.

I am allergic to ...
Jeg er allergisk mot ...

Please give me a prescription for something that will help me.
Vær så snill å gi meg en resept på noe som kan hjelpe meg.

ambulance	**ambulanse**
appendicitis	**blindtarmebetennelse**
aspirin	**globoid; aspirin**
asthma	**astma**
backache	**vondt i ryggen**
bandage	**bandasje**
blister	**blemme**
blood	**blod**
blood pressure	**blodtrykk**
burn	**brannsår**
cancer	**kreft**
check-up	**undersøkelse**
chest	**bryst**
chickenpox	**vannkopper**
clinic	**klinikk**
cold	**forkjølelse**
concussion	**hjernerystelse**
constipation	**forstoppelse**
contact lenses	**kontaktlinser**
cough	**hoste**
cut	**kutt; sår**
dentist	**tannlege**
diabetes	**diabetes; sukkersyke**
diarrhea	**diaré**
dizzy	**svimmel**
doctor	**lege**
earache	**øreverk**
emergency station	**legevakt**
fever	**feber**
filling	**plombe**
first aid	**førstehjelp**
flu	**influensa**

fracture	**brudd**
glasses	**briller**
hayfever	**høysnue**
heart	**hjerte**
heart attack	**hjerteinfarkt**
hemorrhage	**blødning**
hospital	**sykehus**
ill	**syk**
indigestion	**dårlig fordøyelse, fordøyelsesbesvær**
inflammation	**betennelse**
injection	**sprøyte**
insect bite	**stikk**
itch	**kløe**
kidney	**nyre**
lump	**klump**
measles	**meslinger**
migraine	**migrene**
mumps	**kusma**
nausea	**kvalme**
nurse (female)	**sykepleierske**
nurse (male)	**sykepleier**
operation	**operasjon**
optician	**optiker**
pain	**smerte**
pneumonia	**lungebetennelse**
pregnant	**gravid**
prescription	**resept**
rheumatism	**reumatisme**
sore throat	**vondt i halsen**
sprain	**forstue**
sting	**stikk**
stomach	**mage**
temperature	**temperatur**
tonsils	**mandler**
toothache	**tannpine**
ulcer	**magesår**
vaccination	**vaksinasjon**
visiting hours	**visitt-tid**
to vomit	**å kaste opp**
X-ray	**røntgen**

At the Pharmacy (På apoteket)

Do you have anything for mosquitoes?
Har du noe for mygg?

Do you have suntan oil?
Har du solbadolje?

Do you have sunblock?
Har du solkrem med faktor?

Do you have sunglasses?
Har du solbriller?

Do you have anything to protect me from the sun?
Har du noe vil skjerme mot solen?

I have a stomach ache. Do you have anything for that?
Jeg har vondt i magen. Har du noe for det?

I have a sore throat.
Jeg har vondt i halsen.

I have a toothache.
Jeg har tannpine.

I have a headache.
Jeg har hodepine.

I have cut my finger.
Jeg har skåret meg i fingeren.

I have a cold.
Jeg er forkjølet.

I have a cough.
Jeg hoster.

I have diarrhea.
Jeg har diaré.

How many pills do I take?
Hvor mange piller tar jeg?

How often?
Hvor ofte?

What is the dosage for children?
Hva er dosen for barn?

Must I have a prescription?
Må jeg ha resept?

Thank you for your help.
Takk for hjelpen.

conditioner	**hårkondisjoner**
hairbrush	**hårbørste**
nail clippers	**neglesaks**
shampoo	**sjampo**
soap	**såpe**
sun block	**solskjerm**
suntan oil	**solbadolje**
toothbrush	**tannbørste**
toothpaste	**tannpasta**

EMERGENCIES

Fire (**brann**): dial 110

Police (**politi**): dial 112

Rescue (**redningssentral**): dial 112

Medical emergency (**medisinsk nødhjelp**): dial 113

Ambulance (**ambulanse**): dial 113

Credit card loss (**Bankenes meldingstjeneste**): dial
80 03 02 50

Emergency medical attention—see *Legevakten* in telephone directory

Poison information central (**Giftinformasjonssentralen**):
dial 22 59 13 00

I have lost my keys.
Jeg har mistet nøklene mine.

I have left my pocketbook on the bus.
Jeg har glemt igjen min pung på bussen.

Help!	**Hjelp!**
Look out!	**Se opp!**
Fire!	**Brann!**
Thief!	**Tyv!**
He's drowning!	**Han drukner!**
Go away!	**Gå bort! Forsvinn!**
Stop!	**Stopp!**

I'm lost.
Jeg kan ikke finne veien.
Jeg har gått meg vill.
Jeg har gått meg bort.

My little boy / daughter has disappeared.
Min liten gutt / datter har forsvunnet.

Call for ...	**Ring til ...**
an ambulance!	**en ambulanse!**
a doctor!	**legen!**
the police!	**politiet!**

Sound the fire alarm!
Slå brannalarm!

Does anyone here speak English?
Er det noen her som snakker engelsk?

Where is the U. S. Consulate?
Hvor er det amerikanske konsulat?

REFERENCES

US Embassy in Oslo 22-44 85 50

Babysitting—local telephone directory

Norwegian telephone numbers 180

Overseas telephone numbers: dial 181

Public transportation—see *ruteopplysningen* in the local telephone directory

Road conditions (**vegmeldingstjenesten**): dial 175

Railway schedules (**NSB billettbestilling og rutopplysning**): dial 81 50 08 88

Time of day (**telfonuret**): dial 170

Numbers

1	en, et
2	to
3	tre
4	fire
5	fem
6	seks
7	syv, sju
8	åtte
9	ni
10	ti
11	elleve
12	tolv
13	tretten
14	fjorten
15	femten
16	seksten
17	sytten
18	atten
19	nitten
20	tyve, tjue
21	en og tyve, tjue-en
22	to og tyve, tjue-to
23	tre og tyve, tjue-tre
24	fire og tyve, tjue-fire
25	fem og tyve, tjue-fem
26	seks og tyve, tjue-seks

27	syv og tyve, tjue-syv
28	åtte og tyve, tjue-åtte
29	ni og tyve, tjue-ni
30	tretti
40	førti
50	femti
60	seksti
70	sytti
80	åtti
90	nitti
100	hundre
1000	tusen

In Norwegian numbers over 1000 are divided by a period and not by a comma. Decimals are marked with a comma: 1.50 in English is 1,50 in Norwegian.

10.000	ti tusen
20.000	tyve tusen, tjue tusen
30.000	tretti tusen
40.000	førti tusen
50.000	femti tusen
60.000	seksti tusen
70.000	sytti tusen
80.000	åtti tusen
90.000	nitti tusen
100.000	hundre tusen
200.000	to hundre tusen
300.000	tree hundre tusen
400.000	fire hundre tusen
500.000	fem hundre tusen
600.000	seks hundre tusen
700.000	syv hundre tusen
800.000	åtti hundre tusen
900.000	ni hundre tusen
1.000.000	one million

Ordinals *(Ordenstall)*

1st	først
2nd	annen
3rd	tredje
4th	fjerde

5th	femte
6th	sjette
7th	sjuende
8th	åttende
9th	niende
10th	tiende
11th	ellevte
12th	tolvte
13th	trettende
14th	fjortende
15th	femtende
16th	sekstende
17th	syttende
18th	attende
19th	nittende
20th	tyvende, tjuende
21th	en og tyvende, tjueførste
22nd	to og tyvende, tjueandre
23rd	tre og tyvende, tjuetredje
24th	fire og tyvende, tjuefjerde
25th	fem og tyvende, tjuefemte
26th	seks og tyvende, tjuesjette
27th	syv og tyvende, tjuesjuende
28th	åtte og tyvende, tjueåttende
29th	ni og tyvende, tjueniende
30th	trettiende
40th	førtiende
50th	femtiende
60th	sekstiende
70th	syttiende
80th	åttiende
90th	nittiende
100th	hundrede
200th	to hundrede

Weights *(Vekt)*

g	gram
kg	kilo
l	liter
100g	3.5 oz.
1kg	1000g (2.2 lbs)
1l	1 liter (1.06 U.S. quarts)

Measures	*(Mål)*
m	meter
cm	centimeter
1 mile	1,61 km
1 yard	0,91 M
1 inch	(tomme) 2,54 cm

Temperature	*(Temperatur)*
°C	°F
100°	212°
38°	100°
36.9°	98.4° (body temperature)
0°	32° (freezing point)
–20°	–4°

Clothing Sizes (Klestørrelser)

Men's sizes (Herrestørrelser)

Norwegian	*American*
46	36
48	38
50	40
52	42
54	44
56	46
58	48

Men's shirt sizes (Skjortestørrelser for herrer)

Norwegian	*American*
36	14
37	14½
38	15
39	15½
41	16
42	16½
43	17
44–45	17½
46	18

Women's sizes (Damestørrelser)

Norwegian	Misses	American
38	6	
40	8	
42	10	34
44	12	36
46	14	38
48	16	40
50	18	42
52	20	44

Children's sizes (Barnestørrelser)

European (cm.)	American (age)
	4
135	6
150	8
155	10
160	12
165	14

Shoe Sizes (Størrelse på sko)

Norwegian shoes sizes follow the European Paris Point System.

Norwegian	US (women's)	US (men's)
32	2	
33	3	
34	4	
35	5	
36	5.5	
37	6	
37.5	6.5	
38	7	
39	8	6
39.5	8.5	6.5
40	9	7
41	9.5	8
42	10	9
43	11	10
44		11
45		12
46		13
47		14